FAMILY FAVORITES THAT ARE ECONOMICAL AND EASY TO MAKE

From breakfasts and brunches to main dishes, snacks, and dazzling desserts, in this community-style cookbook you will find a dieter's culinary heaven with such savory dishes as:

—Cheese Pancakes with Pineapple Topping
—Vegetable-Shrimp Quiche
—Chicken Enchiladas
—Southern Corn Bread
—Chocolate Soufflé, Peanut Butter Macaroons, and many more!

Each recipe lists complete calorie, protein, fat, carbohydrate, calcium, sodium, and cholesterol counts to suit the individual needs of the weight- and health-conscious. And over 100 recipes can be made in 30 minutes or less!

WEIGHT WATCHERS®
FAVORITE RECIPES

WEIGHT WATCHERS®
FAVORITE RECIPES

Over 280 Winning Dishes from
Weight Watchers Members and Staff

Photography by Guy Powers

A PLUME BOOK

A DIVISION OF PENGUIN BOOKS USA INC., NEW YORK
PUBLISHED IN CANADA BY
PENGUIN BOOKS CANADA LIMITED, MARKHAM, ONTARIO
WEIGHT WATCHERS is a registered trademark of
Weight Watchers International, Inc.

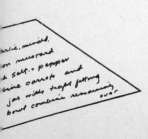

A hardcover edition was published by New American Library
and simultaneously in Canada by The New American Library
of Canada Limited (now Penguin Books Canada Limited).

Designed by Julian Hamer

Food stylist: Susan West

Prop stylist: Dale Goday

Illustrations by Dolores R. Santoliquido

Nutrition analysis by Hill Nutrition Associates, Inc.

PLUME TRADEMARK REG. U.S. PAT. OFF. AND FOREIGN COUNTRIES
REGISTERED TRADEMARK—MARCA REGISTRADA
HECHO EN HARRISONBURG, VA., U.S.A.

SIGNET, SIGNET CLASSIC, MENTOR, ONYX, PLUME,
MERIDIAN and NAL BOOKS are published *in the United
States* by New American Library, a division of Penguin Books
USA Inc., 1633 Broadway, New York, New York 10019, and
in Canada by Penguin Books Canada Limited, 2801 John
Street, Markham, Ontario L3R 1B4

Library of Congress Cataloging-in-Publication Data

Weight Watchers favorite recipes

   Includes index.
   1. Reducing diets—Recipes.   2. Weight Watchers
International.   I. Weight Watchers International.
RM222.2.W3136   1986   641.5′635   86-16174
ISBN 0-453-01012-1
ISBN 0-452-26055-8 (pbk.)

First Plume Printing, March, 1988

       13 14 15 16 17

PRINTED IN THE UNITED STATES OF AMERICA

*This book is dedicated to our "family"—
the Weight Watchers members, staff, franchisees,
area directors, and licensees whose enthusiasm,
warmth, support, and understanding provide
inspiration to so many.*

Contents

Introduction

Dear Readers,

Back in the summer of 1984, we at Weight Watchers International thought how wonderful it would be to publish a cookbook of the favorite recipes of Weight Watchers members and staff. "Why not have a contest," we thought, "and pick the winning recipes."

So notices went out in Weight Watchers meetings all over the United States and Canada and thousands of recipe forms were distributed in the fall and winter of 1984–1985. At first, the recipes began to slowly trickle in to our offices; later they poured in from just about everywhere.

Then the long and difficult selection process began. Each recipe was classified by food category and state or province, while multiple entries were cross-indexed. Next, our kitchen staff took over, carefully reviewing each recipe. After months of testing and tasting, the winning recipes were selected.

Once selected, the winning recipes were revised and rewritten by our editorial staff, who carefully checked to be sure that the ingredients, measurements, and methods conformed to our standards of recipe style, and, of course, to be sure that they were consistent with the Food Plan.

We now had over 250 winning recipes, plus 30 that were developed by our kitchen staff. It was time to write the notes that were to accompany each recipe. But first, we needed to know more about our winners, so our editorial staff contacted hundreds of them by phone and letter.

Talking to the winners was a marvelous experience. Most were absolutely thrilled to hear that their recipes had been chosen for the cookbook, and they were more than happy to share with us the background of their recipes, as well as some personal information about themselves and their families.

We spoke with men and women, young and old, married and single, urban and rural. Our winners are a truly diverse group, reflecting the variety of cultures and experiences that characterize the population of North America, but with a single, common thread—the shared experience of successful weight loss on the Weight Watchers program.

The people we spoke with were extremely pleased with Weight Watchers, and some were so enthusiastic that they persuaded friends and relatives to come to meetings. One woman told us her weight loss was the best thing she'd ever done for

❖❖❖

herself. Another wrote a poem to her Weight Watchers leader when she reached her goal.

We spoke to a man who lost 121 pounds; a Weight Watchers leader who lost 137 pounds; a woman and her husband who each lost 75 pounds. Over and over, we heard the success stories, and whether the loss was 13 pounds or 113 pounds, the warmth, the enthusiasm, the gratitude for Weight Watchers came shining through.

After reaching their goal weight, a number of our winners have gone on to become Weight Watchers leaders, weighers, and receptionists. In addition, most winners lead busy lives as homemakers, career persons, or both. The variety of occupations was astounding. We spoke with a restaurant chef, a biochemist, a dress designer, a locksmith, an artist, and numerous teachers and nurses. Many members volunteer their time and skills in museums, hospitals, nursing homes, churches and synagogues, the PTA, and other local organizations.

Our winners' hobbies range from the traditional (gardening, cooking, sewing, needlepoint) to the artistic (painting, drawing, music, flower-arranging) to the active (hiking, skiing, aerobics, skating, white-water rafting). Travel is also high on the list of interests; some of our winners are world travelers who have been to France, Greece, Mexico, Hawaii, and other parts of the globe.

After gathering all of the information about our newfound friends, we completed the writing and editing of our cookbook early in 1986 and sent the manuscript off to our publisher. Galleys were proofread, recipes were photographed, and everything moved along right on schedule.

Now the weeks and months of work are over, and our dream is a reality. Here, in these pages, Weight Watchers members and staff present their own special favorites—over 280 mouthwatering recipes for you to enjoy while losing (or maintaining) weight.

Start your meal with classic Onion Soup, Spinach Salad with Mustard-Honey Dressing, or Herb-Marinated Tomatoes. For your main course, select spicy Shrimp Creole or a hearty Vegetable-Cheese Lasagna. In an Oriental mood? Try Chinese Steak or Beef 'n' Broccoli Stir-Fry. If company's coming for dinner, why not serve elegant Chicken in Cheddar-Wine Sauce or colorful Green Beans Provençale. And, for family meals, Oven-Barbecued Chicken is perfect.

Just because you're dieting doesn't mean you have to give up dessert. Our creative friends have dreamed up dozens of delectables for you to enjoy while following the Food Plan. Try Carrot Cake, Oatmeal-Raisin Cookies, Apple-Cinnamon Bread Pudding, or Chocolate-Cherry Frozen Pie.

As our gift to you, our readers, we've included 30 recipes developed by the chefs here at Weight Watchers, and we thought you'd like to know a little something about the folks behind these recipes. We'd also like to express our gratitude to them for their countless hours of hard work.

Nina Procaccini, assistant manager of the Weight Watchers test kitchen, is a native of Brooklyn, New York, and worked for several Long Island restaurants before joining Weight Watchers International in 1979. Nina has done recipe development and food styling for six Weight Watchers cookbooks, and she constantly delights and surprises us with innovative recipes and techniques that reflect her ongoing love affair with food.

Christy Foley-McHale spent more than seven years working in restaurants before coming to Weight Watchers over two years ago. Christy, who grew up in Queens and Long Island, and has been cooking since the age of seven, holds a degree in professional chef's studies from the State University of New York.

Judi Rettmer, a native of Queens, New York, is a self-taught chef who has firsthand experience with the Weight Watchers program. She lost 70 pounds by following the Food Plan, and has maintained her goal weight despite her love of cooking and her constant contact with food. Judi won a bronze medal for her pastries in an American Culinary Federation competition, and is the recipient of several honorable mentions in other culinary competitions.

Bianca Brown, a European-trained home economist, worked for many years as a consultant and a food stylist for major food publications before joining Weight Watchers International. Bianca has traveled extensively throughout the world, expanding her knowledge of international cuisine.

This book would not have been possible without the assistance of many other talented and hard-working people.

To Eileen Pregosin, Patricia Barnett, Anne Neiwirth, Harriet Pollock, Elizabeth Resnick-Healy, and April Rozea, we extend our gratitude for researching, writing, and editing the text.

And we thank our dedicated secretarial staff, AnnMarie Clarke, Isabel Fleisher, and Carole B. Langroth, for their skill, patience, and cooperation in typing and revising the manuscript.

We hope you enjoy reading, preparing, and tasting the recipes in this book. They're our winners' favorites, and we're certain they'll become your favorites as well, especially, as one member says, if they're "served with love."

WEIGHT WATCHERS INTERNATIONAL

About the Recipe Symbols

◐ This symbol indicates that the recipe can be prepared in 30 minutes or less.

¢ This symbol indicates a budget recipe.

Rise and Shine
Breakfasts and Brunches

Bread Pudding ☾

A first-time grandmother, Carol moved from Ohio to Florida, where she keeps busy with golf, needlework, and playing the organ. She says this recipe makes a delicious breakfast.

**1 slice white bread,
  cut into cubes
1 small apple, cored, pared,
  and diced
1 cup skim milk
1 egg
1 teaspoon *each* granulated
  sugar and vanilla extract
¼ teaspoon ground cinnamon
Dash ground nutmeg**

Preheat oven to 350°F. Spray 2-cup casserole with nonstick cooking spray; arrange bread cubes and apple in dish and set aside.

In small bowl combine milk, egg, sugar, and vanilla and beat until smooth. Pour milk mixture over bread and apple, being sure bread is well moistened; sprinkle with cinnamon and nutmeg. Bake for 35 to 40 minutes (until pudding is lightly browned and a knife, inserted in center, comes out clean). Remove from oven and let stand 15 minutes before serving.

MAKES 1 SERVING

Each serving provides: 1 Protein Exchange; 1 Bread Exchange; 1 Fruit Exchange; 1 Milk Exchange; 20 calories Optional Exchange
Per serving: 319 calories; 17 g protein; 7 g fat; 45 g carbohydrate; 361 mg calcium; 318 mg sodium; 280 mg cholesterol

VARIATION:

Substitute 2 tablespoons dark raisins for the apple.

Per serving: 317 calories; 17 g protein; 7 g fat; 45 g carbohydrate; 366 mg calcium; 320 mg sodium; 280 mg cholesterol

*Carol O. Jentsch
Lake Mary, Florida*

❖❖

Prepare-Ahead French Toast ❻

George is a retired police officer with a keen interest in Japanese language and culture. In fact, he and his Japanese pen pal have been corresponding for over 20 years, and George has also visited Japan. George's French toast recipe is super-easy and extra-good when the bread is soaked in the egg mixture overnight.

1 egg
2 tablespoons skim milk
Granulated sugar substitute
**   to equal 2 teaspoons sugar***
½ teaspoon vanilla extract
Dash *each* ground cinnamon
**   and ground nutmeg**
1 ounce French bread, cut
**   into 3 slices**
1 tablespoon reduced-calorie
**   pancake syrup (60 calories**
**   per fluid ounce)**

In shallow bowl combine all ingredients except bread and syrup, mixing thoroughly. Add bread slices to egg mixture and let soak, coating all sides; cover with plastic wrap and refrigerate overnight.

Spray 10-inch nonstick skillet with nonstick cooking spray and heat over medium-low heat. Add soaked bread to skillet, pouring any remaining egg mixture over bread; cook, turning once, until golden brown, 2 to 3 minutes on each side. Serve with syrup.

MAKES 1 SERVING

*Do not use low-calorie sweetener with aspartame in this recipe; it may lose sweetness during cooking.

Each serving provides: 1 Protein Exchange; 1 Bread Exchange; 40 calories Optional Exchange
Per serving: 214 calories; 10 g protein; 7 g fat; 27 g carbohydrate; 80 mg calcium; 249 mg sodium; 276 mg cholesterol

George Mengelkoch
Portland, Oregon

Cheese Pancakes with Pineapple Topping ◐

Deborah and her aunt, a former Weight Watchers member, worked together to develop this out-of-the-ordinary pancake recipe. The mother of two children, Deborah likes to cook and crochet.

3 tablespoons all-purpose flour
1 teaspoon double-acting baking powder
Granulated sugar substitute to equal 1 teaspoon sugar*
Dash salt
1 egg
½ cup *each* part-skim ricotta cheese and canned crushed pineapple (no sugar added)
1 teaspoon cornstarch, dissolved in 1 tablespoon water

Onto a sheet of wax paper or a paper plate sift together flour, baking powder, sweetener, and salt; set aside. In medium bowl beat egg; add ricotta cheese and sifted flour mixture and stir until smooth.

Spray 12-inch skillet or a griddle with nonstick cooking spray and heat; drop 3 heaping tablespoonfuls batter into hot skillet (or onto griddle), making 3 pancakes, each about 3 inches in diameter. Cook until bottom is browned and bubbles appear on surface; using a pancake turner, turn pancakes over and cook until other side is browned. Remove pancakes to plate and keep warm. Repeat procedure, spraying pan and making 3 more pancakes.

In small saucepan combine pineapple and dissolved cornstarch; bring to a boil. Cook, stirring constantly, until mixture is slightly thickened. Serve warm pineapple sauce with pancakes.

MAKES 1 SERVING

*Do not use low-calorie sweetener with aspartame in this recipe; it may lose sweetness during cooking.

Each serving provides: 3 Protein Exchanges; 1 Bread Exchange; 1 Fruit Exchange; 10 calories Optional Exchange
Per serving: 423 calories; 23 g protein; 16 g fat; 48 g carbohydrate; 597 mg calcium; 783 mg sodium; 312 mg cholesterol

Deborah Shilling
Ashland, Ohio

❖❖❖

Pineapple Pancakes ◖

Here's a change of pace from the usual pancakes-and-syrup combo. Rosemary's recipe is easy to make, colorful to look at, and delicious to eat.

½ cup canned crushed
    pineapple (no sugar added)
2 teaspoons reduced-calorie
    margarine (tub)
1 teaspoon reduced-calorie
    pancake syrup (60 calories
    per fluid ounce)
⅓ cup plus 2 teaspoons
    buttermilk
1 slice reduced-calorie white
    bread (40 calories per slice),
    toasted and torn into small
    pieces
1 egg
1 tablespoon water
2 teaspoons all-purpose flour
Granulated sugar substitute
    to equal 2 teaspoons sugar*
½ teaspoon vanilla extract
⅛ teaspoon baking soda
Dash pumpkin pie spice

In small saucepan combine pineapple, margarine, and syrup and bring to a boil. Remove from heat; set aside and keep warm.

In blender container combine remaining ingredients and process until smooth, scraping down sides of container as necessary.

Spray 12-inch nonstick skillet or a griddle with nonstick cooking spray and heat; drop batter by heaping tablespoonfuls into skillet (or onto griddle), making 4 equal pancakes. Cook until bottom is browned and bubbles appear on surface; using a pancake turner, turn pancakes over and cook until other side is browned. Remove pancakes to plate and top with warm pineapple mixture.

MAKES 1 SERVING, 4 PANCAKES

*Do not use low-calorie sweetener with aspartame in this recipe; it may lose sweetness during cooking.

Each serving provides: 1 Protein Exchange; ½ Bread Exchange; 1 Fat Exchange; 1 Fruit Exchange; ½ Milk Exchange; 30 calories Optional Exchange
Per serving: 305 calories; 13 g protein; 11 g fat; 41 g carbohydrate; 174 mg calcium; 445 mg sodium; 278 mg cholesterol

Rosemary Harbaugh
Mackinaw, Illinois

Whole Wheat Pancakes ◑◐

Jane, her husband, and their two sons love pancakes, so Jane adapted her mother-in-law's recipe. A patient-account supervisor at a local hospital, Jane enjoys landscape painting. The family belongs to an antique car club and owns a 1928 Model A Ford.

¾ cup buttermilk
1 egg
1 tablespoon plus 1 teaspoon vegetable oil
1 tablespoon firmly packed brown sugar
¾ cup whole wheat flour
1 teaspoon double-acting baking powder
½ teaspoon *each* **baking soda and salt**

In medium mixing bowl combine buttermilk, egg, oil, and sugar and beat until thoroughly combined; add remaining ingredients, stirring until smooth.

Spray 12-inch nonstick skillet or a griddle with nonstick cooking spray and heat over medium heat; using half of the batter, drop batter by heaping tablespoonfuls into skillet (or onto griddle), making 4 pancakes. Cook until bottom is browned and bubbles appear on surface, about 3 minutes; using pancake turner, turn pancakes over and cook until other side is browned. Remove to serving plate and keep warm. Using remaining batter, repeat procedure, spraying pan with cooking spray and making 4 more pancakes.

MAKES 4 SERVINGS, 2 PANCAKES EACH

Each serving provides: 1 Bread Exchange; 1 Fat Exchange; ¼ Milk Exchange; 35 calories Optional Exchange
Per serving: 167 calories; 6 g protein; 7 g fat; 22 g carbohydrate; 127 mg calcium; 550 mg sodium; 70 mg cholesterol

SERVING SUGGESTION:

Top each portion of pancakes with 1 poached egg. Add 1 Protein Exchange to Exchange Information.

Per serving: 245 calories; 12 g protein; 12 g fat; 22 g carbohydrate; 156 mg calcium; 696 mg sodium; 343 mg cholesterol

Jane Alvested
Independence, Missouri

❖✦❖

Curried Poached Egg ◑

John is a commercial artist whose hobby is his family: wife Frances, their daughter, and three sons. Frances inspired John to create this delicacy, which, John says, should be "served with love."

1 teaspoon margarine
½ teaspoon all-purpose flour
¼ cup skim milk
1 ounce Cheddar cheese, shredded
½ English muffin, toasted
½ medium tomato, thinly sliced, divided
1 egg, poached (hot)
¼ to ½ teaspoon curry powder
1 teaspoon chopped fresh parsley

In small saucepan heat margarine over medium heat until bubbly and hot; add flour and cook, stirring constantly, for 1 minute. Gradually stir in milk; cook, stirring constantly, until mixture is smooth and slightly thickened, about 1 minute. Reduce heat to low; add cheese and cook, stirring constantly, until cheese is melted and mixture is smooth.

To serve, place muffin half on plate, cut-side up; top with half of the tomato slices. Set poached egg on tomato slices and top with cheese mixture; sprinkle with curry powder, then parsley. Serve with remaining tomato slices.

MAKES 1 SERVING

Each serving provides: 2 Protein Exchanges; 1 Bread Exchange; 1 Vegetable Exchange; 1 Fat Exchange; ¼ Milk Exchange; 5 calories Optional Exchange
Per serving: 333 calories; 18 g protein; 20 g fat; 21 g carbohydrate; 320 mg calcium; 550 mg sodium; 303 mg cholesterol

John N. Wynkoop
Portland, Oregon

Poached Eggs with Pizzazz ◐◑

Peggy developed this dish as an alternative to eggs Benedict, and added the benefits of vegetables. A former dress shop owner, Peggy is now retired.

2 ounces American cheese,
  shredded
2 tablespoons skim milk
1 English muffin, split in half
  and toasted
10 cooked broccoli spears
2 eggs, poached (hot)

In small nonstick saucepan combine cheese and milk and cook over low heat, stirring frequently, until cheese is melted and mixture is smooth, 3 to 4 minutes.

On each of 2 flameproof plates place 1 muffin half. Arrange 5 broccoli spears on each half, radiating out like spokes of a wheel; top each with 1 poached egg and half of cheese mixture. Broil until cheese mixture is bubbly, 1 to 2 minutes.

MAKES 2 SERVINGS

Each serving provides: 2 Protein Exchanges; 1 Bread Exchange; 2½ Vegetable Exchanges; 5 calories Optional Exchange
Per serving: 312 calories; 21 g protein; 15 g fat; 26 g carbohydrate; 444 mg calcium; 726 mg sodium; 299 mg cholesterol

Peggy Dowell
Claremont, California

Eggs Mexicali ◐ ◑

A Mexican friend gave Jeri-Ann a south-of-the-border egg dish that she adapted to fit the Food Plan. Jeri-Ann is a Weight Watchers receptionist who likes sports, the outdoors, and is the proud mother of a little girl, Rebecca.

1 teaspoon vegetable oil
½ medium tomato, diced
2 tablespoons onion, diced
2 teaspoons minced fresh *or* drained canned mild green chili pepper
2 eggs, beaten
2 corn tortillas (6-inch diameter each), heated and each cut into 4 wedges

In small nonstick skillet heat oil; add tomato, onion, and chili pepper and cook, stirring frequently, until onion is translucent. Add eggs and cook, stirring frequently, just until eggs are set, 1 to 2 minutes.

To serve, on each of 2 plates arrange half of the egg mixture and 4 tortilla wedges.

MAKES 2 SERVINGS

Each serving provides: 1 Protein Exchange; 1 Bread Exchange; ½ Vegetable Exchange; ½ Fat Exchange

Per serving: 152 calories; 8 g protein; 8 g fat; 12 g carbohydrate; 73 mg calcium; 94 mg sodium; 274 mg cholesterol

VARIATION:

For eggs topped with Mexican sauce, add ¼ cup tomato sauce to sautéed vegetables and cook, stirring until heated; remove from heat and set aside. Heat another small nonstick skillet and add eggs; cook, stirring frequently, just until eggs are set, 1 to 2 minutes. On each of 2 plates arrange half of the eggs; top each portion with half of the vegetable mixture and ½ ounce shredded Monterey Jack cheese. Serve each portion with 4 tortilla wedges. Increase Protein Exchange to 1½ Exchanges and Vegetable Exchange to 1 Exchange.

Per serving: 214 calories; 11 g protein; 13 g fat; 14 g carbohydrate; 183 mg calcium; 354 mg sodium; 286 mg cholesterol

Jeri-Ann Cude
Sunnyvale, California

Sesame Zucchini 'n' Eggs ◖

Christine is a homemaker and mother of two who loves to cook and enjoys the challenge of adapting recipes to fit the Weight Watchers food plan. She has found this dish is a good way to use the zucchini from her garden.

2 eggs
1 tablespoon water
¼ teaspoon *each* basil leaves
    and salt
⅛ teaspoon *each* thyme leaves
    and pepper
2 teaspoons margarine
¼ cup diced onion
1 cup sliced zucchini (⅛-inch-
    thick slices)
2 teaspoons sesame seed,
    lightly toasted

In small bowl combine eggs, water, and seasonings; set aside. In 9-inch skillet heat margarine over medium heat until bubbly and hot; add onion and sauté until translucent, about 2 minutes. Add zucchini and continue to sauté, stirring frequently, until zucchini is fork-tender. Add egg mixture and sesame seed and cook, stirring frequently, until eggs are set, about 2 minutes.

MAKES 1 SERVING

Each serving provides: 2 Protein Exchanges; 2½ Vegetable Exchanges; 2 Fat
    Exchanges; 40 calories Optional Exchange
Per serving: 294 calories; 15 g protein; 22 g fat; 10 g carbohydrate; 163 mg
    calcium; 773 mg sodium; 548 mg cholesterol

Christine Bermel
New Fairfield, Connecticut

❖·❖

Battered Leeks ⊖◐

*For an adventure in breakfast eating, try Francis' omelet. It's simple to prepare —
and oh, so delicious!*

4 cups diced thoroughly
   washed leeks (white portion
   with some green), divided
4 eggs
⅔ cup instant nonfat dry milk
   powder, divided
½ teaspoon salt, divided
Pepper
4 cherry tomatoes
Italian (flat-leaf) parsley sprigs

Spray 10-inch nonstick skillet with nonstick cooking spray and set over medium heat; add 2 cups leeks, cover skillet, and cook, stirring occasionally, until leeks are softened, 3 to 4 minutes. In small mixing bowl beat together 2 eggs, ⅓ cup milk powder, ¼ teaspoon salt, and dash pepper; pour into skillet, making sure egg mixture thoroughly coats leeks. Cook until bottom of omelet is golden, 1 to 2 minutes; using pancake turner, carefully turn omelet over. Cook other side just until set, about 1 minute; transfer to serving platter and keep warm. Repeat procedure; garnish omelets with tomatoes and parsley.

MAKES 4 SERVINGS

Each serving provides: 1 Protein Exchange; 2⅛ Vegetable Exchanges;
   ½ Milk Exchange
Per serving: 185 calories; 12 g protein; 6 g fat; 22 g carbohydrate; 232 mg
   calcium; 427 mg sodium; 276 mg cholesterol

*Francis John Marone
Bridgeton, New Jersey*

Omelet Delicious ⊙◑

Experimentation led Donna to create this Cheddary egg dish. It's a Sunday evening favorite in the Allen household, but it also makes a wonderful brunch or lunch.

2 eggs
2 tablespoons water
¼ teaspoon salt
Dash pepper
1 teaspoon margarine
1 tablespoon *each* diced
  green bell pepper and diced
  onion
½ cup chopped mushrooms
1 ounce sharp Cheddar
  cheese, shredded

Using a wire whisk, in small bowl beat together eggs, water, salt, and pepper. In 9-inch skillet heat margarine until bubbly and hot; add egg mixture to skillet and immediately sprinkle bell pepper and onion onto half of omelet. When egg mixture is partially set, sprinkle mushrooms over onion mixture and cook until bottom of omelet is lightly browned and firm; using spatula, fold omelet in half. Sprinkle with cheese; remove from heat, cover, and let stand until cheese is partially melted, about 1 minute.

MAKES 1 SERVING

Each serving provides: 3 Protein Exchanges; 1¼ Vegetable Exchanges; 1 Fat
    Exchange
Per serving: 320 calories; 20 g protein; 25 g fat; 4 g carbohydrate; 271 mg
    calcium; 901 mg sodium; 578 mg cholesterol

Donna J. Allen
Rochester, Minnesota

Oriental Omelet ◑

Sesame oil adds flavor to this simple but delicious Chinese-style omelet.

4 eggs, beaten
¼ cup *each* **chopped red bell pepper, chopped scallions (green onions), and bean sprouts**
2 tablespoons water
1½ teaspoons soy sauce*
½ packet (about ½ teaspoon) instant chicken broth and seasoning mix
1 teaspoon Chinese sesame oil

Preheat oven to 400°F. In medium mixing bowl combine eggs, pepper, scallions, bean sprouts, water, soy sauce, and broth mix.

In 9-inch skillet that has a metal or removable handle heat oil over medium heat *(do not let oil smoke)*; add egg mixture and cook until underside is set, about 1 minute. Transfer skillet to oven and bake until top of omelet is set and golden brown, 8 to 10 minutes.

MAKES 2 SERVINGS

Each serving provides: 2 Protein Exchanges; ¾ Vegetable Exchange; ½ Fat Exchange; 3 calories Optional Exchange
Per serving: 194 calories; 13 g protein; 14 g fat; 4 g carbohydrate; 70 mg calcium; 680 mg sodium; 548 mg cholesterol

*Reduced-sodium soy sauce may be substituted. Reduce calories to 193, calcium to 66 mg, and sodium to 500 mg.

Weight Watchers Kitchens

Tomato-Cheese Strata

Similar to lasagna but without the noodles, this strata recipe is one that Andrea likes to prepare for herself and her husband. Andrea is a hand-weaver and works as a seamstress in a bridal shop.

2 teaspoons vegetable oil
½ cup *each* finely chopped carrot, chopped green bell pepper, chopped onion, and diced zucchini
2 cups drained canned Italian tomatoes, seeded and diced
1 tablespoon chopped fresh parsley
1 teaspoon *each* garlic powder, basil leaves, and salt
½ teaspoon pepper
1 cup part-skim ricotta cheese
1 egg
2 ounces mozzarella cheese, shredded

Preheat oven to 350°F. In 10-inch nonstick skillet heat oil over medium heat; add carrot, green pepper, onion, and zucchini and sauté until vegetables are softened, 1 to 2 minutes. Add tomatoes, parsley, garlic, basil, salt, and pepper and cook, stirring occasionally, until vegetables are thoroughly cooked and mixture thickens, 5 to 8 minutes. Transfer mixture to 9-inch pie plate and spread in an even layer; set aside.

In blender container combine ricotta cheese and egg and process until smooth, scraping down sides of container as necessary. Spread cheese mixture in an even layer over vegetable mixture; sprinkle with mozzarella cheese. Bake until strata is puffed and lightly browned, 25 to 30 minutes; remove from oven and let stand 5 minutes before cutting.

MAKES 4 SERVINGS

Each serving provides: 1½ Protein Exchanges; 2 Vegetable Exchanges; ½ Fat Exchange; 20 calories Optional Exchange
Per serving: 211 calories; 13 g protein; .12 g fat; 14 g carbohydrate; 305 mg calcium; 900 mg sodium; 99 mg cholesterol

Andrea D. Marshall
Coventry, Connecticut

Ham and Cheese Strata

The Weight Watchers program has helped her change the way she eats, says Barbara, who has lost over 25 pounds. She prepares this dish for her family for Sunday brunch.

8 slices reduced-calorie white bread (40 calories per slice), toasted and cut into cubes
4 ounces turkey-ham (100% turkey), cut into thin strips
2 ounces Cheddar cheese, shredded
2 cups skim milk
2 eggs

Preheat oven to 350°F. Spray 9-inch pie plate with nonstick cooking spray. Arrange bread cubes in a single layer over bottom and up sides of pie plate; top evenly with turkey-ham and sprinkle evenly with cheese.

In small bowl beat together milk and eggs and pour into pie plate. Bake for 45 to 55 minutes (until strata is puffed and lightly browned and a knife, inserted in center, comes out clean). Remove strata from oven and let stand 10 minutes before cutting.

MAKES 4 SERVINGS

Each serving provides: 2 Protein Exchanges; 1 Bread Exchange; ½ Milk Exchange
Per serving: 256 calories; 20 g protein; 9 g fat; 24 g carbohydrate; 310 mg calcium; 658 mg sodium; 154 mg cholesterol

Barbara J. Jones
Parma, Ohio

Bacon 'n' Egg Casserole

To make this a do-ahead dish, Connie suggests you prepare it up to the point of baking, then cover and refrigerate it overnight. In the morning you can just bake it as directed and you'll have a wonderful brunch dish.

**2 slices white bread, toasted
and cut into cubes
4 ounces Swiss *or* Cheddar
cheese, shredded
4 ounces sliced Canadian-
style bacon, cut into ½-inch
squares, divided
2 cups skim milk
4 eggs
½ teaspoon *each* salt and
prepared mustard
⅛ teaspoon *each* onion
powder and pepper**

Preheat oven to 350°F. Spray an 8 x 8 x 2-inch baking pan with nonstick cooking spray. Arrange bread cubes over bottom of pan, sprinkle with cheese, and top with 2 ounces bacon.

In medium mixing bowl beat together milk, eggs, and seasonings; pour egg mixture into pan and sprinkle with remaining 2 ounces bacon. Bake for 45 to 50 minutes (until top is browned and a knife, inserted in center, comes out clean).

MAKES 4 SERVINGS

Each serving provides: 3 Protein Exchanges; ½ Bread Exchange; ½ Milk Exchange
Per serving with Swiss cheese: 306 calories; 25 g protein; 16 g fat; 14 g carbohydrate; 466 mg calcium; 948 mg sodium; 317 mg cholesterol
With Cheddar cheese: 314 calories; 24 g protein; 18 g fat; 14 g carbohydrate; 398 mg calcium; 1,050 mg sodium; 321 mg cholesterol

*Connie Enerson
Hettinger, North Dakota*

❖❖

Cheddar-Egg Stuffed Biscuit

Pat manages a lunch program for a school district, and, naturally, loves to cook. She created this recipe especially for herself. Pat is married, and has three sons and one grandchild.

2 tablespoons chopped green
 bell pepper
1 tablespoon *each* chopped
 onion and celery
1 egg, beaten, divided
1 teaspoon imitation bacon
 bits
1 ready-to-bake refrigerated
 buttermilk flaky biscuit
 (1 ounce); keep refrigerated
 until ready to use
½ ounce Cheddar cheese,
 shredded

Preheat oven to 350°F. Spray 8-inch non-stick skillet with nonstick cooking spray and heat; add bell pepper, onion, and celery and cook over medium heat, stirring occasionally, until vegetables are softened, 1 to 2 minutes. Remove 1 teaspoon beaten egg to small cup; cover cup with plastic wrap and set aside. Pour remaining egg into skillet and cook, stirring constantly, until egg is set, about 1 minute. Sprinkle with bacon bits; remove from heat and set aside.

Carefully separate biscuit into 2 thin layers of dough and roll each between 2 sheets of wax paper, forming two 6-inch circles. Using a 5-inch round cookie cutter, cut each circle into a smaller circle, reserving scraps. Sprinkle cheese onto center of 1 circle and top with egg mixture. Place remaining dough circle over filling; crimp edges of dough to seal and fold under biscuit. Use scraps of dough to decorate biscuit.

Spray nonstick baking sheet with nonstick cooking spray and place stuffed biscuit on sheet; using pastry brush, brush biscuit with reserved teaspoon egg. Bake until golden brown, 8 to 10 minutes.

MAKES 1 SERVING

Each serving provides: 1½ Protein Exchanges; 1 Bread Exchange; ½ Vegetable Exchange; 10 calories Optional Exchange
Per serving: 237 calories; 12 g protein; 14 g fat; 15 g carbohydrate; 141 mg calcium; 552 mg sodium; 289 mg cholesterol

Pat Young
Basehor, Kansas

Cheddar-Parmesan Eggs ◐

Jane loves to cook, so she created this recipe to make a wonderful brunch dish. Jane, a part-time nurse, is the mother of two young children.

¼ cup reduced-calorie margarine (tub)
⅓ cup all-purpose flour
1 teaspoon salt
½ teaspoon pepper
2 cups hot water
4 ounces Cheddar cheese, shredded
½ cup skim milk
2 packets instant chicken broth and seasoning mix
1 tablespoon Worcestershire sauce
12 eggs, hard-cooked and cut lengthwise into halves
2 ounces grated Parmesan cheese

In 2-quart saucepan heat margarine over medium heat until bubbly and hot; add flour, salt, and pepper and cook, stirring constantly, for 1 minute. Gradually stir in hot water and cook, stirring constantly, until mixture comes to a boil. Reduce heat to low; add Cheddar cheese, milk, and broth mix and let simmer, stirring constantly, until cheese is melted. Remove from heat and stir in Worcestershire sauce; set aside.

Preheat oven to 350°F. In shallow baking dish that is large enough to hold egg halves in a single layer, arrange eggs, cut-side down; pour sauce over eggs and sprinkle with Parmesan cheese. Bake until eggs are heated through and sauce is bubbly, 15 to 20 minutes.

MAKES 6 SERVINGS

Each serving provides: 3 Protein Exchanges; 1 Fat Exchange; 40 calories Optional Exchange
Per serving: 349 calories; 23 g protein; 24 g fat; 9 g carbohydrate; 352 mg calcium; 1,194 mg sodium; 576 mg cholesterol

VARIATION:

Use a shallow flameproof baking dish. After baking, set oven control to broil and broil until cheese is golden brown, 1 to 2 minutes.

Jane P. Epping
Davenport, Iowa

❖·❖

Turkey Sausage ⊙ ◑

The source of Helen's recipe was her father. The original recipe called for pork, but Helen substituted turkey, and the result is a fast-and-easy dish she serves to her family for breakfast. Helen is a project manager for the San Francisco Redevelopment Agency.

2¼ pounds ground turkey
1½ teaspoons salt
1¼ teaspoons pepper
1 teaspoon ground sage
¾ teaspoon ground ginger
¼ teaspoon ground red
    pepper

In large mixing bowl thoroughly combine all ingredients. Divide mixture into twelve 3-ounce portions and shape each portion into a patty or link (or shape some into patties and some into links).*

Spray a nonstick griddle with nonstick cooking spray and heat. Add sausages and cook, turning, until browned on all sides and cooked throughout.

MAKES 12 SAUSAGE PATTIES (OR LINKS)

*Uncooked sausage patties (or links) may be frozen for future use. Shape, wrap in moisture- and vapor-resistant wrap such as freezer paper, heavy-duty foil, or plastic wrap, and freeze.

To cook sausages while still frozen, spray a skillet with nonstick cooking spray (skillet should be large enough to hold sausages in a single layer); add 1 tablespoon water to skillet and bring to a boil. Add frozen sausages, cover, and cook until water evaporates, about 2 minutes. Remove cover and cook, turning until browned on all sides and cooked throughout.

Each patty (or link) provides: 2 Protein Exchanges
Per serving: 129 calories; 15 g protein; 7 g fat; 0.3 g carbohydrate; 20 mg
    calcium; 340 mg sodium; 52 mg cholesterol

Helen Sause
Alameda, California

Tomato-Cheese Toast ☕◑

Looking for an unusual breakfast idea? Try Gladys's original recipe for a real change of pace. Gladys is a community health nurse whose leisure activities include boating, cross-country skiing, knitting, reading, and gardening.

1 slice whole wheat bread, toasted
½ medium tomato, thinly sliced
⅓ cup cottage cheese
½ teaspoon *each* chopped basil leaves, salt, and pepper

Set toast on plate and arrange tomato slices on toast; top with cheese and sprinkle with seasonings.

MAKES 1 SERVING

Each serving provides: 1 Protein Exchange; 1 Bread Exchange; 1 Vegetable Exchange
Per serving: 157 calories; 12 g protein; 4 g fat; 19 g carbohydrate; 102 mg calcium; 1,529 mg sodium; 11 mg cholesterol

VARIATION:

Omit basil, salt, and pepper. Combine cottage cheese with 1 tablespoon finely chopped scallion (green onion). Arrange tomato slices on toast; top with cheese mixture and sprinkle with dash paprika. Increase Vegetable Exchange to 1⅛ Exchanges.

Per serving: 154 calories; 12 g protein; 4 g fat; 18 g carbohydrate; 78 mg calcium; 435 mg sodium; 11 mg cholesterol

Gladys Rowlett
Kelowna, British Columbia, Canada

Arabian Pocket Bread ⊙

An Egyptian friend gave this recipe to Theodosia when she lived in Wyoming. This traditional Middle Eastern bread is easy to make, and everyone will enjoy it. Theodosia enjoys quilting when she's not busy caring for her six children.

1 packet fast-rising active
   dry yeast
1¼ cups warm water (see
   yeast package directions
   for temperature)
½ teaspoon granulated sugar
4½ cups all-purpose flour,
   divided
2 tablespoons vegetable oil
1 teaspoon salt

Spray large bowl with nonstick cooking spray; set aside. In another large bowl sprinkle yeast over water; add sugar and stir. Let stand until mixture becomes foamy, about 5 minutes; add 1 cup flour, the oil, and salt. Using electric mixer at low speed, beat until combined, 1 to 2 minutes. Stir in all but 2 tablespoons flour, mixing well. Using remaining 2 tablespoons flour, flour work surface; knead dough on floured surface until smooth and elastic, about 5 minutes. Form into ball and place in sprayed bowl; cover with plastic wrap and let stand in warm, draft-free place until doubled in volume, 45 to 60 minutes. Remove dough from bowl and punch down. Cut into 16 equal pieces and shape each into a ball.

Preheat oven to 450°F. Using rolling pin, roll balls into circles, each about 5 inches in diameter; set on nonstick baking sheet, leaving about 2 inches between each. Bake until golden brown, 5 to 7 minutes. Remove breads to wire rack; let cool at least 5 minutes.

MAKES 16 SERVINGS, 1 POCKET EACH

Each serving provides: 1½ Bread Exchanges; 15 calories Optional Exchange
Per serving: 145 calories; 4 g protein; 2 g fat; 27 g carbohydrate; 7 mg calcium; 138 mg sodium; 0 mg cholesterol

Theodosia Ann Peters
Mt. Pleasant, Michigan

Banana-Date Muffins

A busy mother of six, Huguette has lost over 50 pounds. She does bookkeeping for her husband, a truck driver. These muffins are her creation and are very easy to make.

2 cups plus 1 tablespoon
   all-purpose flour
2 tablespoons double-acting
   baking powder
¾ teaspoon ground cinnamon
½ teaspoon salt
½ cup *each* granulated sugar
   and reduced-calorie
   margarine (tub)
1 egg
1 teaspoon vanilla extract
3 medium bananas, peeled
   and mashed
¾ ounce ready-to-eat wheat
   bran flake cereal
12 pitted dates, diced

Preheat oven to 400°F. Onto sheet of wax paper or a paper plate sift together flour, baking powder, cinnamon, and salt; set aside.

In medium mixing bowl combine sugar, margarine, egg, and vanilla and, using electric mixer, beat until light and fluffy. Add bananas and stir to combine; add flour mixture and beat until well blended. Stir in cereal and dates. Spray twelve 2½-inch-diameter muffin-pan cups with nonstick cooking spray; fill each cup with an equal amount of batter (each will be about ⅔ full). Bake for 20 to 25 minutes (until muffins are lightly browned and a toothpick, inserted in center, comes out dry). Remove muffins to wire rack to cool.

MAKES 12 SERVINGS, 1 MUFFIN EACH

Each serving provides: 1 Bread Exchange; 1 Fat Exchange; 1 Fruit Exchange; 45 calories Optional Exchange
Per serving: 208 calories; 3 g protein; 5 g fat; 39 g carbohydrate; 119 mg calcium; 407 mg sodium; 23 mg cholesterol

Huguette Weber
St. Isidore, Ontario, Canada

Oatmeal 'n' Raisin Muffins ©

Marsha is a busy homemaker who enjoys crafts, sewing, music, reading, and cooking. She and her husband turned one of their favorite snacks, oatmeal cookies, into a muffin they could enjoy while following the Food Plan.

1 cup plus 2 tablespoons all-purpose flour
2 teaspoons double-acting baking powder
¼ teaspoon *each* ground cinnamon and salt
¼ cup *each* margarine, firmly packed brown sugar, and granulated sugar
1 egg
1 cup skim milk
4½ ounces uncooked quick *or* old-fashioned oats
¾ cup dark raisins

Preheat oven to 375°F. Line twelve 2½-inch-diameter muffin-pan cups with paper baking cups and set aside.

In small bowl combine flour, baking powder, cinnamon, and salt; set aside. Using electric mixer, in mixing bowl cream margarine with sugars until light and fluffy; add egg and beat until combined. Alternately beat in flour mixture and milk, a little of each at a time, beating well after each addition. Stir in oats and raisins. Fill each baking cup with an equal amount of batter (each will be about ⅔ full). Bake for 20 to 25 minutes (until muffins are lightly browned and a toothpick, inserted in center, comes out dry). Remove muffins to wire rack to cool.

MAKES 12 SERVINGS, 1 MUFFIN EACH

Each serving provides: 1 Bread Exchange; 1 Fat Exchange; ½ Fruit Exchange; 55 calories Optional Exchange
Per serving: 192 calories; 4 g protein; 5 g fat; 33 g carbohydrate; 81 mg calcium; 180 mg sodium; 23 mg cholesterol

Marsha M. Williams
Post Falls, Idaho

Orange-Bran Muffins ⓒ

Loretta is a cook at a well-known Minneapolis deli, where her recipes are often used. In her spare time she enjoys crafts, folk-art painting, redecorating, and gardening. Her muffin recipe is an old favorite, revised to fit the Food Plan.

1½ cups all-purpose flour
½ teaspoon *each* double-acting baking powder and baking soda
¼ teaspoon salt
2 eggs
¼ cup vegetable oil
2 tablespoons granulated sugar
1 tablespoon firmly packed dark brown sugar
1 teaspoon grated orange peel
¾ cup buttermilk
3 ounces ready-to-eat wheat bran flake cereal
¾ cup golden raisins

Preheat oven to 350°F. Onto sheet of wax paper or a paper plate sift together flour, baking powder, baking soda, and salt; set aside. Using electric mixer, in medium mixing bowl combine eggs, oil, sugars, and orange peel, beating until smooth; alternately add flour mixture and buttermilk, a little of each at a time, stirring after each addition until thoroughly combined. Add cereal and raisins and stir to combine. Spray twelve 2½-inch-diameter muffin-pan cups with nonstick cooking spray. Fill each with an equal amount of batter (each will be about ⅔ full). Bake for 25 to 30 minutes (until muffins are lightly browned and a toothpick, inserted in center, comes out dry). Remove muffins to wire rack and let cool for at least 10 minutes before serving.

MAKES 12 SERVINGS, 1 MUFFIN EACH

Each serving provides: 1 Bread Exchange; 1 Fat Exchange; ½ Fruit Exchange; 35 calories Optional Exchange
Per serving: 179 calories; 4 g protein; 6 g fat; 29 g carbohydrate; 43 mg calcium; 192 mg sodium; 46 mg cholesterol

Loretta Lundy
Minneapolis, Minnesota

❖❖❖

Chocolate-Peanut Butter Bar

Marion's sweet-and-chewy bar is great for a fast-and-easy breakfast or as a delicious snack. Born in the United Kingdom, Marion has attended Weight Watchers meetings on both sides of the Atlantic. She feels that no matter where you go in the world, when you are at a Weight Watchers meeting you are among friends.

2 tablespoons black coffee or water (hot)
1 tablespoon chunky peanut butter
1 packet (1 serving) reduced-calorie chocolate dairy drink mix
¾ ounce uncooked old-fashioned oats
2 tablespoons dark raisins

Using a fork, in small mixing bowl combine coffee (or water) and peanut butter, mixing until peanut butter is softened; add remaining ingredients and mix thoroughly (mixture will be stiff and sticky). Transfer mixture to sheet of wax paper or plastic wrap and, using hands, press mixture together and shape into a log about 5 inches long and 1½ inches wide. Tightly wrap log in the wax paper (or plastic wrap) and freeze overnight.

MAKES 1 SERVING

Each serving provides: 1 Protein Exchange; 1 Bread Exchange; 1 Fat Exchange; 1 Fruit Exchange; 1 Milk Exchange
Per serving with coffee: 302 calories; 15 g protein; 11 g fat; 42 g carbohydrate; 226 mg calcium; 79 mg sodium; 0 mg cholesterol
If coffee is not used, reduce calories to 301 and calcium to 225 mg.

SERVING SUGGESTION:

For a softer bar, remove from freezer about 1 hour before serving and store in refrigerator.

Marion J. Findlay
Bellerose, New York

Simply Bananas ◐

Leona loves fruit and grows her own alfalfa sprouts, so this unusual combination came naturally. Because she works nights in a nursing home, Leona enjoys having this fast, easy, and delicious dish when she gets home.

½ small orange (unpeeled)
1½ cups shredded lettuce
¼ cup alfalfa sprouts
⅓ cup cottage cheese
½ medium banana, peeled and
  sliced
1 teaspoon sunflower seed

Using a vegetable peeler or a zester, remove 2 thin strips of orange peel from orange; set aside for garnish. Over bowl to catch juices, remove remaining peel and section orange; set sections and juice aside.

Line salad plate with shredded lettuce; arrange sprouts in center and top with a scoop of cottage cheese. Surround cottage cheese with banana slices and orange sections. Sprinkle cheese and fruit with reserved juice from orange, then with sunflower seed; garnish with reserved orange peel.

MAKES 1 SERVING

Each serving provides: 1 Protein Exchange; 3½ Vegetable Exchanges; 1½ Fruit Exchanges; 20 calories Optional Exchange
Per serving: 187 calories; 12 g protein; 5 g fat; 26 g carbohydrate; 135 mg calcium; 289 mg sodium; 10 mg cholesterol

Leona W. Gaunya
South Berwick, Maine

✧✧✧

Vanilla Yogurt Crunch ❿

Debra is a writer whose poetry and fiction have been published. She feels that being on the Weight Watchers program has given her a great deal of motivation. Her yogurt dish is delicious with breakfast or as a snack and is easy to prepare.

1 envelope unflavored gelatin
1 cup boiling water
2 cups plain low-fat yogurt
Granulated low-calorie
**   sweetener with aspartame**
**   to equal 10 teaspoons sugar**
2 teaspoons vanilla extract
3 ounces ready-to-eat crunchy
**   nutlike cereal nuggets**

In 1-quart heatproof bowl sprinkle gelatin over water; stir until gelatin is dissolved. Stir in yogurt, sweetener, and vanilla and, using a wire whisk, beat until smooth, about 1 minute; divide into 4 serving dishes, cover, and refrigerate until set, about 1 hour. Just before serving, sprinkle each portion with ¾ ounce cereal nuggets.

MAKES 4 SERVINGS, ABOUT ¾ CUP EACH

Each serving provides: 1 Bread Exchange; 1 Milk Exchange
Per serving: 166 calories; 11 g protein; 2 g fat; 26 g carbohydrate; 216 mg
    calcium; 229 mg sodium; 7 mg cholesterol

Debra Frigen Monroe
Manhattan, Kansas

Breakfast in a Glass—I ⊙◑

Beth's search for an easy-to-prepare, fast, and delicious breakfast led to these two frothy creations. A Weight Watchers leader who lost 137 pounds, Beth enjoys dancing and singing.

½ cup *each* plain low-fat
   yogurt and orange juice
   (no sugar added)
1 egg
1 teaspoon honey
¼ teaspoon vanilla extract
Granulated low-calorie
   sweetener with aspartame
   to equal 1 teaspoon sugar
3 to 4 ice cubes

In blender container combine all ingredients except ice cubes and process until smooth; with motor running, add ice cubes, 1 at a time, processing for a few seconds after each addition. Continue processing until mixture is smooth and thickened.

MAKES 1 SERVING

Each serving provides: 1 Protein Exchange; 1 Fruit Exchange; 1 Milk
   Exchange; 20 calories Optional Exchange
Per serving: 234 calories; 13 g protein; 7 g fat; 28 g carbohydrate; 247 mg
   calcium; 150 mg sodium; 281 mg cholesterol

Beth Gaines
Nashville, Tennessee

Breakfast in a Glass—II ⊙◑

1 egg
½ medium banana, peeled
½ cup skim milk
1 teaspoon wheat germ
½ teaspoon honey
¼ teaspoon vanilla extract
Granulated low-calorie
   sweetener with aspartame
   to equal 1 teaspoon sugar
3 to 4 ice cubes

In blender container combine all ingredients except ice cubes and process until smooth; with motor running add ice cubes, 1 at a time, processing for a few seconds after each addition. Continue processing until mixture is smooth and thickened.

MAKES 1 SERVING

Each serving provides: 1 Protein Exchange; 1 Fruit Exchange; ½ Milk
   Exchange; 20 calories Optional Exchange
Per serving: 200 calories; 12 g protein; 6 g fat; 24 g carbohydrate; 183 mg
   calcium; 134 mg sodium; 276 mg cholesterol

Beth Gaines
Nashville, Tennessee

To Whet Your Appetite
Appetizers,
Hors d'Oeuvres,
and Soups

Fruit Appetizer

This refreshing first course is a favorite at family dinners. Karann, a dietary supervisor at a hospital, adapted it from a friend's recipe.

1 tablespoon plus 1½ tea-
   spoons uncooked pearl
   tapioca
Dash salt
½ cup *each* water and orange
   juice (no sugar added)
⅓ cup pineapple juice
   (no sugar added)
1 cup strawberries, cut into
   halves
2 medium peaches, blanched,
   peeled, pitted, and sliced
2 small oranges, peeled and
   sectioned
2 small apples, cored, pared,
   and diced
⅛ medium pineapple, pared
   and diced

In small saucepan combine tapioca and salt; add water and bring to a boil. Reduce heat to medium-low and let simmer, stirring frequently, until tapioca turns clear, 10 to 15 minutes. Add orange juice and pineapple juice and stir to combine; remove from heat and set aside.

In medium bowl combine strawberries, peaches, oranges, apples, and pineapple; pour tapioca mixture over fruits and mix well. Cover with plastic wrap and refrigerate until chilled, at least 1 hour.

MAKES 8 SERVINGS

Each serving provides: 1 Fruit Exchange; 20 calories Optional Exchange
Per serving: 66 calories; 1 g protein; 0.2 g fat; 16 g carbohydrate; 21 mg
   calcium; 17 mg sodium; 0 mg cholesterol

Karann Hessing
Oskaloosa, Iowa

Beefy Tomato Warmer ⊝◑

Donna's ready-in-a-jiffy soup is great for those chilly days when you want something more than just tea or coffee. A full-time homemaker and mother, Donna enjoys needlework and cooking.

1 cup *each* tomato juice
   and water
1 packet instant beef broth
   and seasoning mix
1 teaspoon Worcestershire
   sauce
¼ teaspoon basil leaves

In 1-quart saucepan combine all ingredients and bring to a boil. Reduce heat to low, cover, and let simmer until flavors are blended, 2 to 3 minutes.

MAKES 2 SERVINGS

Each serving provides: 30 calories Optional Exchange
Per serving: 29 calories; 2 g protein; 1 g fat; 7 g carbohydrate; 15 mg
   calcium; 841 mg sodium; 0 mg cholesterol

Donna J. Allen
Rochester, Minnesota

Cauliflower Soup ©

Cindy and her mom collaborated to create this soup. Although it's a great winter-time warmer, you can have it in any season since the ingredients are available year round.

½ cup chopped onion
3 ounces pared potato, diced
1 cup *each* water and
   skim milk
1 tablespoon plus 1 teaspoon
   all-purpose flour
1 teaspoon salt (optional)
Dash *each* white pepper
   and ground nutmeg
1 cup frozen cauliflower,
   cooked until tender-crisp
2 ounces American cheese,
   diced
1 tablespoon chopped fresh
   parsley

In 2-quart saucepan combine onion and potato; add water, cover pan, and bring liquid to a boil. Cook over high heat until potato is tender-crisp, 5 to 7 minutes.

In small bowl combine milk and flour, stirring until flour is dissolved. Stir milk mixture into potato mixture; add salt if desired, pepper, and nutmeg and mix well. Reduce heat to medium and cook uncovered, stirring occasionally, until liquid is smooth and thick, 5 to 10 minutes. Add cauliflower, cheese, and parsley to saucepan; cook, stirring occasionally, until cheese is melted and cauliflower is cooked through, 2 to 3 minutes.

MAKES 2 SERVINGS

Each serving provides: 1 Protein Exchange; ½ Bread Exchange; 1½ Vegetable Exchanges; ½ Milk Exchange; 20 calories Optional Exchange
Per serving without salt: 253 calories; 14 g protein; 10 g fat; 29 g carbohydrate; 375 mg calcium; 524 mg sodium; 29 mg cholesterol
If salt is used, increase calcium to 382 mg and sodium to 1,590 mg.

Cindy Howland
Pittsfield, Maryland

Chicken and Escarole Soup ⓒ

Mary's Italian-style variation on that old standard, chicken soup, is a hearty broth loaded with chicken, vegetables, and noodles. Her family and friends love it — you will, too!

8 ounces skinned and boned chicken breasts
1½ quarts water
4 packets instant chicken broth and seasoning mix
2 cups diced carrots
1 cup diced celery
½ cup chopped onion
3 cups chopped escarole
1½ ounces uncooked noodles (medium width)
1 tablespoon chopped fresh parsley
Dash pepper

In 4-quart saucepan combine chicken with water and broth mix; bring to a boil. Reduce heat to low, cover, and let simmer for 20 minutes. Using a slotted spoon, remove chicken from liquid to work surface; dice chicken and set aside. Add carrots, celery, and onion to saucepan, cover, and cook over medium heat for 10 minutes. Return chicken to saucepan; add remaining ingredients and cook until noodles are tender, 8 to 10 minutes.

MAKES 4 SERVINGS

Each serving provides: 1½ Protein Exchanges; ½ Bread Exchange; 3¼ Vegetable Exchanges; 10 calories Optional Exchange
Per serving: 156 calories; 17 g protein; 1 g fat; 19 g carbohydrate; 61 mg calcium; 925 mg sodium; 43 mg cholesterol

VARIATION:

1 cup hot cooked long-grain rice may be substituted for the noodles. Do not add rice with remaining ingredients. Cook escarole mixture until hot, 8 to 10 minutes; add rice and stir to combine. Serve immediately.

Per serving: 170 calories; 17 g protein; 1 g fat; 23 g carbohydrate; 63 mg calcium; 925 mg sodium; 33 mg cholesterol

Mary Theresa Basso
Bronx, New York

Cream of Mushroom Soup

Nancy, the mother of two teenagers, works in a school library, and is also a receptionist at Weight Watchers meetings. Her hearty soup is chock full of chunky vegetables. Savor its creamy goodness soon!

2 cups chopped cauliflower
1 cup water
¼ cup *each* sliced carrot, sliced celery, and chopped onion
1 packet instant chicken broth and seasoning mix
1 cup skim milk
1 tablespoon plus 1 teaspoon reduced-calorie margarine (tub)
2 cups sliced mushrooms
1 garlic clove, minced
1 tablespoon chopped fresh parsley

In 2½-quart saucepan combine cauliflower, water, carrot, celery, onion, and broth mix and bring to a boil. Reduce heat to low and let simmer until vegetables are tender, about 15 minutes. Remove from heat, add milk, and stir to combine.

Pour half of vegetable mixture into blender container and process until smooth. Transfer mixture to 2-quart bowl and repeat procedure with remaining vegetable mixture; set aside.

In 2½-quart saucepan heat margarine over medium heat until bubbly and hot; add mushrooms and garlic and sauté until lightly browned. Add pureed vegetable mixture and parsley to mushrooms and cook, stirring occasionally, until mixture is thoroughly heated, 2 to 3 minutes.

MAKES 4 SERVINGS

Each serving provides: 2¼ Vegetable Exchanges; ½ Fat Exchange; ¼ Milk Exchange; 3 calories Optional Exchange
Per serving: 70 calories; 4 g protein; 2 g fat; 9 g carbohydrate; 101 mg calcium; 299 mg sodium; 1 mg cholesterol

Nancy Sanders
Youngstown, Ohio

Creamy Vegetable-Beef Soup ☉

Sharon's sister, who lives in Honolulu, sent her this recipe, which they then altered to fit the Food Plan. Sharon, who lost over 40 pounds on the Weight Watchers program, is a kindergarten teacher whose interests include crafts and archaeology.

½ cup *each* chopped onion
   and diced celery
2 garlic cloves, minced
1 can (16 ounces) French-style
   green beans, undrained
   (about 1½ cups)
1½ cups tomato juice
1¼ cups canned ready-to-
   serve beef broth
½ cup sliced carrot
1 bay leaf
1 teaspoon curry powder
½ teaspoon salt
Dash pepper
1 cup skim milk

Spray 3-quart saucepan with nonstick cooking spray and heat over medium heat; add onion, celery, and garlic and cook, stirring occasionally, until vegetables are softened, 1 to 2 minutes. Stir in remaining ingredients except milk; bring to a boil. Reduce heat to low, cover, and let simmer until carrots are tender, 15 to 20 minutes; remove from heat and let cool 5 to 10 minutes. Remove and discard bay leaf.

Pour half of mixture into blender container and process at low speed until smooth; transfer mixture to 1½-quart bowl and process remaining soup. Pour soup back into saucepan; add milk and cook over low heat, stirring occasionally, until soup is thoroughly heated, 3 to 5 minutes (*do not boil*).

MAKES 4 SERVINGS, ABOUT 1¼ CUPS EACH

Each serving provides: 1½ Vegetable Exchanges; ¼ Milk Exchange; 30 calories Optional Exchange
Per serving: 81 calories; 5 g protein; 1 g fat; 16 g carbohydrate; 134 mg calcium; 1,362 mg sodium; 1 mg cholesterol

Sharon Marshall
Danville, Virginia

Hearty Kidney Bean Soup

Peggy created this filling soup to use up leftovers—and her family really goes for it. Peggy, a CPA and a mother, enjoys sewing, skiing, and horseback riding.

9 ounces sorted uncooked red kidney beans or white kidney (cannellini) beans, rinsed
2 quarts water, divided
4 cups canned crushed tomatoes
1 cup *each* diced carrots, celery, and onions
¼ cup chopped fresh Italian (flat-leaf) parsley
2 packets instant chicken broth and seasoning mix
1 large garlic clove, minced
2 cups shredded green cabbage
½ cup dry white table wine
1 teaspoon salt
¼ teaspoon pepper

In large bowl combine beans and 1 quart water; cover and let stand overnight.

Drain beans, discarding soaking liquid. In 4-quart saucepan combine beans and remaining 1 quart water and bring to a boil; add tomatoes, carrots, celery, onions, parsley, broth mix, and garlic. Reduce heat and let simmer, stirring occasionally, until beans are tender, 1 to 1½ hours. Add remaining ingredients and let simmer 30 minutes longer.

MAKES 8 SERVINGS

Each serving provides: 1½ Protein Exchanges; 2¼ Vegetable Exchanges; 20 calories Optional Exchange
Per serving: 169 calories; 9 g protein; 1 g fat; 30 g carbohydrate; 95 mg calcium; 705 mg sodium; 0 mg cholesterol

Peggy Hayes
Half Moon Bay, California

New England Clam Chowder ◖

Here's a slimmed-down version of Maureen's favorite soup. A bank teller and mother of two, Maureen enjoys doing needle crafts in her spare time.

2 teaspoons margarine
½ cup chopped onion
6 ounces pared potatoes,
   cut into ½-inch cubes
4 ounces drained canned
   clams, chopped (reserve
   ¼ cup liquid)
¾ cup water
1 cup skim milk
Dash *each* salt and white
   pepper

In 1-quart saucepan heat margarine until bubbly and hot; add onion and sauté until softened. Add potatoes, reserved clam liquid, and water and bring to a boil; cook until potatoes are tender, about 8 minutes. Stir in milk, clams, salt, and pepper and heat *(do not boil)*.

MAKES 2 SERVINGS

Each serving provides: 2 Protein Exchanges; 1 Bread Exchange; ½ Vegetable Exchange; 1 Fat Exchange; ½ Milk Exchange; 5 calories Optional Exchange
Per serving: 219 calories; 16 g protein; 6 g fat; 26 g carbohydrate; 200 mg calcium; 368 mg sodium; 41 mg cholesterol

Maureen A. West
Frankfort, New York

Peanut Butter Soup ⊙◐

A recipe for Indonesian peanut sauce inspired Dorothy to create this unusual vegetable soup with a peanut butter kick. Dorothy's a native New Yorker who enjoys sewing, cooking, and going to museums.

2 tablespoons *each* diced onion and celery
½ cup *each* canned ready-to-serve chicken *or* beef broth and water
1 tablespoon chunky peanut butter
3 medium tomatoes, blanched, peeled, seeded, and chopped
Dash *each* salt, pepper, and hot sauce

Spray small saucepan with nonstick cooking spray and heat; add onion and celery and cook, stirring frequently, for 2 minutes. Stir in broth, water, and peanut butter; bring mixture to a boil. Reduce heat; let simmer for 8 minutes. Add tomatoes, salt, and pepper and, stirring frequently, return mixture to a boil. Transfer to soup bowl, add hot sauce, and stir to combine.

MAKES 1 SERVING

Each serving provides: 1 Protein Exchange; 6½ Vegetable Exchanges; 1 Fat Exchange; 20 calories Optional Exchange
Per serving: 189 calories; 9 g protein; 9 g fat; 21 g carbohydrate; 46 mg calcium; 795 mg sodium; 0 mg cholesterol

SERVING SUGGESTION:

Serve with saltines or crispbread for a hearty start to a meal.

Dorothy Wisker
Whitestone, New York

Shrimp-Corn Chowder

Delores, a housewife and mother of two, loves to cook and travel. She recommends this creamy chowder with lunch or dinner.

6 ounces pared potatoes, diced
1½ cups boiling water
1 tablespoon plus 1 teaspoon reduced-calorie margarine (tub)
¼ cup chopped scallions (green onions)
2 garlic cloves, minced
2 cups skim milk
⅓ cup reduced-calorie creamed cheese spread
1 tablespoon minced fresh parsley
½ teaspoon salt
⅛ teaspoon thyme leaves, crushed
Dash white pepper
1 cup drained canned whole-kernel corn
5 ounces cooked shelled and deveined shrimp, cut into 1-inch pieces (reserve 4 whole shrimp, tails left on, for garnish)
Parsley sprigs

In 1-quart saucepan add potatoes to boiling water and cook over high heat until potatoes are fork-tender, 10 to 15 minutes. Remove from heat and let cool, reserving cooking liquid.

In 3-quart saucepan heat margarine over medium heat until bubbly and hot; add scallions and garlic and sauté until scallions are softened, about 1 minute. Remove from heat and set aside.

In blender container combine potatoes, cooking liquid, milk, and creamed cheese spread and process until smooth; add to scallion mixture along with minced parsley, salt, thyme, and pepper. Cook over medium heat until mixture comes just to a boil. Reduce heat to low and let simmer, stirring occasionally, until mixture is slightly thickened, 15 to 20 minutes. Stir in corn and shrimp pieces and continue cooking until shrimp are heated through, 2 to 3 minutes. Serve garnished with whole shrimp and parsley sprigs.

MAKES 4 SERVINGS

Each serving provides: 1½ Protein Exchanges; 1 Bread Exchange; ⅛ Vegetable Exchange; ½ Fat Exchange; ½ Milk Exchange; 5 calories Optional Exchange
Per serving: 191 calories; 17 g protein; 4 g fat; 23 g carbohydrate; 220 mg calcium; 473 mg sodium; 56 mg cholesterol*

*This figure does not include reduced-calorie creamed cheese spread; nutrition analysis not available.

Delores A. Peterson
Mahomet, Illinois

Versatile Lentil Soup ☻

Elaine lives in rural Ontario and enjoys cooking, painting, and cross-country skiing. She says this hearty soup is a delicious way to add fiber to your diet, and suggests freezing extra portions for future use.

4½ ounces sorted uncooked lentils, rinsed
1½ quarts water
1 cup diced carrots
½ cup *each* **diced celery, diced onion, diced zucchini, and sliced green beans**
4 packets instant beef broth and seasoning mix
2 garlic cloves, minced
¼ teaspoon pepper

In 4-quart saucepan combine lentils with water; bring to a boil. Reduce heat and let simmer for 20 minutes. Add remaining ingredients to lentils and stir to combine; cover and let simmer, stirring occasionally, until lentils and vegetables are tender, about 30 minutes longer.

MAKES 6 SERVINGS

Each serving provides: 1 Protein Exchange; 1 Vegetable Exchange; 5 calories Optional Exchange
Per serving: 99 calories; 7 g protein; 0.3 g fat; 18 g carbohydrate; 36 mg calcium; 520 mg sodium; 0 mg cholesterol

Elaine Douglas
Northbrook, Ontario, Canada

Deviled Eggs

Our chef suggests using a pastry bag fitted with a wide tip; a narrow one may clog. If you don't have a pastry bag, spoon the yolk mixture into the whites and, using the tip of a knife, create decorative swirls in the yolks.

4 eggs, hard-cooked and
    chilled
3 tablespoons whipped cream
    cheese
2 teaspoons mayonnaise
½ teaspoon salt
¼ to ½ teaspoon Dijon-style
    mustard
Dash white pepper
1 to 2 drops hot sauce
2 tablespoons minced scallion
    (green onion)
1 tablespoon finely chopped
    capers
Parsley sprigs (optional)

Cut eggs lengthwise into halves. Carefully remove yolks from egg halves to a small bowl and set whites aside; mash yolks. Add remaining ingredients except scallion, capers, and parsley and mix into a smooth paste; fold in scallion and capers.

Using a spoon or pastry bag fitted with a wide tip, fill each reserved white half with ⅛ of the yolk mixture. Arrange eggs on serving platter and, if desired, garnish with parsley; serve immediately or cover loosely and refrigerate until ready to serve.

MAKES 4 SERVINGS, 2 HALVES EACH

Each serving provides: 1 Protein Exchange; ½ Fat Exchange; 25 calories
  Optional Exchange
Per serving: 122 calories; 7 g protein; 10 g fat; 1 g carbohydrate; 38 mg
  calcium; 446 mg sodium; 283 mg cholesterol

Weight Watchers Kitchens

Bean Dip

This Mexican-style appetizer can be made mild or hot by adjusting the amount of jalapeño pepper. Serve with corn chips, melba rounds, or your favorite cracker.

2 teaspoons olive oil
¼ cup finely chopped green bell pepper
2 tablespoons finely chopped onion
1 garlic clove, minced
½ teaspoon seeded and minced drained canned jalapeño pepper
4 ounces drained canned pink beans *or* red kidney beans, mashed
¼ cup sour cream
5 large pitted black olives, chopped
½ teaspoon *each* chopped fresh cilantro (Chinese parsley) and salt

In 10-inch nonstick skillet heat oil over medium heat; add bell pepper, onion, garlic, and jalapeño pepper and sauté until vegetables are softened, 1 to 2 minutes. Add beans and cook, stirring frequently, until beans are thoroughly heated, 2 to 3 minutes. Transfer to small mixing bowl; add remaining ingredients and mix well. Transfer to serving dish; cover with plastic wrap and refrigerate until flavors are blended and mixture is well chilled, at least 30 minutes.

MAKES 4 SERVINGS

Each serving provides: ½ Protein Exchange; ⅛ Vegetable Exchange; ½ Fat Exchange; 40 calories Optional Exchange
Per serving: 97 calories; 3 g protein; 6 g fat; 8 g carbohydrate; 37 mg calcium; 511 mg sodium (estimated); 6 mg cholesterol

Weight Watchers Kitchens

Creamed Pimiento Cheese ◐

Mary is a high school history teacher and a girls' volleyball and track coach. She loves sports, sewing, and reading. She also loves to adapt recipes to fit the Food Plan, which is what she's done here with her delicious cheese spread.

⅔ cup reduced-calorie
   creamed cheese spread,
   softened
2 tablespoons *each* minced
   onion and green bell pepper
1 tablespoon *each* diced
   drained canned pimiento
   and reduced-calorie
   mayonnaise
2 teaspoons ketchup
1 egg, hard-cooked
   and chopped

Using a fork, in small bowl combine all ingredients, mixing until smooth. Cover and refrigerate until chilled.

MAKES 4 SERVINGS

Each serving provides: ½ Protein Exchange; ⅛ Vegetable Exchange; 45 calories Optional Exchange
Per serving: 76 calories; 7 g protein; 4 g fat; 3 g carbohydrate; 41 mg calcium; 163 mg sodium; 70 mg cholesterol*

*This figure does not include reduced-calorie creamed cheese spread; nutrition analysis not available.

SERVING SUGGESTION:

Serve as a spread on melba rounds, as a dip with crudités, or, for an attractive hors d'oeuvre, stuffed into celery ribs, cherry tomatoes, or Chinese snow peas (stem ends and strings removed).

Mary P. Echols
Bivins, Texas

Salmon Spread

Doris, a Weight Watchers leader who lost 50 pounds on Program, walks three miles a day. She enjoys cooking and collecting recipes and converting them to fit the Food Plan. This tasty spread can be prepared in advance, covered, and stored in the refrigerator for up to a week.

11 ounces skinned drained canned salmon, flaked
1 cup reduced-calorie creamed cheese spread
1 tablespoon *each* minced onion and lemon juice
1 teaspoon horseradish mustard *or* ½ teaspoon *each* prepared horseradish and prepared mustard
Dash salt (optional)
2 tablespoons finely chopped fresh parsley, thoroughly dried with paper towels
42 melba rounds

Using a fork, in medium mixing bowl thoroughly combine all ingredients except parsley and melba rounds. Cover with plastic wrap and refrigerate until chilled, about 1 hour.

Transfer salmon mixture to serving platter and form into a mound; using rubber scraper smooth sides and shape into a ball. Sprinkle parsley over surface of ball, pressing to adhere. Serve with melba rounds.

MAKES 14 SERVINGS

Each serving provides: 1 Protein Exchange; ½ Bread Exchange; 5 calories Optional Exchange
Per serving without salt: 85 calories; 8 g protein; 2 g fat; 8 g carbohydrate; 60 mg calcium; 126 mg sodium; 8 mg cholesterol*
If salt is used, increase to 136 mg.

*This figure does not include reduced-calorie creamed cheese spread; nutrition analysis not available.

SERVING SUGGESTION:

Try this spread on crispbread, as a dip for breadsticks, or as a tasty sandwich filling.

Doris M. Thesing
Lewiston, Minnesota

❖❖

Party Cheese-Nut Ball

Shaping the cheese ball will be easier if the mixture is thoroughly chilled beforehand. Serve this elegant hors d'oeuvre accompanied by assorted crackers and slices of fresh fruit.

6 ounces Cheddar cheese, shredded
½ cup cream cheese, softened
1 tablespoon *each* finely diced onion, green bell pepper, and drained canned pimiento
½ teaspoon Worcestershire sauce
¼ teaspoon lemon juice
⅛ teaspoon ground red pepper
2 ounces chopped walnuts or pecans

In 1-quart bowl combine cheeses, mixing until well blended; add remaining ingredients except nuts and stir to combine. Cover bowl with plastic wrap and refrigerate until mixture is well chilled, about 1 hour.

On sheet of wax paper spread nuts. Shape cheese mixture into a ball and roll in chopped nuts. Transfer to serving plate.

MAKES 12 SERVINGS

Each serving provides: ½ Protein Exchange; 65 calories Optional Exchange
Per serving with walnuts: 121 calories; 5 g protein; 11 g fat; 1 g carbohydrate; 115 mg calcium; 119 mg sodium; 25 mg cholesterol
With pecans: 123 calories; 5 g protein; 11 g fat; 1 g carbohydrate; 112 mg calcium; 118 mg sodium; 25 mg cholesterol

VARIATION:

2 ounces chopped almonds may be substituted for the walnuts or pecans. Reduce Optional Exchange to 60 calories.

Per serving: 119 calories; 5 g protein; 10 g fat; 2 g carbohydrate; 123 mg calcium; 119 mg sodium; 25 mg cholesterol

Weight Watchers Kitchens

Sesame Cheese Ball

A demand for party recipes at her Weight Watchers meeting prompted Nancy to adapt this old favorite. Nancy has been a Weight Watchers leader for four years and, in her spare time, she enjoys gardening, sewing, and cooking.

2²/₃ cups reduced-calorie creamed cheese spread

5 ounces sharp Cheddar cheese, coarsely shredded

1 tablespoon *each* finely chopped scallion (green onion) and drained canned pimiento

2 teaspoons Worcestershire sauce

1 teaspoon lemon juice

¼ teaspoon salt

2 tablespoons plus 2 teaspoons sesame seed, toasted

In medium bowl combine all ingredients except sesame seed, mixing until smooth. Cover and refrigerate until mixture is firm, at least 4 hours.

Form cheese mixture into a ball. Onto sheet of wax paper or plastic wrap sprinkle sesame seed; roll cheese ball in seeds until ball is thoroughly coated. Serve immediately or cover and refrigerate until ready to serve.

MAKES 8 SERVINGS

Each serving provides: 1½ Protein Exchanges; 50 calories Optional Exchange
Per serving: 168 calories; 15 g protein; 10 g fat; 4 g carbohydrate; 195 mg calcium; 365 mg sodium; 19 mg cholesterol*

*This figure does not include reduced-calorie creamed cheese spread; nutrition analysis not available.

SERVING SUGGESTION:

Serve with crispbread or melba rounds.

Nancy J. Brown
Marionville, Missouri

Breadstick Dippers ©

Paulette is a registered nurse and mother of a young daughter. She also works as a receptionist/weigher once a week at a Weight Watchers meeting. Paulette adapted her niece's recipe and suggests serving these breadsticks warm with a dip at your next party.

2¼ cups all-purpose flour, divided
1 tablespoon granulated sugar
2 teaspoons double-acting baking powder
1 teaspoon salt
1 cup skim milk
¼ cup reduced-calorie margarine (tub), melted

Preheat oven to 425°F. Into medium mixing bowl sift together 2 cups flour, the sugar, baking powder, and salt; add milk and, using a wooden spoon, mix to form dough. Using 2 tablespoons of the remaining flour, lightly flour work surface; turn dough out onto floured surface and knead, adding remaining 2 tablespoons flour as needed, until dough becomes smooth and elastic, about 5 minutes. Using rolling pin, roll dough into 12 x 8-inch rectangle, about ½ inch thick. Cut dough in half lengthwise; cut each half crosswise into 18 equal slices. Dip dough slices into margarine, being sure to use all of the margarine; place dough slices on baking sheet, leaving a space of about 1 inch between each. Bake until golden brown, 10 to 15 minutes.

MAKES 12 SERVINGS, 3 STICKS EACH

Each serving provides: 1 Bread Exchange; ½ Fat Exchange; 15 calories Optional Exchange
Per serving: 114 calories; 3 g protein; 2 g fat; 20 g carbohydrate; 65 mg calcium; 306 mg sodium; 0.4 mg cholesterol

Paulette J. Howe
Hugo, Minnesota

Cheddar-Onion Hors d'Oeuvres ◑

Several part-time jobs, including one as a weigher at Weight Watchers meetings, keep Shirley very busy. She also manages to find time for reading and cooking. This recipe is a big hit with Shirley's card club.

4 ready-to-bake refrigerated
  buttermilk flaky biscuits
  (1 ounce each)*
2 eggs
1 teaspoon Worcestershire
  sauce
½ teaspoon Dijon-style
  mustard
Dash pepper
½ cup finely chopped onion
2 ounces Cheddar cheese,
  shredded

Preheat oven to 450°F. Spray sixteen 1½- or 2-inch miniature muffin-pan cups with non-stick cooking spray. Carefully separate each biscuit into 4 thin layers of dough. Firmly press 1 layer onto bottom and up the sides of each cup; set aside.

In small mixing bowl beat together eggs, Worcestershire sauce, mustard, and pepper; add onion and cheese and mix well. Spoon ⅛ of mixture (about a scant tablespoonful) into each biscuit-lined cup and partially fill remaining cups with water (this will prevent pan from burning and/or warping). Bake until hors d'oeuvres are puffed and lightly browned, 10 to 12 minutes.

MAKES 8 SERVINGS, 2 HORS D'OEUVRES EACH

*Keep biscuits refrigerated until ready to use. Separate dough into layers as soon as biscuits are removed from refrigerator; they will be difficult to work with if allowed to come to room temperature.

Each serving provides: ½ Protein Exchange; ½ Bread Exchange; ⅛ Vegetable Exchange
Per serving: 95 calories; 4 g protein; 6 g fat; 7 g carbohydrate; 61 mg calcium; 224 mg sodium; 76 mg cholesterol

Shirley Gorg
Spring Lake Park, Minnesota

Herbed Spinach Balls ❻

These tasty little balls are great for parties or snacks—even Tanya's three daughters love them. Tanya lost 70 pounds on the Weight Watchers program and is now a leader at three weekly meetings. She plays piano in her spare time.

1 package (10 ounces) frozen
   chopped spinach, thawed
   and well drained (about
   1 cup)
½ cup finely chopped onion
1 egg, beaten
2 tablespoons plus
   2 teaspoons reduced-calorie
   margarine (tub), melted
⅓ cup plus 2 teaspoons plain
   dried bread crumbs
2 tablespoons grated
   Parmesan cheese
¼ teaspoon *each* garlic
   powder, thyme leaves,
   rubbed sage, and salt
Dash pepper

Preheat oven to 350°F. In medium mixing bowl combine spinach, onion, egg, and margarine, mixing well. Add remaining ingredients and mix again until thoroughly combined.

Using rounded teaspoonfuls, shape spinach mixture into 16 equal balls. Spray nonstick baking sheet with nonstick cooking spray; arrange balls on sheet. Bake until balls are cooked through and lightly browned, 18 to 20 minutes.

MAKES 4 SERVINGS, 4 SPINACH BALLS EACH

Each serving provides: ½ Bread Exchange; ¾ Vegetable Exchange; 1 Fat
   Exchange; 35 calories Optional Exchange
Per serving: 126 calories; 6 g protein; 7 g fat; 12 g carbohydrate; 140 mg
   calcium; 401 mg sodium; 71 mg cholesterol

Tanya L. Clarke
Longview, Washington

Shrimp Louis Salad

Chicken, Cheese, 'n' Biscuits

Fruited Pork Chops

Baked Squash

Mushroom Curry
Italian Vegetables

Seafood-Linguine Mornay

Northwest Cioppino

"Gum Drops"

Mushrooms in Pastry ◑

Luanne encases delectable mushrooms in pockets of dough to serve as party appetizers. Originally from Brooklyn, New York, she now lives in Ohio with her husband and young daughter.

1 tablespoon plus 1 teaspoon
   margarine, softened
2 teaspoons Dijon-style
   mustard
½ teaspoon parsley flakes
¼ teaspoon tarragon leaves
4 ready-to-bake refrigerated
   buttermilk flaky biscuits
   (1 ounce each)
1 cup thinly sliced mushrooms

Preheat oven to 350°F. In small bowl combine margarine, mustard, parsley, and tarragon and mix until thoroughly combined; set aside.

Using a rolling pin, roll each biscuit between 2 sheets of wax paper, forming 4 circles about 6 inches in diameter each. Spray nonstick baking sheet with nonstick cooking spray; carefully remove wax paper from biscuit circles and transfer circles to sprayed sheet. Spread ¼ of margarine mixture onto center of each circle and top each with ¼ cup mushrooms. Moisten edges of dough with water, then fold each circle over, turnover style; using tines of a fork, press edges to seal. Bake until lightly browned, 10 to 15 minutes.

MAKES 4 SERVINGS, 1 MUSHROOM-FILLED PASTRY EACH

Each serving provides: 1 Bread Exchange; ½ Vegetable Exchange; 1 Fat Exchange
Per serving: 126 calories; 2 g protein; 8 g fat; 14 g carbohydrate; 3 mg calcium; 413 mg sodium; 0 mg cholesterol

Luanne Kleiman
Columbus, Ohio

Smoky Frank Tidbits ◑

These hors d'oeuvres went over big with members at Janice's Weight Watchers meeting, prompting her to submit the recipe. Janice loves flower-gardening and her part-time job in a flower shop.

⅔ cup pineapple juice
   (no sugar added)
2 teaspoons cornstarch
1 tablespoon plus 1 teaspoon
   ketchup
1 teaspoon firmly packed
   brown sugar
½ teaspoon bottled liquid
   smoke
8 ounces turkey frankfurters,
   cut into 48 equal pieces

In small saucepan combine pineapple juice and cornstarch, stirring to dissolve cornstarch. Add remaining ingredients except frankfurters and cook over medium heat, stirring constantly, until mixture comes to a boil and thickens. Add frankfurters and cook until heated through, about 3 minutes.

MAKES 8 SERVINGS

Each serving provides: 1 Protein Exchange; 20 calories Optional Exchange
Per serving: 82 calories; 4 g protein; 5 g fat; 5 g carbohydrate; 40 mg
   calcium; 316 mg sodium; 24 mg cholesterol
These figures do not include liquid smoke; nutrition analyses not available.

Janice Brooks
Sisseton, South Dakota

Zucchini Hors d'Oeuvres from the Microwave ⊙◑

Donna dreamed up this delicious appetizer to use on her job as a demonstrator of microwave ovens. The mother of three boys, Donna keeps extra-busy with her many part-time jobs.

2 medium zucchini (about 5 ounces each), cut into ¼-inch-thick slices
2 tablespoons plus 2 teaspoons reduced-calorie margarine (tub)
2 tablespoons *each* grated Parmesan cheese and chopped scallion (green onion)
¼ teaspoon oregano leaves
Dash *each* garlic powder and pepper
1 tablespoon seasoned dried bread crumbs
¼ teaspoon paprika

On large microwave-safe serving plate arrange zucchini slices in a single layer; cover with plastic wrap and microwave on High until tender-crisp, 1 to 2 minutes.* Remove plate from oven and set aside.

In small bowl combine remaining ingredients except bread crumbs and paprika. Spread an equal amount of mixture over each zucchini slice; sprinkle each slice with an equal amount of bread crumbs, then paprika; microwave on High until hot, 30 seconds to 1 minute. Let stand for 1 minute before serving.

MAKES 8 SERVINGS

*Cooking time may be different in your microwave oven. To help ensure good results, be sure to check the instructions accompanying your unit regarding length of time to cook zucchini.

Each serving provides: ½ Vegetable Exchange; ½ Fat Exchange; 10 calories Optional Exchange
Per serving: 32 calories; 1 g protein; 2 g fat; 2 g carbohydrate; 25 mg calcium; 89 mg sodium; 1 mg cholesterol

Donna Reinschmidt
Los Gatos, California

From the Salad Bar
Salads and Dressings

Carrot and Raisin Salad

A Weight Watchers leader for several years, Linda loves to exercise. She developed this salad after some experimentation and has shared the recipe with her members.

2 cups grated carrots
½ cup canned crushed
pineapple (no sugar added)
2 tablespoons dark raisins
1 tablespoon lemon juice
(optional)
¼ cup plain low-fat yogurt
2 tablespoons reduced-calorie
mayonnaise
Granulated low-calorie
sweetener with aspartame
to equal 1 teaspoon sugar
(optional)
2 teaspoons shredded
coconut

In medium bowl combine carrots, pineapple, raisins, and, if desired, lemon juice. Using a wire whisk, in small bowl combine remaining ingredients except coconut; pour over carrot mixture and toss until well coated. Cover bowl with plastic wrap and refrigerate for at least 1 hour. Just before serving, toss again and sprinkle with coconut.

MAKES 2 SERVINGS

Each serving provides: 2 Vegetable Exchanges; 1½ Fat Exchanges; 1 Fruit
    Exchange; ¼ Milk Exchange; 10 calories Optional Exchange
Per serving with lemon juice and sweetener: 180 calories; 4 g protein; 5 g
    fat; 32 g carbohydrate; 96 mg calcium; 178 mg sodium; 7 mg cholesterol
With lemon juice: 179 calories; 3 g protein; 5 g fat; 32 g carbohydrate; 96 mg
    calcium; 178 mg sodium; 7 mg cholesterol
With sweetener: 179 calories; 4 g protein; 5 g fat; 32 g carbohydrate; 95 mg
    calcium; 176 mg sodium; 7 mg cholesterol
Without lemon juice and sweetener: 178 calories; 3 g protein; 5 g fat; 32 g
    carbohydrate; 95 mg calcium; 176 mg sodium; 7 mg cholesterol

Linda Maxwell
Taylorville, Illinois

Carrot Salad in Tomato Marinade ◑

Glenda's salad recipe combines the crunch of fresh vegetables with a tangy dressing. Be sure to chill the salad for several hours, or overnight, to let the flavors blend.

¼ cup tomato sauce
1 tablespoon plus
   1½ teaspoons white wine
   vinegar
1 tablespoon plus 1 teaspoon
   vegetable oil
¾ teaspoon Worcestershire
   sauce
¼ teaspoon *each* salt and
   prepared mustard
Dash pepper
2 cups thinly sliced carrots,
   blanched
¼ cup *each* chopped green
   bell pepper, celery, and
   onion

In small saucepan combine tomato sauce, vinegar, oil, Worcestershire sauce, salt, mustard, and pepper and bring to a boil. Reduce heat to low and let simmer, stirring frequently, until flavors are blended, 5 to 7 minutes; let cool.

In medium glass or stainless-steel bowl (not aluminum*) combine carrots, bell pepper, celery, and onion; pour tomato mixture over vegetables and toss to coat. Cover with plastic wrap and refrigerate until chilled, at least 2 hours.

MAKES 4 SERVINGS

*It's best to marinate in glass or stainless-steel containers; acidic ingredients such as vinegar may react with aluminum, causing color and flavor changes in foods.

Each serving provides: 1½ Vegetable Exchanges; 1 Fat Exchange
Per serving: 77 calories; 1 g protein; 5 g fat; 8 g carbohydrate; 24 mg calcium; 269 mg sodium; 0 mg cholesterol

Glenda E. Bennett
Le Claire, Iowa

Cauliflower Salad

Toinette is a busy homemaker and mother who is very involved in her church, civic associations, the Scouts, and the PTA. She also runs a small catering business in her home, especially for friends. This salad is one of her specialties, and a family favorite.

1 medium head iceberg lettuce (about 2½ pounds), torn into bite-size pieces
4 cups cauliflower florets
1 cup thinly sliced red onion (separated into rings)
¾ cup reduced-calorie mayonnaise
⅓ cup *each* grated Parmesan cheese and imitation bacon bits

Line bottom of large shallow bowl with lettuce; top with cauliflower florets and onion slices. Using a rubber scraper, spread mayonnaise over entire surface of salad; sprinkle with Parmesan cheese and bacon bits *(do not toss)*. Cover with plastic wrap and refrigerate overnight. Just before serving, toss salad to combine.

MAKES 12 SERVINGS

Each serving provides: 1½ Vegetable Exchanges; 1½ Fat Exchanges; 25 calories Optional Exchange
Per serving: 95 calories; 4 g protein; 6 g fat; 8 g carbohydrate; 114 mg calcium; 294 mg sodium; 7 mg cholesterol

Toinette Augustine
Bay Village, Ohio

Cucumber-Sour Cream Salad ⊙

Since this delicious salad will keep in the refrigerator for up to a week, make enough to have on hand as a refreshing change of pace. Fresh dill, readily available in most markets, gives this cool side dish its unique flavor.

2 medium cucumbers, pared
½ teaspoon salt
3 tablespoons sour cream
1 tablespoon distilled white
   vinegar
2 teaspoons to 1 tablespoon
   chopped fresh dill
½ teaspoon granulated sugar
⅛ teaspoon white pepper

Cut cucumbers lengthwise into halves and, using the tip of a teaspoon, scoop out and discard seeds. Cut cucumbers crosswise into very thin slices and transfer to medium bowl; sprinkle with salt, tossing well to combine. Let cucumber mixture stand at room temperature for 20 minutes. Squeeze out and discard accumulated liquid from cucumbers.

In small bowl combine remaining ingredients; pour over cucumbers and toss well. Serve immediately or cover and refrigerate until chilled; toss again before serving.

MAKES 4 SERVINGS

Each serving provides: 1 Vegetable Exchange; 30 calories Optional Exchange
Per serving: 38 calories; 1 g protein; 2 g fat; 4 g carbohydrate; 30 mg
   calcium; 80 mg sodium; 5 mg cholesterol

Weight Watchers Kitchens

Green Bean Salad ©

This salad recipe was passed down through Doris's family for several generations, beginning with her German great-grandmother. Doris, a substitute teacher's aide and mother of two, enjoys camping and hiking.

2 cups *each* **trimmed and diagonally sliced green beans (1-inch pieces) and water**
2 tablespoons *each* **finely diced onion and vegetable oil**
1 tablespoon red wine vinegar
1 teaspoon salt
Dash pepper

In 1-quart saucepan combine green beans and water and bring to a boil. Reduce heat and let simmer until beans are tender, about 10 minutes. Drain beans and transfer to medium bowl; add remaining ingredients and toss until thoroughly coated. Cover with plastic wrap and refrigerate until chilled; toss salad again just before serving.

MAKES 4 SERVINGS

Each serving provides: 1 Vegetable Exchange; 1½ Fat Exchanges
Per serving: 80 calories; 1 g protein; 7 g fat; 4 g carbohydrate; 25 mg calcium; 554 mg sodium; 0 mg cholesterol

Doris Clements
Aloha, Oregon

Herb-Marinated Tomatoes ⊙

Looking for a new way to prepare tomatoes? Try Cherie's recipe—her family loves it. It's also a great way to use up all those home-grown tomatoes at the end of the summer. Cherie, a preschool teacher, has two preschoolers of her own.

**2 medium tomatoes, cut into
¼-inch-thick slices
1 tablespoon plus 1 teaspoon
red wine vinegar
2 teaspoons olive *or* vegetable
oil
¼ teaspoon salt
⅛ teaspoon *each* powdered
mustard, tarragon leaves,
and thyme leaves, crumbled
Dash *each* oregano leaves
and freshly ground pepper
4 romaine *or* iceberg lettuce
leaves**

In shallow 1-quart glass or stainless-steel bowl (not aluminum*) arrange tomato slices, overlapping slices slightly. In small bowl combine remaining ingredients except lettuce; pour over tomatoes. Cover bowl with plastic wrap and refrigerate for at least 1 hour, basting tomatoes several times with marinade.

To serve, line 2 salad plates with 2 lettuce leaves each; top each portion of lettuce with half of the tomato slices and half of the marinade.

MAKES 2 SERVINGS

*It's best to marinate in glass or stainless-steel containers; acidic ingredients such as vinegar may react with aluminum, causing color and flavor changes in foods.

Each serving provides: 2½ Vegetable Exchanges; 1 Fat Exchange
Per serving: 69 calories; 1 g protein; 5 g fat; 6 g carbohydrate; 22 mg calcium; 283 mg sodium; 0 mg cholesterol

*Cherie H. Klein
Issaquah, Washington*

Jicama-Mushroom Salad

A receptionist and weigher for Weight Watchers, Genie lost 30 pounds on the Program. Her husband is very supportive and will try anything she cooks, so Genie experimented with jicama when members at her Weight Watchers meeting began talking about it. This salad is one of her delicious creations.

3 cups cubed pared jicama (1-inch cubes)
1 quart water
⅓ cup *each* sliced mushrooms, chopped onion, chopped celery, and plain low-fat yogurt
¼ cup chopped green bell pepper
2 tablespoons plus 2 teaspoons reduced-calorie mayonnaise
2 teaspoons prepared spicy brown mustard
1 teaspoon prepared horseradish
¼ teaspoon *each* salt and pepper
1 teaspoon chopped fresh parsley

In 2½-quart saucepan add jicama to water and bring to a boil; reduce heat and let simmer until tender, about 45 minutes (jicama should remain slightly crunchy).

Drain jicama and rinse with running cold water; transfer to medium bowl. Add remaining ingredients except parsley and toss until thoroughly combined. Cover bowl with plastic wrap; refrigerate until mixture is chilled, at least 1 hour. When ready to serve, transfer mixture to serving bowl and sprinkle with parsley.

MAKES 4 SERVINGS

Each serving provides: 2⅛ Vegetable Exchanges; 1 Fat Exchange; 15 calories Optional Exchange
Per serving: 88 calories; 3 g protein; 3 g fat; 12 g carbohydrate; 58 mg calcium; 264 mg sodium; 4 mg cholesterol

Genie McCook
Texarkana, Texas

Spinach Salad with Mustard-Honey Dressing ◐

Rachel says she started cooking at the age of eight and hasn't stopped since. Her salad recipe is a reflection of her interest in weight-conscious eating, a concern shared by her physician husband. And the dedication to weight control runs in the family—Rachel's mother was a Weight Watchers leader.

1 cup torn spinach leaves, washed well and drained
½ cup *each* torn iceberg lettuce leaves and sliced mushrooms
1 medium tomato, chopped
¼ cup plain low-fat yogurt
Granulated low-calorie sweetener with aspartame to equal 1 teaspoon sugar (optional)
½ teaspoon *each* Dijon-style mustard and honey
Dash ground ginger
1 hard-cooked egg, diced

In medium bowl combine spinach, lettuce, mushrooms, and tomato. In small bowl combine remaining ingredients except egg; pour over spinach mixture and toss until well coated. Serve sprinkled with diced egg.

MAKES 1 SERVING

Each serving provides: 1 Protein Exchange; 6 Vegetable Exchanges; ½ Milk Exchange; 10 calories Optional Exchange
Per serving with sweetener: 180 calories; 13 g protein; 7 g fat; 18 g carbohydrate; 217 mg calcium; 241 mg sodium; 277 mg cholesterol
If sweetener is not used, decrease calories to 178.

Rachel Green Panish
Glen Oaks, New York

Tomato-Egg Accordion Salad ⊙ ◑

Think salad is boring? Mary's attractive and tasty dish is sure to change your mind. Mary lost 53 pounds on the Weight Watchers program. Way to go, Mary!

1 medium tomato
2 iceberg *or* romaine lettuce leaves, torn into bite-size pieces
1 tablespoon reduced-calorie Thousand Island dressing (30 calories per table-spoon), divided
1 egg, hard-cooked and shelled

Set tomato stem-end down and cut into 8 evenly spaced slices, cutting to within ½ inch from bottom *(do not cut all the way through)*. Arrange lettuce on salad plate and place tomato, stem-end down, on lettuce; spread tomato slices slightly apart and drizzle half of dressing evenly over cut sides of tomato slices. Cut egg crosswise into 7 slices and insert 1 egg slice between each tomato slice; drizzle with remaining dressing.

MAKES 1 SERVING

Each serving provides: 1 Protein Exchange; 2½ Vegetable Exchanges; 30 calories Optional Exchange
Per serving: 138 calories; 8 g protein; 7 g fat; 11 g carbohydrate; 52 mg calcium; 277 mg sodium; 274 mg cholesterol

Mary Perdue
Clifton, Texas

Waldorf-Style Salad

Charlene adapted her mother-in-law's recipe for the classic Waldorf Salad and came up with this delicious version. With the crunch of sunflower seed and the use of reduced-calorie mayonnaise, she thinks it tastes even better than the original. When she's not working as a directory-assistance operator, Charlene enjoys crafts, quilting, and painting.

2 tablespoons lemon juice
2 small Red Delicious apples,
  cored and diced
1 cup diced celery
¼ cup dark raisins
2 tablespoons plus 2
  teaspoons reduced-calorie
  mayonnaise
4 iceberg or romaine lettuce
  leaves
1 tablespoon plus 1 teaspoon
  sunflower seed

In small mixing bowl sprinkle lemon juice over apples and toss lightly to combine; add celery, raisins, and mayonnaise and mix until thoroughly coated. Cover with plastic wrap and refrigerate for at least 30 minutes.

To serve, line 4 salad plates with 1 lettuce leaf each; top each with an equal amount of apple mixture and sprinkle each with 1 teaspoon sunflower seed.

MAKES 4 SERVINGS

Each serving provides: ¾ Vegetable Exchange; 1 Fat Exchange; 1 Fruit Exchange; 20 calories Optional Exchange
Per serving: 111 calories; 2 g protein; 4 g fat; 18 g carbohydrate; 30 mg calcium; 105 mg sodium; 3 mg cholesterol

Charlene K. Harsh
Canton, Ohio

Special Slaw ©

Kathi, who usually doesn't like slaw, tasted a particularly good one at a Dallas restaurant. The key ingredient was garlic. Here's her version. Kathi enjoys reading, but her number-one hobby is spending time with her three grandchildren.

3½ cups shredded green
   cabbage
½ cup *each* diced onion
   and buttermilk
⅓ cup reduced-calorie
   mayonnaise
2 to 4 garlic cloves, minced
3 tablespoons white wine
   vinegar
1 teaspoon celery seed
Dash pepper

In medium bowl combine cabbage and onion. In small mixing bowl combine remaining ingredients, mixing well. Pour buttermilk mixture over cabbage mixture; toss to combine. Cover bowl with plastic wrap and refrigerate for several hours.

MAKES 8 SERVINGS

Each serving provides: 1 Vegetable Exchange; 1 Fat Exchange; 10 calories
   Optional Exchange
Per serving: 47 calories; 1 g protein; 3 g fat; 4 g carbohydrate; 42 mg
   calcium; 98 mg sodium; 4 mg cholesterol

Kathi Thompson
Dallas, Texas

Coleslaw with Yogurt Dressing Ⓒ

Charlene's experience as a clothes fitter came in handy when she lost weight—all her clothes had to be taken in! Charlene says the Weight Watchers program turned her life around. Try her colorful, crunchy coleslaw for a summer barbecue.

3 cups shredded green
  cabbage
1 cup shredded red cabbage
½ cup *each* grated carrot and
  chopped celery
¼ cup *each* diced green bell
  pepper, diced scallions
  (green onions), seeded and
  chopped cucumber, and
  sliced radishes
½ cup plain low-fat yogurt
2 tablespoons red wine
  vinegar, or to taste
1 tablespoon plus 1 teaspoon
  vegetable oil
Granulated low-calorie
  sweetener with aspartame
  to equal 2 teaspoons sugar
Dash *each* salt, pepper, and
  garlic powder

In large salad bowl combine green and red cabbage, carrot, celery, bell pepper, scallions, cucumber, and radishes. In small bowl combine remaining ingredients; pour over vegetables and toss until well coated. Cover salad bowl with plastic wrap and refrigerate until chilled. Toss again just before serving.

MAKES 4 SERVINGS

Each serving provides: 3 Vegetable Exchanges; 1 Fat Exchange; ¼ Milk
  Exchange
Per serving: 91 calories; 3 g protein; 5 g fat; 9 g carbohydrate; 101 mg
  calcium; 86 mg sodium; 2 mg cholesterol

Charlene L. Skow
Bellevue, Washington

Potato Salad

Robin credits Weight Watchers for his 121-pound weight loss. A longtime member, he enjoys listening to music. Try his delicious potato-egg dish—it's a wonderful change from the typical potato salad.

2 eggs, hard-cooked and
   chopped
3 ounces peeled cooked
   potato, cut into cubes and
   chilled
½ cup chopped celery
1 tablespoon diced drained
   canned pimiento
1 teaspoon minced onion
2 tablespoons plain low-fat
   yogurt
1 tablespoon reduced-calorie
   mayonnaise
Granulated low-calorie
   sweetener with aspartame
   to equal 2 teaspoons sugar
   (optional)
1 teaspoon prepared yellow
   mustard
⅛ teaspoon salt
Dash pepper

In medium bowl combine eggs, potato, celery, pimiento, and onion. In small bowl combine remaining ingredients, mixing thoroughly. Pour yogurt mixture over potato mixture and toss gently to coat. Cover with plastic wrap and refrigerate for at least 1 hour.

MAKES 1 SERVING

Each serving provides: 2 Protein Exchanges; 1 Bread Exchange; 1⅛ Vegetable Exchanges; 1½ Fat Exchanges; ¼ Milk Exchange
Per serving with sweetener: 312 calories; 17 g protein; 16 g fat; 25 g carbohydrate; 145 mg calcium; 672 mg sodium; 555 mg cholesterol
If sweetener is not used, decrease calories to 308 and protein to 16 g.

Robin Risser
Mansfield, Ohio

Rice Salad ☾

A Weight Watchers member for over six years, James lost 73 pounds on the Program. In addition to attending school, he is a soloist in a choir and plays the organ. James created this dish as an alternative to potato salad.

1 cup *each* **cooked long-grain rice and chopped celery**
2 eggs, hard-cooked and chopped
½ cup chopped cucumber
¼ cup chopped onion
4 radishes, chopped
3 tablespoons plain low-fat yogurt
2 tablespoons reduced-calorie mayonnaise
2 teaspoons pickle relish
1 teaspoon prepared brown mustard
¼ teaspoon *each* **salt and pepper**

In medium bowl combine rice, celery, eggs, cucumber, onion, and radishes. In small bowl or cup combine remaining ingredients; pour over rice mixture and toss to coat. Cover with plastic wrap and refrigerate until flavors are blended, at least 1 hour. Toss again just before serving.

MAKES 2 SERVINGS

Each serving provides: 1 Protein Exchange; 1 Bread Exchange; 2 Vegetable Exchanges; 1½ Fat Exchanges; 25 calories Optional Exchange
Per serving: 277 calories; 10 g protein; 10 g fat; 35 g carbohydrate; 114 mg calcium; 585 mg sodium; 280 mg cholesterol

James A. Shannon
Mendota, Illinois

Cranberry Holiday Salad ℂ

This sweet, crunchy salad is a family recipe that Carole converted to fit the Food Plan. Carole, who lives on a hobby farm with her husband and dog, has five married sons. In addition to cooking, she enjoys interior decorating, knitting, crocheting, counted cross-stitching, oil painting, and flower arranging for weddings.

1 envelope (four ½-cup servings) low-calorie cherry-flavored gelatin (8 calories per ½ cup)
2 cups boiling water
1 cup cold water
3 small apples, cored and quartered
2 cups fresh or frozen cranberries (no sugar added)*
1 small orange, peeled and sectioned
1 cup *each* canned crushed pineapple (no sugar added) and chopped celery
Granulated low-calorie sweetener with aspartame to equal 2 teaspoons sugar

In medium heatproof bowl sprinkle gelatin over boiling water and stir until dissolved; stir in cold water and set aside.

In work bowl of food processor combine apples, cranberries, and orange sections and process until finely chopped (*do not puree*); add to dissolved gelatin. Stir in pineapple, celery, and sweetener and pour into 13 x 9 x 2-inch pan. Cover and refrigerate until set, at least 3 hours.

MAKES 8 SERVINGS

*If frozen berries are used, thaw after measuring.

Each serving provides: ¼ Vegetable Exchange; 1 Fruit Exchange; 4 calories Optional Exchange
Per serving: 69 calories; 1 g protein; 0.3 g fat; 17 g carbohydrate; 21 mg calcium; 16 mg sodium; 0 mg cholesterol

Carole A. Burslie
McIntosh, Minnesota

Cranberry Relish Mold ☻

Here's a colorful accompaniment to holiday dinners. Marjory likes to use fresh cranberries in season, and thinks this relish goes best with turkey, chicken, and ham. A part-time travel agent, Marjory is also a volunteer at a local museum, where she has contributed recipes for a cookbook that the museum published.

2 cups fresh *or* frozen
   cranberries (no sugar
   added)*
1 small orange, peeled and
   chopped
Granulated low-calorie
   sweetener with aspartame
   to equal 6 teaspoons sugar
1 envelope (eight ½-cup
   servings) *or* 2 envelopes
   (four ½-cup servings each)
   low-calorie orange- *or*
   raspberry-flavored gelatin
   (8 calories per ½ cup)
2 cups boiling water
½ cup *each* canned crushed
   pineapple (no sugar added),
   drained, and cold water

In work bowl of food processor or blender container combine cranberries, orange, and sweetener and process until finely chopped, scraping down sides of container as necessary *(do not puree).*

In large heatproof mixing bowl dissolve gelatin in boiling water; stir in cranberry mixture, pineapple, and cold water. Rinse an 8-cup mold with cold water; transfer gelatin mixture to mold. Cover with plastic wrap and refrigerate until set, at least 3 hours (may be refrigerated overnight).

MAKES 8 SERVINGS

*If cranberries are frozen, there is no need to thaw them before using.

Each serving provides: ½ Fruit Exchange; 8 calories Optional Exchange
Per serving: 40 calories; 2 g protein; 0.1 g fat; 8 g carbohydrate; 12 mg calcium; 5 mg sodium; 0 mg cholesterol

Marjory I. Graham
Chadds Ford, Pennsylvania

Creamy Egg Salad ☺ ◑

Laurinda's delicious egg salad is made extra-creamy by adding the reduced-calorie creamed cheese spread. Laurinda's hobbies include walking, swimming, counted cross-stitching, and spending time with her husband, Dwayne, and daughter, Megan.

1 egg, hard-cooked and chopped
⅓ cup reduced-calorie creamed cheese spread
2 teaspoons reduced-calorie mayonnaise
1 teaspoon minced onion
⅛ teaspoon salt
Dash pepper

In small bowl combine all ingredients, mixing well. Serve immediately or cover and refrigerate until chilled.

MAKES 1 SERVING

Each serving provides: 2 Protein Exchanges; 1 Fat Exchange; 25 calories Optional Exchange
Per serving: 186 calories; 17 g protein; 11 g fat; 5 g carbohydrate; 93 mg calcium; 592 mg sodium; 277 mg cholesterol*

SERVING SUGGESTIONS:

1. Serve mixture between 2 slices reduced-calorie white, wheat, or rye bread (40 calories per slice). Add 1 Bread Exchange to Exchange Information.

Per serving: 266 calories; 21 g protein; 11 g fat; 23 g carbohydrate; 133 mg calcium; 782 mg sodium; 277 mg cholesterol*

2. Line a plate with 4 iceberg lettuce leaves; top with egg mixture and arrange 3 medium tomato wedges, 4 green bell pepper rings, and 2 tablespoons alfalfa sprouts around egg mixture. Add 2¾ Vegetable Exchanges to Exchange Information.

Per serving: 214 calories; 18 g protein; 12 g fat; 10 g carbohydrate; 127 mg calcium; 601 mg sodium; 277 mg cholesterol*

*This figure does not include reduced-calorie creamed cheese spread; nutrition analysis not available.

Laurinda VanRoekel
Corsica, South Dakota

Greek Country Salad ◑

A trip to Greece was the inspiration for this salad. Susan, a Weight Watchers leader, adapted it from versions she tried there. Close your eyes, take a bite — and you can almost hear the bouzouki music playing.

2 cups torn lettuce leaves
4 ounces drained canned
   chick-peas (garbanzo
   beans)
1 medium tomato, cut into
   wedges
½ medium cucumber, scored
   and thinly sliced
½ medium green bell pepper,
   seeded and thinly sliced
12 pitted black olives, sliced
2 ounces feta cheese,
   crumbled
1 tablespoon olive oil
2 teaspoons drained capers,
   rinsed
1 teaspoon *each* white wine
   vinegar and lemon juice
½ teaspoon chopped fresh dill
Dill sprig

In medium salad bowl combine lettuce, chick-peas, tomato, cucumber, green pepper, and olives; top with feta cheese. Cover and refrigerate until chilled.

To serve, in small bowl combine remaining ingredients, except dill sprig, mixing well; pour dressing over salad and toss to coat. Arrange on serving platter and garnish with dill sprig.

MAKES 2 SERVINGS

Each serving provides: 2 Protein Exchanges; 4 Vegetable Exchanges; 1½ Fat
   Exchanges; 30 calories Optional Exchange
Per serving: 275 calories; 10 g protein; 18 g fat; 21 g carbohydrate; 243 mg
   calcium; 761 mg sodium (estimated); 25 mg cholesterol

Susan E. Slesinger
Lakewood, California

Stuffed Pasta Shell Salad

This is not only a family favorite, it's a neighborhood favorite as well. Corky used to make it in large quantities for block parties and no one ever knew it fit a weight-reduction program. Corky, who moved to Connecticut from the Midwest, enjoys traveling and exploring the East Coast.

8 uncooked jumbo macaroni shells (1½ ounces), cooked according to package directions and drained
2 tablespoons reduced-calorie Italian dressing (30 calories per tablespoon)
⅔ cup cottage cheese
½ cup part-skim ricotta cheese
2 tablespoons minced scallions (green onions)
2 teaspoons grated Parmesan cheese
1 teaspoon lemon juice
⅛ teaspoon grated lemon peel
Dash *each* salt and pepper

In shallow glass or stainless-steel bowl (not aluminum*) combine macaroni shells and dressing; toss to coat. Cover with plastic wrap and let marinate in refrigerator until chilled.

In small bowl combine remaining ingredients. Using slotted spoon, remove shells from bowl, reserving dressing. Spoon ⅛ of cheese mixture into each shell; set shells on serving platter and drizzle with reserved dressing.

MAKES 2 SERVINGS, 4 SHELLS EACH

*It is best to marinate in glass or stainless-steel containers; acidic ingredients such as the vinegar in salad dressing may react with aluminum, causing color and flavor changes in foods.

Each serving provides: 2 Protein Exchanges; 1 Bread Exchange; ⅛ Vegetable Exchange; 40 calories Optional Exchange
Per serving: 275 calories; 19 g protein; 10 g fat; 26 g carbohydrate; 244 mg calcium; 655 mg sodium; 31 mg cholesterol

Corky Fennell
West Hartford, Connecticut

Capered Chicken Salad

This tasty dish is a great way to use up leftover chicken, and it makes a nice party platter, too. Capers, olives, and Dijon mustard add just the right amount of "zing."

14 ounces skinned and boned cooked chicken breasts, cut into ½-inch cubes

2 eggs, hard-cooked and chopped

6 ounces peeled cooked potatoes, cut into ½-inch cubes

½ cup diced dill pickle

¼ cup chopped scallions (green onions)

2 tablespoons diced red bell pepper

4 pitted black olives, sliced

⅓ cup plus 2 teaspoons sour cream

1 tablespoon plus 1 teaspoon mayonnaise

1 tablespoon chopped drained capers

2 teaspoons Dijon-style mustard

⅛ teaspoon *each* salt and pepper

In medium mixing bowl combine chicken, eggs, potatoes, pickle, scallions, bell pepper, and olives.

In small bowl combine remaining ingredients, mixing well; pour dressing over chicken mixture and mix well. Cover bowl with plastic wrap and refrigerate until salad is chilled. Mix again just before serving.

MAKES 4 SERVINGS

Each serving provides: 4 Protein Exchanges; ½ Bread Exchange; ½ Vegetable Exchange; 1 Fat Exchange; 55 calories Optional Exchange
Per serving: 333 calories; 36 g protein; 15 g fat; 11 g carbohydrate; 72 mg calcium; 650 mg sodium; 234 mg cholesterol

Weight Watchers Kitchens

Chicken Salad

Kathleen and her husband raise beef cattle on their farm, but chicken is one of her favorite foods when she's trying to control her weight. This colorful salad is easy to prepare—and delicious, too.

6 ounces skinned and boned boiled chicken, diced
20 small red seedless grapes, cut into halves
1 small Red Delicious or McIntosh apple, cored and diced
½ cup diced celery
¼ cup diced onion
1 tablespoon plus 1 teaspoon reduced-calorie mayonnaise
1 teaspoon *each* distilled white vinegar and lemon juice
Dash *each* salt and pepper
2 medium tomatoes
4 lettuce leaves

In medium mixing bowl combine all ingredients except tomatoes and lettuce; cover with plastic wrap and refrigerate until thoroughly chilled, at least 1 hour.

Set tomatoes stem-end down and cut each into 8 wedges, cutting to within ½ inch from bottom (*do not cut all the way through*); press wedges open to resemble a flower. Line 2 salad plates with 2 lettuce leaves each. Set tomatoes on lettuce leaves and fill each with half of the chicken salad.

MAKES 2 SERVINGS

Each serving provides: 3 Protein Exchanges; 3¼ Vegetable Exchanges; 1 Fat Exchange; 1 Fruit Exchange
Per serving: 291 calories; 27 g protein; 10 g fat; 26 g carbohydrate; 62 mg calcium; 254 mg sodium; 79 mg cholesterol

Kathleen Pithoud
Bloomingdale, Indiana

Chinese Chicken Salad

Eileen has added her own special touches to create this colorful and tasty salad. Besides cooking, Eileen loves gardening, crocheting, and crafts. She has six children and twelve grandchildren.

½ cup canned pineapple chunks (no sugar added); drain and reserve juice
1 tablespoon *each* rice *or* cider vinegar and soy sauce*
1½ teaspoons Dijon-style mustard
1 teaspoon peanut *or* vegetable oil
Dash five-spice powder
6 ounces skinned and boned cooked chicken breasts, cut into thin strips
2 cups shredded lettuce
¼ cup sliced scallions (green onions)
2 tablespoons coarsely chopped fresh parsley
¼ cup sliced red bell pepper
1½ ounces drained canned water chestnuts, sliced
1 medium scallion (green onion), trimmed and cut lengthwise into 4 thin strips
½ teaspoon sesame seed, toasted

In medium glass or stainless-steel bowl (not aluminum†) combine reserved pineapple juice, vinegar, soy sauce, mustard, oil, and five-spice powder; add chicken and toss to coat. Cover with plastic wrap and refrigerate for 1 hour, tossing mixture occasionally. In another bowl combine lettuce, sliced scallions, and parsley and toss to combine; cover with plastic wrap and refrigerate until ready to use.

To serve, line serving platter with lettuce mixture. Spoon chicken mixture onto lettuce mixture and top chicken with pineapple chunks, bell pepper, and water chestnuts; garnish with scallion strips and sprinkle with sesame seed.

MAKES 2 SERVINGS

Each serving provides: 3 Protein Exchanges; 2½ Vegetable Exchanges; ½ Fat Exchange; ½ Fruit Exchange; 25 calories Optional Exchange
Per serving: 245 calories; 29 g protein; 6 g fat; 19 g carbohydrate; 83 mg calcium; 849 mg sodium; 72 mg cholesterol

*Reduced-sodium soy sauce may be substituted. Reduce calories to 244, carbohydrate to 18 g, calcium to 75 mg, and sodium to 488 mg.
†It's best to marinate in glass or stainless-steel containers; acidic ingredients such as vinegar and pineapple juice may react with aluminum, causing color and flavor changes in foods.

Eileen Claeys
Long Grove, Iowa

Curried Tropical Chicken Salad

Dorothy is a Weight Watchers leader who enjoys experimenting in the kitchen. Here she adds zip to an old favorite with interesting flavors and textures.

12 ounces skinned and boned cooked chicken, diced

1½ cups cooked long-grain rice

1 cup drained canned crushed pineapple (no sugar added)

½ cup *each* finely chopped celery and sliced scallions (green onions)

40 small *or* 24 large seedless green grapes, cut into halves

3 ounces drained canned water chestnuts, sliced

1 cup plain low-fat yogurt

2 tablespoons reduced-calorie mayonnaise

1 tablespoon soy sauce*

1 teaspoon Dijon-style mustard

¼ teaspoon *each* curry powder, salt, and salt-free low-pepper no-garlic herb seasoning

Dash pepper, or to taste

16 lettuce leaves

In medium mixing bowl combine chicken, rice, pineapple, celery, scallions, grapes, and water chestnuts, mixing well. In small mixing bowl combine remaining ingredients except lettuce, mixing well; pour dressing over chicken mixture and mix until thoroughly combined. Cover with plastic wrap and refrigerate for at least 30 minutes.

To serve, line 4 plates with 4 lettuce leaves each and top each portion of lettuce with ¼ of the chilled chicken salad.

MAKES 4 SERVINGS

Each serving provides: 3 Protein Exchanges; 1 Bread Exchange; 1½ Vegetable Exchanges; ½ Fat Exchange; 1 Fruit Exchange; ½ Milk Exchange; 10 calories Optional Exchange

Per serving: 407 calories; 31 g protein; 10 g fat; 49 g carbohydrate; 185 mg calcium; 695 mg sodium; 82 mg cholesterol

*Reduced-sodium soy sauce may be substituted. Reduce calories to 406, calcium to 181 mg, and sodium to 514 mg.

Dorothy L. Young
Shawnee, Kansas

Pineapple-Chicken Salad ◑

Sharon, married and the mother of two young children, is a legal secretary who also finds time to teach choir at her church. Her delicious salad is lovely to look at — and a great way to use up leftover chicken.

1 small pineapple
6 ounces diced cooked chicken
2 ounces julienne-cut Cheddar cheese (thin strips)
¼ cup *each* sliced celery, diagonally sliced carrot, diced green bell pepper, sliced scallions (green onions), and golden raisins
3 cups torn lettuce leaves
½ cup plain low-fat yogurt
2 tablespoons plus 2 teaspoons mayonnaise
¼ teaspoon salt
Dash pepper, or to taste

Using heavy knife, cut pineapple in half lengthwise *(do not remove leaves)*; using spoon or paring knife, scoop or cut out fruit from each pineapple half, leaving a ¼-inch-thick shell. Dice pineapple and measure 1 cup; refrigerate remaining pineapple for use at another time.

In medium mixing bowl combine 1 cup pineapple with the chicken, cheese, vegetables, and raisins, mixing well. Line each pineapple shell with 1½ cups lettuce; top each with half of the chicken mixture. In small bowl combine yogurt, mayonnaise, and seasonings and drizzle half of mixture over each portion of chicken mixture. Each salad-stuffed shell serves 2.

MAKES 4 SERVINGS

Each serving provides: 2 Protein Exchanges; 2 Vegetable Exchanges; 2 Fat Exchanges; 1 Fruit Exchange; ¼ Milk Exchange
Per serving: 283 calories; 19 g protein; 16 g fat; 18 g carbohydrate; 207 mg calcium; 346 mg sodium; 60 mg cholesterol

VARIATION:

Prepare chicken mixture as directed, but discard pineapple shells. Fill each of four 2-ounce pita breads with ¾ cup lettuce, ¼ of the chicken mixture, and ¼ of the mayonnaise mixture. Great for toting! Add 2 Bread Exchanges to Exchange Information.

Per serving: 457 calories; 24 g protein; 16 g fat; 54 g carbohydrate; 217 mg calcium; 709 mg sodium; 60 mg cholesterol

Sharon M. Martin
Bluford, Illinois

Tofu-Turkey Salad ◓◑

This dish was a spur-of-the-moment creation, using what was in the house. Dolly, a real estate appraiser, is especially fond of tofu. Her hobbies include pottery, aerobics, and cross-country skiing.

3 ounces skinned and boned cooked turkey breast, cut into cubes
3 ounces firm-style tofu (soybean curd), cut into cubes
1 small apple, cored and grated
¼ cup *each* diced celery and grated onion
1 tablespoon plus 1 teaspoon reduced-calorie mayonnaise
2 teaspoons apple cider vinegar
1 teaspoon chopped fresh parsley
⅛ teaspoon salt
Dash pepper
8 lettuce leaves

In medium mixing bowl combine turkey, tofu, apple, celery, and onion. In small measuring cup or bowl combine mayonnaise, vinegar, parsley, salt, and pepper, mixing well; pour dressing over salad and, using a wooden spoon, toss gently to coat thoroughly. Line 2 salad plates with 4 lettuce leaves each and top each portion of lettuce with half of turkey mixture.

MAKES 2 SERVINGS

Each serving provides: 2 Protein Exchanges; 1½ Vegetable Exchanges; 1 Fat Exchange; ½ Fruit Exchange
Per serving: 172 calories; 17 g protein; 6 g fat; 13 g carbohydrate; 106 mg calcium; 263 mg sodium; 33 mg cholesterol

Dolly Magarik
Albany, New York

❖❖

Turkey Salad ◑

Mary created this salad to use up leftover Thanksgiving or Christmas turkey, but now she serves it often, not just at holiday time. Mary has three grown children, and owns and operates a campground.

12 ounces skinned and boned cooked turkey, cut into 1-inch cubes
6 ounces drained canned water chestnuts, sliced
1 cup diced celery
2 tablespoons reduced-calorie mayonnaise
8 iceberg or romaine lettuce leaves
1 small carrot (about 2 ounces), pared and diced
1 medium green or red bell pepper, seeded and diced
4 eggs, hard-cooked, chilled, and cut into quarters

In medium bowl combine turkey, water chestnuts, celery, and mayonnaise, mixing well; cover and refrigerate until chilled.

Chill 4 salad plates. Line each chilled plate with 2 lettuce leaves; top each portion of lettuce with ¼ of the chilled turkey mixture. Around each portion of turkey decoratively arrange ¼ each of the carrot and bell pepper pieces and 4 egg quarters.

MAKES 4 SERVINGS

Each serving provides: 4 Protein Exchanges; ½ Bread Exchange; 1¾ Vegetable Exchanges; ½ Fat Exchange; 10 calories Optional Exchange
Per serving: 290 calories; 32 g protein; 12 g fat; 12 g carbohydrate; 81 mg calcium; 226 mg sodium; 342 mg cholesterol

SERVING SUGGESTION:

Serve each portion with 10 small or 6 large seedless green or red grapes. Add ½ Fruit Exchange to Exchange Information.

Per serving: 325 calories; 33 g protein; 12 g fat; 21 g carbohydrate; 86 mg calcium; 227 mg sodium; 342 mg cholesterol

Mary Stafford
St. Paul, Indiana

Turkey-Taco Salad ⓒ

Susan dreamed up this inexpensive and filling Mexican-style salad, which her family loves. A former home economics and math teacher, Susan is now a full-time homemaker and mother of three.

15 ounces ground turkey
¾ cup water
1 envelope (1¼ ounces) taco seasoning mix
1¾ cups shredded lettuce
½ cup *each* shredded carrot, diced celery, and diced green bell pepper
¼ cup chopped onion
1 ounce *each* Cheddar and Monterey Jack cheese, shredded
2 medium tomatoes, seeded and diced
4 corn tortillas (6-inch diameter each), heated and cut into 6 wedges each

Spray 10-inch nonstick skillet with nonstick cooking spray and heat over medium heat; add turkey and, using back of a wooden spoon to crumble meat, cook, stirring occasionally, until turkey is browned and cooked through, 5 to 8 minutes. Add water and taco seasoning mix and stir to combine thoroughly; bring liquid to a boil. Reduce heat to low and let simmer, stirring occasionally, for 15 to 20 minutes.

While meat mixture is simmering, in medium mixing bowl combine lettuce, carrot, celery, bell pepper, and onion. Line serving platter with lettuce mixture; top with turkey mixture and sprinkle with cheese. Arrange diced tomatoes around outer edge of platter and serve salad with tortilla wedges.

MAKES 4 SERVINGS

Each serving provides: 3½ Protein Exchanges; 1 Bread Exchange; 2¾ Vegetable Exchanges
Per serving: 330 calories; 26 g protein; 16 g fat; 22 g carbohydrate; 211 mg calcium; 774 mg sodium; 85 mg cholesterol

Susan E. Carpenter
Olympia, Washington

Creamy Shrimp Salad ◐

Jackie loves shrimp and here she incorporates it with other ingredients to create a delicious salad that's perfect for lunch or dinner.

2 tablespoons skim milk
1 tablespoon plus 1½ tea-
    spoons seafood cocktail
    sauce
1 tablespoon plain low-fat
    yogurt
½ to 1 teaspoon lemon juice
4 ounces cooked shelled and
    deveined small shrimp
½ cup diced tomato
¼ cup *each* diced green bell
    pepper and onion
1½ ounces drained canned
    water chestnuts, diced
2 tablespoons diced red bell
    pepper
½ teaspoon salt (optional)
Dash pepper
1 cup shredded lettuce

In small bowl combine milk, seafood cocktail sauce, yogurt, and lemon juice; set aside.

In medium bowl combine remaining ingredients except lettuce; add milk mixture and toss lightly to coat. Serve on bed of shredded lettuce.

MAKES 1 SERVING

Each serving provides: 4 Protein Exchanges; ½ Bread Exchange; 4¼ Vegetable Exchanges; ¼ Milk Exchange; 25 calories Optional Exchange
Per serving with salt: 257 calories; 32 g protein; 2 g fat; 28 g carbohydrate; 261 mg calcium; 1,585 mg sodium; 172 mg cholesterol
If salt is not used, decrease calcium to 254 mg and sodium to 519 mg.

Jackie L. Jones
Provo, Utah

Shrimp Louis Salad ◑

Lynda prefers to eat very little beef or pork, concentrating on seafood and poultry, and this dish is a favorite meal of hers. She has encouraged many friends to join Weight Watchers and feels that the meeting provides a wonderful service.

1 cup cottage cheese
¼ cup tomato juice
1 egg, hard-cooked and
    chopped
1 teaspoon prepared mustard
8 romaine lettuce leaves,
    shredded
2 cups seeded and sliced
    cucumbers
12 ounces cooked shelled and
    deveined shrimp, chilled,
    divided
¼ avocado (2 ounces), pared
    and thinly sliced
8 pitted black olives, sliced

In blender container combine cottage cheese, tomato juice, egg, and mustard; process until smooth. Transfer mixture to a 2-cup serving bowl; cover and refrigerate until chilled.

When ready to serve, line a shallow serving bowl with lettuce leaves; decoratively arrange cucumbers, all but 1 shrimp, the avocado, and olives on lettuce. Serve salad with dressing on the side; garnish with remaining shrimp.

MAKES 4 SERVINGS

Each serving provides: 4 Protein Exchanges; 1½ Vegetable Exchanges; 40 calories Optional Exchange
Per serving: 220 calories; 30 g protein; 8 g fat; 6 g carbohydrate; 162 mg calcium; 478 mg sodium; 204 mg cholesterol

Lynda M. Kuehn
Quesnel, British Columbia,
Canada

Shrimp Salad San Joaquin

A self-employed locksmith, Elaine is extremely busy with her Fresno-based business. She does like to take time out for cooking, however, and her cool and colorful shrimp salad is a delight.

12 ounces cooked shelled and deveined small shrimp (tails left on)
1 cup chopped scallions (green onions)
2 tablespoons olive *or* vegetable oil
2 to 3 small garlic cloves, minced
1⅓ cups water
4 packets instant chicken broth and seasoning mix
1½ teaspoons hot sauce
½ teaspoon crushed red pepper
4 ounces uncooked instant rice
2 medium tomatoes, seeded and cut into thin strips
1 cup diced green bell peppers
1½ teaspoons salt (optional)
Dash pepper, or to taste
Italian (flat-leaf) parsley sprigs and thin lime slices

In large glass or stainless-steel bowl (not aluminum*) combine shrimp, scallions, oil, and garlic and toss to coat thoroughly. Cover with plastic wrap and refrigerate overnight.

In 1-quart saucepan combine water, broth mix, hot sauce, and red pepper, stirring to dissolve broth mix; bring to a boil and stir in rice. Remove pan from heat, cover, and let stand 5 minutes; using a fork, fluff rice. Add tomatoes, bell peppers, salt if desired, and pepper; toss to combine. Add rice mixture to shrimp mixture; toss to combine. Cover with plastic wrap and refrigerate until chilled, at least 1 hour. Serve garnished with parsley sprigs and lime slices.

MAKES 4 SERVINGS

*It's best to marinate in glass or stainless-steel containers; aluminum may react with some foods, such as shrimp, causing color and flavor changes.

Each serving provides: 3 Protein Exchanges; 1 Bread Exchange; 2 Vegetable Exchanges; 1½ Fat Exchanges; 10 calories Optional Exchange
Per serving with salt: 280 calories; 20 g protein; 8 g fat; 32 g carbohydrate; 84 mg calcium; 1,796 mg sodium; 128 mg cholesterol
If salt is not used, decrease calcium to 79 mg and sodium to 972 mg.

J. Elaine Willhoite
Fresno, California

Buttermilk-Cheese Dressing ◐

Elsa loves blue cheese salad dressing so she developed this milder Program version. It will keep for up to two weeks in the refrigerator, so feel free to double or triple the recipe. Elsa, who has six children and two grandchildren, does a lot of walking and also enjoys gardening.

¾ cup buttermilk
2 tablespoons reduced-calorie mayonnaise
1 tablespoon well-chilled blue or feta cheese, crumbled*

In jar that has a tight-fitting cover combine all ingredients; cover and shake well.

MAKES 4 SERVINGS, ABOUT ¼ CUP EACH

*The cheese will crumble more easily if it is well chilled.

Each serving provides: ½ Fat Exchange; ¼ Milk Exchange; 20 calories Optional Exchange
Per serving with blue cheese: 46 calories; 2 g protein; 3 g fat; 3 g carbohydrate; 64 mg calcium; 134 mg sodium; 6 mg cholesterol
If feta cheese is used, reduce calories to 44 and sodium to 128 mg.

VARIATION:

Instead of 1 tablespoon of blue or feta cheese, use 1½ teaspoons of each.

Per serving: 45 calories; 2 g protein; 3 g fat; 3 g carbohydrate; 64 mg calcium; 131 mg sodium; 6 mg cholesterol

Elsa I. Ralston
Vernon, British Columbia, Canada

Caper Dressing

This recipe is the result of Gail's search for an elegant sauce to enhance a salmon loaf, but it's also wonderful over salad, hard-cooked eggs, tuna, or baked potato. Gail is a member of the Herb Society of America as well as the editor of her local chapter's monthly newsletter.

¼ cup plain low-fat yogurt
2 tablespoons plus 2 tea-
   spoons reduced-calorie
   mayonnaise
1½ teaspoons chopped
   drained capers*

In small bowl combine all ingredients, mixing well; cover with plastic wrap and refrigerate for at least 30 minutes before serving.

MAKES 4 SERVINGS, ABOUT 2 TABLESPOONS EACH

*Capers can usually be found in the gourmet or ethnic section of the supermarket, or they may be kept with the pickles and relishes. They are well worth the search and the price, since, when it comes to flavor, a little goes a long way.

Each serving provides: 1 Fat Exchange; 10 calories Optional Exchange
Per serving: 36 calories; 1 g protein; 3 g fat; 2 g carbohydrate; 26 mg
   calcium; 112 mg sodium; 4 mg cholesterol

SERVING SUGGESTION:

If desired, garnish with drained whole capers and a parsley sprig and serve as a dip with assorted fresh vegetables.

Gail Bartter
Berea, Ohio

Oriental Dressing ◐

Merrill enjoys salad and was tired of the same old dressings, so he decided to experiment a bit. Result: a tangy dressing that adds excitement to a salad. Merrill works in the real estate field and is married.

¼ cup oil (olive, peanut, vegetable, *or* soybean)

2 tablespoons *each* rice vinegar, water, diced celery, and diced onion

1 tablespoon teriyaki *or* soy sauce*

1½ teaspoons lime juice (no sugar added)

1 teaspoon ketchup

1 slice pared ginger root (about ¼ inch thick)

In blender container combine all ingredients and process until smooth, 1 to 2 minutes, scraping down sides of container as necessary; transfer dressing to container, cover tightly, and refrigerate until chilled. Shake or stir just before serving.

MAKES 8 SERVINGS, ABOUT 2 TABLESPOONS EACH

Each serving provides: 1½ Fat Exchanges; 1 calorie Optional Exchange
Per serving with teriyaki sauce: 65 calories; 0.1 g protein; 7 g fat; 1 g carbohydrate; 2 mg calcium; 84 mg sodium; 0 mg cholesterol
With soy sauce: 64 calories; 0.2 g protein; 7 g fat; 1 g carbohydrate; 3 mg calcium; 175 mg sodium; 0 mg cholesterol

*Reduced-sodium soy sauce may be substituted. Reduce calcium to 2 mg and sodium to 85 mg.

Merrill L. Johnson-Lannen
Brooklyn, New York

Onion-Yogurt Dip ☾

Patricia has prepared this dip for her family and for parties, and it's always a hit. A busy mother of two, in her spare time Patricia likes to sew, knit, and do needlepoint.

½ cup plain low-fat yogurt
2 tablespoons plus
   2 teaspoons mayonnaise
2 tablespoons chopped
   scallion (green onion)
2 teaspoons parsley flakes
1 teaspoon Worcestershire
   sauce
½ packet (about ½ teaspoon)
   instant onion broth and
   seasoning mix
⅛ teaspoon garlic powder

In small mixing bowl combine all ingredients, mixing until thoroughly blended; transfer to serving dish, cover with plastic wrap, and refrigerate for at least 1 hour. Stir again just before serving.

MAKES 4 SERVINGS, ABOUT 3 TABLESPOONS EACH

Each serving provides: 2 Fat Exchanges; ¼ Milk Exchange; 1 calorie Optional Exchange
Per serving: 87 calories; 2 g protein; 8 g fat; 3 g carbohydrate; 56 mg calcium; 182 mg sodium; 7 mg cholesterol

VARIATION:

To turn dip into dressing, when combining ingredients add 3 tablespoons skim milk. Increase Optional Exchange to 5 calories.

Per serving: 91 calories; 2 g protein; 8 g fat; 3 g carbohydrate; 70 mg calcium; 188 mg sodium; 7 mg cholesterol

Patricia A. Douglas
Chippewa Falls, Wisconsin

Ricotta Dip ◐

When Linda reached goal, she wrote a poem and dedicated it to her Weight Watchers leader. Now a leader herself (and still writing poems), Linda is very excited about being a part of this cookbook. She is married and has four children.

¼ cup part-skim ricotta
   cheese
1 tablespoon ketchup
2 teaspoons prepared
   horseradish
1 teaspoon onion flakes
Dash to ¼ teaspoon garlic
   powder
Dash *each* salt and pepper
   (optional)

In small bowl combine all ingredients, mixing well; cover with plastic wrap and refrigerate until chilled.

MAKES 1 SERVING, ABOUT ¼ CUP

Each serving provides: 1 Protein Exchange; 15 calories Optional Exchange
Per serving without salt: 112 calories; 8 g protein; 5 g fat; 10 g carbohydrate; 181 mg calcium; 265 mg sodium; 19 mg cholesterol
If salt is used, increase sodium to 396 mg.

SERVING SUGGESTIONS:

1. Serve as a dip with crisp, raw vegetables.

2. To transform this into a salad dressing, process mixture in blender container until smooth; serve over a mixed green salad.

Linda G. Cathorall
Bunker Hill, Illinois

Mainly Meatless
Eggs, Cheese, and Legumes

Black Bean-Chili Soup

A Weight Watchers leader who lost 80 pounds, Susan encourages her members to try new recipes and to adapt family favorites to the Food Plan. And that's exactly what she and her husband have done here. Because the soup freezes well, Susan likes to make a big potful at a time.

12 ounces sorted uncooked black turtle beans (frijoles negros), rinsed
Water
2 tablespoons plus 2 teaspoons olive oil
2 cups chopped onions
2 tablespoons chopped seeded green chili pepper
6 garlic cloves, minced
2 cups canned Italian tomatoes (with liquid); drain, seed, and dice tomatoes, reserving liquid
2 teaspoons ground cumin
1 teaspoon *each* **chili powder and ground coriander**
½ teaspoon crushed red pepper
2 cups plain low-fat yogurt

In medium mixing bowl combine beans with enough water to cover beans by 2 inches. Cover bowl with plastic wrap and let stand overnight.

In 4-quart saucepan heat oil over medium heat; add onions, chili pepper, and garlic and sauté, stirring occasionally, until onions are softened. Drain beans, discard soaking liquid, and add beans to saucepan along with 1 quart plus 3 cups water and the remaining ingredients except yogurt; mix well and bring to a boil. Reduce heat to low, cover pan, and let simmer, stirring occasionally, until beans are tender, about 2 hours. Remove from heat and let cool.

Pour 1 to 2 cups soup into blender container and process until smooth. Transfer mixture to a 1-quart bowl and repeat procedure, 1 to 2 cups at a time, until half of the soup has been processed. Pour soup back into saucepan with unprocessed soup and cook over medium heat until soup is heated through, 5 to 10 minutes. Serve each portion topped with ¼ cup yogurt.

MAKES 8 SERVINGS

Each serving provides: 2 Protein Exchanges; 1 Vegetable Exchange; 1 Fat Exchange; ½ Milk Exchange
Per serving: 253 calories; 14 g protein; 6 g fat; 37 g carbohydrate; 197 mg calcium; 154 mg sodium; 3 mg cholesterol

Susan E. Slesinger
Lakewood, California

Cheese Soup with Popcorn ☾◑

Popcorn makes this soup special and different, says Roxanne, who serves it often. The original recipe came from her sister-in-law, and Roxanne adapted it to fit the Food Plan.

1 tablespoon margarine
⅓ cup *each* diced carrot, celery, and onion
1 tablespoon all-purpose flour
1 cup *each* skim milk and water
1 packet instant chicken broth and seasoning mix
2 ounces *each* Cheddar *or* American cheese, cubed, and diagonally sliced turkey frankfurters
Dash *each* salt, pepper, and paprika
2 cups prepared plain popcorn

In 2-quart saucepan heat margarine until bubbly and hot; add vegetables and cook, stirring frequently, until onion is translucent, 2 to 3 minutes. Sprinkle flour over vegetables and stir quickly to combine; continue to stir and cook for 1 minute. Gradually stir in milk; stirring constantly, add water and broth mix and bring just to a boil. Reduce heat and simmer, stirring constantly, for 2 minutes. Add cheese and cook over low heat, continuing to stir, until cheese is melted; add frankfurters and seasonings and cook until heated through. Divide soup into 2 soup bowls; serve each portion with 1 cup popcorn to be sprinkled on soup.

MAKES 2 SERVINGS

Each serving provides: 2 Protein Exchanges; ½ Bread Exchange; 1 Vegetable Exchange; 1½ Fat Exchanges; ½ Milk Exchange; 20 calories Optional Exchange
Per serving with Cheddar cheese: 335 calories; 17 g protein; 21 g fat; 20 g carbohydrate; 414 mg calcium; 1,100 mg sodium; 57 mg cholesterol
With American cheese: 327 calories; 16 g protein; 21 g fat; 20 g carbohydrate; 385 mg calcium; 1,329 mg sodium; 53 mg cholesterol

Roxanne Salchow
St. Paul, Minnesota

Onion Soup ⊖ ◑

Janet's slimmed-down version of classic French onion soup is perfect all by itself, or as an accompaniment to a meal. The mother of two children, Janet enjoys bowling and volleyball.

4 packets instant beef broth and seasoning mix
1 quart water
2 cups thinly sliced onions
4 slices French bread (½ ounce each), toasted*
4 ounces *each* mozzarella cheese, shredded, and grated Parmesan cheese

In 2- or 3-quart saucepan sprinkle broth mix over water and bring to a boil; add onions and stir to combine. Reduce heat to low and let simmer until onions are tender, about 15 minutes.

In each of 4 flameproof soup crocks place 1 slice of bread, then pour ¼ of the soup into each crock. Sprinkle each portion with 1 ounce mozzarella cheese and 1 ounce Parmesan cheese; broil until cheese melts and is lightly browned, about 5 minutes.

MAKES 4 SERVINGS

*Day-old French bread may be used. Since this is already harder than fresh bread, there's no need to toast it.

Each serving provides: 2 Protein Exchanges; ½ Bread Exchange; 1 Vegetable Exchange; 10 calories Optional Exchange
Per serving: 287 calories; 21 g protein; 15 g fat; 17 g carbohydrate; 563 mg calcium; 1,463 mg sodium; 45 mg cholesterol

B. Janet Maidment
Petrolia, Ontario, Canada

Microwave French Onion Soup ☯◐

A busy mother of five who is employed full-time, Mary depends on her microwave oven to get a meal on the table pronto! This recipe was given to her by a friend, and Mary adapted it to fit the Food Plan.

½ cup sliced onion
2 teaspoons reduced-calorie
  margarine (tub)
1 packet instant beef broth
  and seasoning mix,
  dissolved in 1 cup boiling
  water
Dash white pepper
2 slices French bread
  (½ ounce each), toasted
2 ounces mozzarella cheese,
  shredded

In 12-ounce microwave-safe soup bowl combine onion and margarine; cover with plastic wrap and microwave on High until onion is golden, about 5 minutes.* Remove plastic wrap from bowl; stir in dissolved broth mix and pepper. Place toast slices on soup, top with cheese, and microwave uncovered on High until cheese is melted, 1 to 2 minutes longer.*

MAKES 1 SERVING

*Cooking time may be different in your microwave oven. To help ensure good results, check for doneness while cooking.

Each serving provides: 2 Protein Exchanges; 1 Bread Exchange; 1 Vegetable
  Exchange; 1 Fat Exchange; 10 calories Optional Exchange
Per serving: 313 calories; 16 g protein; 17 g fat; 24 g carbohydrate; 326 mg
  calcium; 1,204 mg sodium; 45 mg cholesterol

Mary A. Dinucci
Columbus, Indiana

Potato-Cheese Frittata ☯◑

Anna adapted her mother's frittata recipe, and the result is a delicious egg dish that can be served for lunch or dinner. Try substituting mozzarella cheese for the Cheddar, suggests Anna. "Gooey and delicious!"

1 teaspoon vegetable oil
3 ounces sliced pared potato
¼ cup diced onion
2 eggs
1 ounce Cheddar cheese,
   shredded
⅛ teaspoon salt
Dash pepper

In 7-inch nonstick skillet heat oil over medium heat; add potato slices and sauté, turning occasionally, until lightly browned. Add onion and cook, continuing to turn, until potato and onion are thoroughly cooked, about 4 minutes longer.

In small bowl combine eggs, cheese, salt, and pepper. Pour egg mixture into skillet and cook until eggs begin to set. Using spatula, lift cooked edges of egg mixture and tilt pan to allow uncooked portions to flow underneath; cook until underside is browned. Loosen sides of egg mixture and slide onto plate. Invert skillet over plate, then invert plate and skillet together so that egg mixture returns to skillet; cook until browned on bottom.

MAKES 1 SERVING

Each serving provides: 3 Protein Exchanges; 1 Bread Exchange; ½ Vegetable
   Exchange; 1 Fat Exchange
Per serving with Cheddar cheese: 394 calories; 21 g protein; 25 g fat; 20 g
   carbohydrate; 279 mg calcium; 596 mg sodium; 578 mg cholesterol
With mozzarella cheese: 359 calories; 20 g protein; 22 g fat; 20 g carbo-
   hydrate; 221 mg calcium; 526 mg sodium; 570 mg cholesterol

Anna Pace
Waterbury, Connecticut

Peanutty California Sandwich ◐◑

Peanut butter is a favorite of Toni's, and the addition of sprouts makes it a real California-style sandwich. Toni does research at the University of California and is an avid skier and aerobics student in her spare time.

⅓ cup cottage cheese
1 tablespoon smooth *or*
  chunky peanut butter
2 slices reduced-calorie whole
  wheat bread (40 calories
  per slice), toasted
2 tablespoons dark raisins
¼ cup alfalfa sprouts

In small bowl combine cheese and peanut butter, mixing well. Spread mixture on 1 slice toast; sprinkle with raisins, then top with sprouts and remaining slice toast.

MAKES 1 SERVING

Each serving provides: 2 Protein Exchanges; 1 Bread Exchange; ½ Vegetable Exchange; 1 Fat Exchange; 1 Fruit Exchange
Per serving: 303 calories; 18 g protein; 11 g fat; 37 g carbohydrate; 98 mg calcium; 549 mg sodium; 10 mg cholesterol

Toni Piccinini
San Francisco, California

Cheese "Calzone" ◑

Edwina's Italian background prompted her to try to create a calzone using pita bread. Married, with two children, Edwina is a teacher whose hobbies are cooking, Romance languages, soccer, and playing the piano.

2 ounces mozzarella cheese, cubed
½ cup part-skim ricotta cheese
1 pita bread (2 ounces)

Preheat oven to 400°F. In small bowl combine cheeses, mixing well. Using a sharp knife, cut halfway around edge of pita; open to form pocket. Spread cheese mixture inside pita; wrap in foil and bake until cheeses melt, about 20 minutes.

MAKES 1 SERVING

Each serving provides: 4 Protein Exchanges; 2 Bread Exchanges
Per serving: 503 calories; 30 g protein; 22 g fat; 44 g carbohydrate; 638 mg calcium; 728 mg sodium; 82 mg cholesterol

Edwina Rohrbach
West Hempstead, New York

Stuffed Pita Scramble ⊖⊕

Weekdays, energetic Sheri works in a bank; weekends, in a gourmet food shop, while her husband cares for their six children. What to do with leftovers? Try Sheri's suggestion and scramble up a speedy lunch or dinner.

1 teaspoon margarine
½ cup sliced zucchini
2 tablespoons chopped onion
2 ounces boiled ham *or* skinned and boned roast turkey, cubed
1 egg, beaten
1 ounce Cheddar *or* Swiss cheese, shredded
1 pita bread (1 ounce)
2 tomato slices

In 8-inch nonstick skillet heat margarine over medium heat until bubbly and hot; add zucchini and onion and sauté, stirring constantly, until zucchini is tender, 2 to 3 minutes. Add ham (or turkey) and cook, stirring constantly, until heated through, about 1 minute. Add egg and cook, stirring frequently, just until egg is set, 1 to 2 minutes. Stir in cheese and cook until cheese melts.

Cut pita in half crosswise, forming 2 pockets; stuff each pocket with half of the egg mixture and 1 tomato slice.

MAKES 1 SERVING

Each serving provides: 4 Protein Exchanges; 1 Bread Exchange; 1½ Vegetable Exchanges; 1 Fat Exchange
Per serving with ham and Cheddar cheese: 417 calories; 29 g protein; 22 g fat; 24 g carbohydrate; 260 mg calcium; 1,157 mg sodium; 334 mg cholesterol
With ham and Swiss cheese: 409 calories; 30 g protein; 21 g fat; 25 g carbohydrate; 328 mg calcium; 1,055 mg sodium; 330 mg cholesterol
With turkey and Cheddar cheese: 430 calories; 34 g protein; 22 g fat; 24 g carbohydrate; 269 mg calcium; 517 mg sodium; 347 mg cholesterol
With turkey and Swiss cheese: 422 calories; 35 g protein; 20 g fat; 24 g carbohydrate; 337 mg calcium; 415 mg sodium; 344 mg cholesterol

Sheri Farley
Palo Alto, California

Vegetable-Shrimp Quiche

An insurance agent and mother of two, Michelle began attending Weight Watchers meetings before her second child was born. Her quiche is an adaptation of several different recipes. Michelle's family loves it—so will you!

4 ready-to-bake refrigerated buttermilk flaky biscuits (1 ounce each)
4 eggs
4 ounces Swiss cheese, shredded
2½ cups parboiled cauliflower florets
4 ounces cooked shelled and deveined shrimp, chopped
1 cup chopped mushrooms
½ cup minced onion
Dash *each* salt and pepper

Preheat oven to 350°F. Roll each biscuit between 2 sheets of wax paper, forming four 5-inch circles. Spray 10-inch pie plate with nonstick cooking spray. Line pie plate with biscuit circles, covering bottom and sides; where biscuits overlap, press together to seal, forming a crust. Bake crust for 5 minutes; remove pie plate to wire rack and let cool.

In medium mixing bowl beat eggs; stir in cheese. Add cauliflower, shrimp, mushrooms, onion, salt, and pepper and mix well. Pour mixture into prepared crust and bake until filling is set, 50 minutes to 1 hour (until a knife, inserted in center, comes out clean).

MAKES 4 SERVINGS

Each serving provides: 3 Protein Exchanges; 1 Bread Exchange; 2 Vegetable Exchanges
Per serving: 333 calories; 25 g protein; 17 g fat; 20 g carbohydrate; 360 mg calcium; 515 mg sodium; 343 mg cholesterol

VARIATION:

For Vegetable-Ham Quiche, substitute 4 ounces diced boiled ham for the shrimp.
Per serving: 341 calories; 24 g protein; 19 g fat; 20 g carbohydrate; 330 mg calcium; 816 mg sodium; 315 mg cholesterol

Michelle Nielson
Marion, Iowa

❖❖

Spinach Pie ©

Margaret adapted a favorite Greek dish to fit the Food Plan. It makes a delicious luncheon entrée.

2 tablespoons margarine
¾ cup chopped onions
2 garlic cloves, minced
2 tablespoons all-purpose
  flour
1 cup skim milk
¼ teaspoon salt
Dash *each* ground nutmeg
  and pepper
8 eggs, beaten
1½ cups well-drained cooked
  spinach
2 ounces *each* Cheddar
  cheese, shredded, and
  grated Parmesan cheese

In small saucepan melt margarine over medium heat; add onions and garlic and sauté until onions are softened, about 1 minute. Add flour and stir quickly to combine. Gradually stir in milk; cook, stirring constantly, until sauce is smooth. Add salt, nutmeg, and pepper, mixing well; cook, stirring occasionally, until mixture is thickened, 5 to 10 minutes. Remove from heat and let cool to lukewarm, about 5 minutes.

Preheat oven to 350°F. Transfer sauce to medium mixing bowl; add eggs and mix well. Add spinach and cheeses and mix until thoroughly combined. Spray 9-inch pie plate with nonstick cooking spray and pour in spinach mixture; bake until top is puffed and lightly browned, 40 to 45 minutes (until a knife, inserted in center, comes out clean). Remove from oven and let cool 5 minutes before serving.

MAKES 6 SERVINGS

Each serving provides: 2 Protein Exchanges; ¾ Vegetable Exchange; 1 Fat Exchange; 25 calories Optional Exchange
Per serving: 263 calories; 18 g protein; 17 g fat; 9 g carbohydrate; 356 mg calcium; 515 mg sodium; 384 mg cholesterol

Margaret Rashash
Sonoma, California

Legume-Cheese Pie ☉

Barbara lost 40 pounds over eleven years ago and has kept them off. A Weight Watchers receptionist for more than ten years, she created this recipe when legumes were added to the Food Plan.

¾ ounce mozzarella cheese, shredded*
¼ ounce grated Parmesan cheese*
4 ounces drained cooked lentils
½ cup *each* cooked sliced carrot, cut green beans, and sliced mushrooms
¼ cup tomato sauce
½ teaspoon onion flakes
¼ teaspoon salt
¼ teaspoon oregano leaves, divided
3 tomato slices

Preheat oven to 325°F. In small cup combine cheeses; transfer half of mixture to 1-quart bowl and add lentils, carrot, green beans, mushrooms, tomato sauce, onion flakes, salt, and ⅛ teaspoon oregano, mixing to combine.

Spray 8- or 9-inch pie plate with nonstick cooking spray and spread lentil mixture evenly over surface of plate; top with tomato slices and sprinkle tomatoes with remaining cheese mixture and ⅛ teaspoon oregano. Bake until cheese is melted, 20 to 30 minutes.

MAKES 1 SERVING

*To help make weighing easy, weigh the mozzarella cheese first; then add Parmesan cheese to the mozzarella until scale registers 1 ounce.

Each serving provides: 3 Protein Exchanges; 4½ Vegetable Exchanges
Per serving: 305 calories; 20 g protein; 7 g fat; 44 g carbohydrate; 312 mg calcium; 1,193 mg sodium; 22 mg cholesterol

Barbara Lennane
Sloatsburg, New York

Tofu-Tamale Pie ⊙

Sheryl and a friend created this unusual entrée together because they both love tofu. Sheryl lost 25 pounds over five years ago, and is now working as Coordinating Director for Operations for Weight Watchers of Greater Iowa, a Weight Watchers franchise. She enjoys jogging, tennis, sewing, and reading.

1 tablespoon plus 1 teaspoon vegetable oil
1 cup chopped onions
2 cups sliced zucchini
1 cup sliced mushrooms
12 ounces firm-style tofu (soybean curd), cut into cubes
3 cups canned crushed tomatoes
1 tablespoon chili powder
½ teaspoon salt
¼ teaspoon pepper
16 pitted black olives, sliced
1 cup drained canned whole-kernel corn
1½ ounces uncooked yellow or white cornmeal
4 ounces sharp Cheddar cheese, shredded

In 12-inch skillet that has an oven-safe or removable handle heat oil over medium-high heat; add onions and sauté until translucent. Add zucchini and mushrooms and sauté 5 minutes; add tofu, tomatoes, chili powder, salt, and pepper. Reduce heat and let simmer 15 minutes.

Preheat oven to 400°F. Stir olives, corn, and cornmeal into tofu mixture and cook, stirring frequently, until mixture thickens, 5 to 10 minutes. Sprinkle with cheese, transfer to oven, and bake until cheese is melted, about 5 minutes. Let stand 5 minutes before serving.

MAKES 4 SERVINGS

Each serving provides: 2 Protein Exchanges; 1 Bread Exchange; 3½ Vegetable Exchanges; 1 Fat Exchange; 20 calories Optional Exchange
Per serving: 383 calories; 19 g protein; 22 g fat; 33 g carbohydrate; 404 mg calcium; 879 mg sodium; 30 mg cholesterol

Sheryl H. Knuth
Omaha, Nebraska

Pasta Primavera ◑

Here is Nancy's version of the classic Italian pasta dish. It's perfect for company dinners; just increase the amounts of each ingredient.

½ cup evaporated skimmed milk
1 egg
¼ cup part-skim ricotta cheese
1 tablespoon reduced-calorie margarine (tub)
1 garlic clove, minced
1 ounce grated Parmesan *or* Romano cheese
⅛ teaspoon *each* basil leaves and oregano leaves
Dash pepper
⅓ cup *each* cooked broccoli florets, cauliflower florets, and sliced carrot
½ cup cooked linguine *or* fettuccine (hot)

In blender container combine milk, egg, and ricotta cheese and process until smooth, scraping down sides of container as necessary; set aside.

In 10-inch nonstick skillet heat margarine over medium heat until bubbly and hot; add garlic and sauté until softened, about 1 minute. Reduce heat to low and add egg mixture, Parmesan (or Romano) cheese, basil, oregano, and pepper; cook, stirring constantly, until sauce is thickened, 3 to 5 minutes *(do not boil)*. Add broccoli, cauliflower, and carrot to sauce and cook, stirring constantly, until vegetables are heated through, about 1 minute. Arrange pasta on serving platter and top with vegetable-cheese mixture.

MAKES 1 SERVING

Each serving provides: 3 Protein Exchanges; 1 Bread Exchange; 2 Vegetable Exchanges; 1½ Fat Exchanges; 1 Milk Exchange
Per serving: 574 calories; 40 g protein; 26 g fat; 47 g carbohydrate; 1,060 mg calcium; 984 mg sodium; 321 mg cholesterol

Nancy Bishop
Pittsburgh, Pennsylvania

Ratatouille-Pasta Gratinée ℂ

Janet prefers meatless dishes to those containing meat; so, while she was on the Program, she created this dish to enjoy. Her hobbies include singing, needlework, and calligraphy.

2 cups *each* diced eggplant and sliced zucchini
1½ teaspoons salt, divided
1 tablespoon plus 1 teaspoon vegetable oil
1 cup sliced onions
1½ cups canned Italian tomatoes (with liquid); drain, seed, and dice tomatoes, reserving liquid
2 tablespoons tomato paste
1 teaspoon oregano leaves
½ teaspoon *each* basil leaves and garlic powder
Dash pepper
2 cups cooked spaghetti *or* fusilli (hot)
8 ounces mozzarella cheese, shredded

Set large colander in sink; add eggplant and zucchini, sprinkle with 1 teaspoon salt, and let stand 30 minutes. Rinse vegetables under running cold water; drain and pat dry with paper towels.

In 12-inch nonstick skillet heat oil over medium-high heat; add eggplant, zucchini, and onions and sauté until vegetables are softened, 1 to 2 minutes. Add tomatoes, reserved liquid, tomato paste, remaining ½ teaspoon salt, the oregano, basil, garlic powder, and pepper and cook, stirring, until tomato paste is dissolved. Reduce heat to low and continue to cook, stirring occasionally, until vegetables are thoroughly cooked and flavors are blended, 15 to 20 minutes.

On flameproof serving platter arrange spaghetti (or fusilli); top with vegetable mixture and sprinkle with cheese. Broil until cheese is melted and lightly browned, 2 to 3 minutes.

MAKES 4 SERVINGS

Each serving provides: 2 Protein Exchanges; 1 Bread Exchange; 3¼ Vegetable Exchanges; 1 Fat Exchange
Per serving: 338 calories; 16 g protein; 18 g fat; 31 g carbohydrate; 372 mg calcium; 840 mg sodium; 44 mg cholesterol

Janet E. Saadian
Alexandria, Virginia

Ziti and Vegetable Medley ❸

Adele wanted a meatless dish that she could freeze and reheat, and this was the result. Traveling, attending Broadway and off-Broadway shows, reading, and knitting are Adele's chief interests, outside of her work as a school secretary.

1 tablespoon vegetable oil
1 cup *each* thinly sliced carrots, sliced onions, sliced zucchini, sliced mushrooms, and broccoli florets
4 ounces Muenster cheese, shredded, divided
1 cup *each* tomato juice and cooked whole wheat ziti macaroni
1 teaspoon *each* chopped fresh basil and Italian (flat-leaf) parsley
Dash pepper

In 10-inch skillet or a wok heat oil; add carrots and cook, stirring quickly and frequently, until carrots are tender, 1 to 2 minutes. Add onions, zucchini, mushrooms, and broccoli and continue stir-frying until vegetables are tender-crisp. Remove skillet (or wok) from heat and stir in 2 ounces cheese, the tomato juice, ziti, basil, parsley, and pepper.

Preheat oven to 350°F. Transfer macaroni mixture to 2-quart casserole and sprinkle with remaining 2 ounces cheese. Bake until cheese is melted and mixture is bubbly, about 20 minutes.

MAKES 2 SERVINGS

Each serving provides: 2 Protein Exchanges; 1 Bread Exchange; 5 Vegetable Exchanges; 1½ Fat Exchanges; 25 calories Optional Exchange
Per serving: 454 calories; 23 g protein; 25 g fat; 39 g carbohydrate; 500 mg calcium; 836 mg sodium; 54 mg cholesterol

Adele Ruderman
Cedarhurst, New York

Vegetable-Cheese Lasagna

Jane worked hard to perfect this recipe. It's her favorite entrée for company dinners. Her family and her guests love it—you will, too.

1 tablespoon plus 1 teaspoon margarine
3 cups thinly sliced mushrooms
1 tablespoon plus 1 teaspoon olive oil
1 cup chopped onions
6 garlic cloves, minced
1½ cups tomato sauce
1 cup canned Italian tomatoes (with liquid); drain and dice tomatoes, reserving liquid
1½ teaspoons salt, divided
1 teaspoon *each* oregano leaves and basil leaves
½ teaspoon pepper, divided
1 bay leaf
2 packages (10 ounces each) frozen chopped spinach, thawed and well drained (about 2 cups)
2 cups part-skim ricotta cheese
1 egg, beaten
8 ounces uncooked lasagna macaroni (12 x 3-inch pieces), cooked according to package directions
11 ounces shredded Monterey Jack cheese, divided

In 10-inch skillet heat margarine over medium heat until bubbly and hot; add mushrooms and sauté, stirring occasionally, until mushrooms are lightly browned and cooked through, 2 to 3 minutes. Remove from heat and set aside. In 3-quart saucepan heat oil over medium heat; add onions and garlic and sauté until onions are softened, 1 to 2 minutes. Add tomato sauce, tomatoes, ¾ teaspoon salt, the oregano and basil, ¼ teaspoon pepper, and the bay leaf; mix well. Reduce heat to low, cover, and let simmer, stirring occasionally, for 25 to 30 minutes; remove and discard bay leaf. In medium mixing bowl combine spinach, ricotta cheese, egg, remaining ¾ teaspoon salt, and remaining ¼ teaspoon pepper, mixing well.

Preheat oven to 350°F. In bottom of 13 x 9 x 2-inch baking dish spread ½ cup tomato mixture; arrange half of the lasagna macaroni lengthwise in dish, overlapping edges slightly. Spread half of the spinach mixture evenly over macaroni and top with half of the mushrooms; spread ½ cup of the tomato mixture over mushrooms and sprinkle with half of the Monterey Jack cheese. Arrange remaining macaroni crosswise in dish, cutting macaroni to fit and overlapping edges slightly. Spread remaining spinach mixture over macaroni, top with remaining mushrooms, tomato mixture, and Monterey Jack cheese. Bake until lasagna is cooked through and cheese is lightly browned, 40 to 50 min-

(continued)

utes. Remove from oven and let stand 15 minutes before serving.

MAKES 8 SERVINGS

Each serving provides: 2½ Protein Exchanges; 1 Bread Exchange; 2½ Vegetable Exchanges; 1 Fat Exchange; 25 calories Optional Exchange

Per serving: 437 calories; 25 g protein; 22 g fat; 36 g carbohydrate; 584 mg calcium; 1,109 mg sodium; 87 mg cholesterol

Jane P. Epping
Davenport, Iowa

Tofu-Cheese Manicotti ☾

This Italian-style specialty contains tofu, a favorite of Jacqueline's, and it meets her requirements for a recipe: it is simple and quick to prepare.

9 ounces firm-style tofu (soybean curd)
3 ounces mozzarella cheese, shredded
2 ounces *each* Cheddar cheese, shredded, and grated Parmesan cheese
2 eggs, lightly beaten
2 teaspoons chopped fresh parsley
½ teaspoon basil leaves
¼ teaspoon *each* salt and pepper
⅛ teaspoon ground nutmeg
8 uncooked manicotti shells (4 ounces), cooked according to package directions and drained
2 cups tomato sauce

Preheat oven to 350°F. In work bowl of food processor process tofu until crumbly (*do not puree*). Transfer to medium bowl; add remaining ingredients except manicotti shells and tomato sauce and stir to combine. Fill each shell with an equal amount of the tofu mixture, reserving any remaining filling.

Spray 13 x 9 x 2-inch baking dish with nonstick cooking spray; arrange stuffed shells crosswise in dish. Combine tomato sauce with remaining tofu mixture and pour over manicotti. Bake until thoroughly heated, about 35 minutes.

MAKES 4 SERVINGS, 2 MANICOTTI EACH

Each serving provides: 3 Protein Exchanges; 1 Bread Exchange; 1 Vegetable Exchange; 50 calories Optional Exchange

Per serving: 409 calories; 27 g protein; 20 g fat; 33 g carbohydrate; 534 mg calcium; 1,344 mg sodium; 180 mg cholesterol

Jacqueline L. Thackery
Columbus, Indiana

Spinach Manicotti

If you like spinach, you'll love Margaret's special manicotti. It's great with a salad for lunch or dinner.

1 tablespoon plus 1 teaspoon *each* margarine and all-purpose flour
1 cup skim milk
¼ cup canned ready-to-serve chicken broth
¾ teaspoon salt, divided
White pepper and ground nutmeg
2 cups part-skim ricotta cheese
1 package (10 ounces) frozen chopped spinach, thawed and well drained (about 1 cup)
2 ounces grated Parmesan cheese
½ teaspoon garlic powder
8 uncooked manicotti shells (4 ounces), cooked according to package directions and drained
2 ounces mozzarella cheese, shredded

In small saucepan heat margarine over medium heat until bubbly and hot; add flour and cook, stirring constantly, for 1 minute. Reduce heat to low; gradually stir in milk and broth. Continue to stir and cook until mixture is smooth; add ¼ teaspoon salt and dash each white pepper and nutmeg and let simmer, stirring occasionally, until mixture is thickened, 10 to 15 minutes.

While mixture is simmering, in medium bowl combine ricotta cheese, spinach, Parmesan cheese, garlic powder, remaining ½ teaspoon salt, ⅛ teaspoon pepper, and dash nutmeg, mixing well.

Preheat oven to 350°F. In bottom of 13 x 9 x 2-inch flameproof baking dish spread ⅓ cup sauce. Stuff ⅛ of spinach mixture into each manicotti shell and arrange stuffed shells in dish; top with remaining sauce and sprinkle with mozzarella. Cover dish and bake until manicotti are heated through, 20 to 25 minutes. Turn oven control to broil, uncover pan, and broil until cheese is melted and lightly browned, 3 to 5 minutes.

MAKES 4 SERVINGS, 2 MANICOTTI EACH

Each serving provides: 3 Protein Exchanges; 1 Bread Exchange; ½ Vegetable Exchange; 1 Fat Exchange; ¼ Milk Exchange; 40 calories Optional Exchange
Per serving: 464 calories; 31 g protein; 22 g fat; 37 g carbohydrate; 770 mg calcium; 1,079 mg sodium; 62 mg cholesterol

Margaret Rashash
Sonoma, California

Mozzarella-Zucchini Special ◑◐

Linda is a Weight Watchers receptionist who lost 35 pounds on the Program. Fresh zucchini from her summer vegetable garden inspired this recipe, which has since become her favorite lunch.

2 teaspoons reduced-calorie
   margarine (tub)
¼ cup thinly sliced celery
1 small garlic clove, minced
1 cup sliced zucchini
½ cup canned crushed
   tomatoes
Dash *each* oregano leaves
   and pepper
2 ounces mozzarella cheese,
   shredded

In 8-inch nonstick skillet heat margarine until bubbly and hot; add celery and garlic and sauté until garlic is lightly browned *(be careful not to burn)*. Add zucchini and sauté until tender-crisp; stir in tomatoes and seasonings and let simmer until zucchini is tender and almost all of the liquid has evaporated, about 5 minutes. Transfer zucchini mixture to microwave-safe plate, sprinkle with cheese, and microwave on High until cheese is melted, about 1 minute.*

MAKES 1 SERVING

*Cooking time may be different in your microwave oven. To help ensure good results, be sure to check for doneness while cooking.

Each serving provides: 2 Protein Exchanges; 3½ Vegetable Exchanges; 1 Fat Exchange
Per serving: 243 calories; 14 g protein; 17 g fat; 12 g carbohydrate; 360 mg calcium; 518 mg sodium; 44 mg cholesterol

VARIATION:

To melt cheese under a broiler, transfer zucchini mixture to flameproof plate and broil until cheese is melted, 2 to 3 minutes.

*Linda K. Smith
Harrisonburg, Virginia*

Baked Stuffed Zucchini ◐

Evelyn revised her sister's recipe to fit the Food Plan. In the summer, she uses fresh zucchini to prepare this dish, then freezes it to enjoy during the winter months.

1 medium zucchini (about
   5 ounces)
1 quart boiling water
1 egg, beaten
2 ounces reduced-calorie
   American-flavor pasteurized
   process cheese product
   (up to 50 calories per
   ounce), cut into ½-inch
   pieces
3 unsalted saltines, made into
   crumbs
⅛ teaspoon salt (optional)
Dash pepper
1 teaspoon *each* grated
   Parmesan cheese and
   imitation bacon bits

In 2-quart saucepan add zucchini to 1 quart boiling water and cook over high heat until zucchini is fork-tender, about 5 minutes. Using tongs or slotted spoon, remove zucchini from saucepan; rinse with cold water.

Preheat oven to 350°F. Cut zucchini in half lengthwise and, using a teaspoon, scoop out pulp, reserving shells. Finely chop pulp and transfer to small mixing bowl; add egg, process cheese, cracker crumbs, salt if desired, and pepper and mix well. Spoon half of mixture into each reserved zucchini shell and place stuffed zucchini in 8 x 8 x 2-inch baking pan; sprinkle ½ teaspoon each Parmesan cheese and bacon bits over each stuffed shell. Bake until cheese is melted and lightly browned, 15 to 20 minutes.

MAKES 1 SERVING

Each serving provides: 2 Protein Exchanges; ½ Bread Exchange; 2 Vegetable
    Exchanges; 20 calories Optional Exchange
Per serving without salt: 253 calories; 24 g protein; 12 g fat; 14 g carbo-
    hydrate; 389 mg calcium; 1,176 mg sodium; 292 mg cholesterol
If salt is used, increase calcium to 391 mg and sodium to 1,443 mg.

Evelyn Masters
Yorktown, Indiana

Cheddar-Egg Stuffed Biscuit

Cheese Soup with Popcorn
Onion Soup
Shrimp-Corn Chowder

Pineapple-Chicken Salad

Shrimp Salad San Joaquin

Instant Fruit "Ice Cream"
Cantaloupe "Ice Cream"

Stuffed Squash Casserole ☉

Jennifer modified a recipe given to her by a friend to create this delicious casserole filled with rice and cheese.

2 teaspoons margarine
½ cup finely chopped onion
2 garlic cloves, minced
1 cup cooked long-grain rice
⅔ cup cottage cheese, pureed
2 eggs, beaten
1 tablespoon chopped fresh
  parsley
1 teaspoon basil leaves
½ teaspoon salt
¼ teaspoon pepper
2 medium zucchini (about
  5 ounces each), sliced
  lengthwise into ⅛-inch-
  thick slices
2 slices American cheese
  (1 ounce each)

Preheat oven to 350°F. In 8-inch nonstick skillet heat margarine over medium heat until bubbly and hot; add onion and garlic and sauté until onion is softened, 1 to 2 minutes. Transfer to medium bowl; add remaining ingredients except zucchini and American cheese, mixing well.

Spray 8 x 8 x 2-inch casserole with non-stick cooking spray; arrange zucchini slices in bottom. Using spatula, evenly spread cottage cheese mixture over zucchini; top with American cheese slices. Bake until zucchini is tender and cheese is melted, 25 to 30 minutes.

MAKES 2 SERVINGS

Each serving provides: 3 Protein Exchanges; 1 Bread Exchange; 2½ Vegetable Exchanges; 1 Fat Exchange
Per serving: 445 calories; 25 g protein; 22 g fat; 36 g carbohydrate; 316 mg calcium; 1,357 mg sodium; 311 mg cholesterol

VARIATION:

2 ounces Cheddar, Swiss, Muenster, or Monterey Jack cheese, shredded, may be substituted for the American cheese.

Per serving with Cheddar cheese: 453 calories; 26 g protein; 22 g fat; 37 g carbohydrate; 346 mg calcium; 1,128 mg sodium; 314 mg cholesterol
With Swiss cheese: 445 calories; 27 g protein; 21 g fat; 37 g carbohydrate; 414 mg calcium; 1,026 mg sodium; 311 mg cholesterol
With Muenster cheese: 443 calories; 26 g protein; 21 g fat; 36 g carbohydrate; 345 mg calcium; 1,130 mg sodium; 312 mg cholesterol
With Monterey Jack cheese: 444 calories; 26 g protein; 22 g fat; 36 g carbohydrate; 353 mg calcium; 1,104 mg sodium; 309 mg cholesterol

Jennifer Ramelmeier
Columbia, Maryland

Cauliflower and Cheese Bake ⊙◑

Phyllis prepares this tasty casserole for her family as well as for guests. You can substitute Cheddar or Swiss for the pasteurized process cheese spread.

2 tablespoons reduced-calorie
  margarine (tub)
6 saltines, made into crumbs
1 package (10 ounces) frozen
  cauliflower, cooked according to package directions
  and drained (about 2 cups)
4 ounces pasteurized process
  cheese spread, cut into
  ½-inch cubes

In small skillet melt margarine; add cracker crumbs and cook over low heat, stirring constantly, until crumbs are lightly browned. Remove skillet from heat and set aside.

Preheat oven to 350°F. Spray 1-quart casserole with nonstick cooking spray; arrange cauliflower in casserole, top with cheese, and sprinkle with crumb mixture. Cover casserole and bake until cheese is melted, about 20 minutes.

MAKES 2 SERVINGS

Each serving provides: 2 Protein Exchanges; ½ Bread Exchange; 2 Vegetable
  Exchanges; 1½ Fat Exchanges
Per serving: 290 calories; 14 g protein; 19 g fat; 18 g carbohydrate; 388 mg
  calcium; 1,108 mg sodium; 39 mg cholesterol
With Cheddar: 349 calories; 18 g protein; 26 g fat; 13 g carbohydrate; 442
  mg calcium; 599 mg sodium; 60 mg cholesterol
With Swiss: 334 calories; 20 g protein; 23 g fat; 15 g carbohydrate; 578 mg
  calcium; 395 mg sodium; 52 mg cholesterol

Phyllis J. Harber
New Haven, Indiana

Chili Relleno Casserole ©

Barbara is an enthusiastic kindergarten teacher and Weight Watchers leader who lost 30 pounds on the Program. This is a family recipe that she revised, eliminating the oil. While on a white-water rafting trip, Barbara made this dish over a campfire and got raves from all 24 people on the trip.

½ **cup drained canned mild whole green chili peppers**
2 **ounces Cheddar cheese, shredded**
2 **eggs, separated**

Preheat oven to 350°F. Spray 1½-quart casserole with nonstick cooking spray. Arrange chili peppers in an even layer in bottom of casserole and sprinkle with cheese; set aside.

Using electric mixer at high speed, in small mixing bowl beat egg whites until stiff but not dry. In separate small mixing bowl lightly beat egg yolks; using rubber scraper, carefully fold egg yolks into egg whites. Spread mixture over chili peppers, making sure mixture touches sides of casserole. Bake until topping is puffed and lightly browned, 25 to 30 minutes.

MAKES 1 SERVING

Each serving provides: 4 Protein Exchanges; 1 Vegetable Exchange
Per serving: 404 calories; 27 g protein; 30 g fat; 6 g carbohydrate; 470 mg calcium; 490 mg sodium; 608 mg cholesterol

Barbara McKinney Streander
Tucson, Arizona

Kale 'n' Cheese Bake

Jean is a member who lost 38 pounds on the Weight Watchers program. She and her family live nine miles from British Columbia in a house they built themselves. This recipe of Jean's is a family favorite.

2 pounds kale*
2 quarts water
5 ounces Cheddar cheese,
  shredded
1¼ cups part-skim ricotta
  cheese
2 eggs, beaten
¼ to ½ teaspoon basil leaves
¼ teaspoon pepper
⅛ teaspoon garlic powder
1 tablespoon plus 1 teaspoon
  grated Parmesan cheese

Wash kale thoroughly and drain; remove and discard stems and chop leaves. In 5-quart saucepan combine kale and water and bring to a boil. Reduce heat to medium and cook until tender, about 5 minutes. Drain kale and transfer to large bowl (there should be about 1 quart cooked kale); add remaining ingredients except Parmesan cheese.

Preheat oven to 350°F. Spray 2-quart casserole with nonstick cooking spray. Transfer kale mixture to casserole; smooth surface and sprinkle with Parmesan cheese. Bake until golden brown and set, 35 to 45 minutes. Remove from oven and let stand 5 minutes before cutting.

MAKES 4 SERVINGS

Each serving provides: 3 Protein Exchanges; 2 Vegetable Exchanges; 10
  calories Optional Exchange
Per serving: 410 calories; 29 g protein; 23 g fat; 28 g carbohydrate; 812 mg
  calcium; 479 mg sodium; 199 mg cholesterol

*Spinach or Swiss chard leaves may be substituted.

Per serving with spinach: 347 calories; 28 g protein; 22 g fat; 13 g carbohydrate; 730 mg calcium; 561 mg sodium; 199 mg cholesterol
With Swiss chard: 340 calories; 25 g protein; 22 g fat; 13 g carbohydrate;
  621 mg calcium; 865 mg sodium; 199 mg cholesterol

Jean Westgate
Everson, Washington

Spaghetti Squash and Spinach Casserole

Mary Beth started cooking when she joined Weight Watchers, and she enjoys inventing her own recipes. This spaghetti squash dish is one of her favorites. Mary Beth's interests are skiing, photography, knitting, and crocheting. She also plays the guitar and flute.

2 eggs
4 cups cooked spaghetti
   squash
1 package (10 ounces) frozen
   chopped spinach, thawed
   and well drained (about
   1 cup)
1 cup drained canned sliced
   mushrooms
½ cup finely chopped red
   bell pepper
¼ cup bean sprouts
1 packet (four ¼-cup servings)
   reduced-calorie chicken
   gravy mix, prepared
   according to package directions (10 calories per ¼ cup
   prepared gravy)
6 ounces mozzarella cheese,
   shredded

Preheat oven to 375°F. In medium mixing bowl beat eggs; add squash, mixing well. Spray shallow 1-quart casserole with non-stick cooking spray and spread squash mixture evenly over bottom of dish; bake until set, 15 to 20 minutes.

In medium mixing bowl combine remaining ingredients except cheese, mixing well. Spread spinach mixture over squash; sprinkle with cheese. Bake until cheese is melted and lightly browned, 20 to 25 minutes; remove from oven and let stand 5 minutes before cutting.

MAKES 4 SERVINGS

Each serving provides: 2 Protein Exchanges; 3¼ Vegetable Exchanges; 10 calories Optional Exchange
Per serving: 238 calories; 16 g protein; 13 g fat; 16 g carbohydrate; 349 mg calcium; 561 mg sodium; 170 mg cholesterol

Mary Beth Healey
Missoula, Montana

Special Eggplant Loaf ☺

This dish is a specialty that Jacqueline learned from her mother-in-law. Jacqueline adapted it for the Food Plan and her whole family enjoys it. A registered nurse, Jacqueline likes to sew and make stained glass.

1 medium eggplant (about 1 pound), pared and cut into 1-inch cubes
2 cups water
¾ teaspoon salt, divided
12 saltines, made into crumbs
1 tablespoon plus 1 teaspoon reduced-calorie margarine (tub), melted
⅔ cup reduced-calorie creamed cheese spread
2 eggs
2 ounces Cheddar cheese, shredded
½ cup diced onion
¼ teaspoon pepper
Dash *each* Worcestershire sauce and hot sauce

Preheat oven to 350°F. In 2½-quart saucepan combine eggplant, water, and ½ teaspoon salt; bring water to a boil and cook for 5 minutes. Drain well and set aside.

In medium bowl combine cracker crumbs and margarine, stirring to combine; remove and reserve ½ cup crumb mixture. To crumb mixture in bowl add creamed cheese spread, eggs, Cheddar cheese, onion, pepper, Worcestershire sauce, hot sauce, and remaining ¼ teaspoon salt, mixing well; add eggplant and stir to combine.

Spray 9 x 5 x 3-inch loaf pan with nonstick cooking spray; transfer eggplant mixture to pan and sprinkle with reserved crumb mixture. Bake until lightly browned, about 45 minutes; let loaf cool in pan 5 minutes before serving.

MAKES 2 SERVINGS

Each serving provides: 3 Protein Exchanges; 1 Bread Exchange; 3½ Vegetable Exchanges; 1 Fat Exchange; 25 calories Optional Exchange
Per serving: 443 calories; 28 g protein; 24 g fat; 31 g carbohydrate; 379 mg calcium; 1,246 mg sodium; 304 mg cholesterol*

*This figure does not include reduced-calorie creamed cheese spread; nutrition analysis not available.

Jacqueline L. Thackery
Columbus, Indiana

Spicy Lentil Stew ⊙

Carol, who runs her own antique business and is an avid swimmer, offers us this vegetarian chili that is sure to spice up any menu.

2 teaspoons margarine
1 cup diced onions
1½ pounds drained cooked
    lentils (reserve 2 cups
    cooking liquid)
2 cups drained canned whole
    tomatoes, chopped
1 cup tomato juice
1 tablespoon chili powder,
    or to taste
1 teaspoon salt
½ teaspoon ground cumin
1 bay leaf

In 2-quart saucepan heat margarine until bubbly and hot; add onions and sauté, stirring occasionally, until tender. Add remaining ingredients and stir to combine; bring mixture to boil. Reduce heat and let simmer, stirring occasionally, until mixture thickens and flavors blend, 45 minutes to 1 hour. Remove and discard bay leaf before serving.

MAKES 4 SERVINGS, ABOUT 1½ CUPS EACH

Each serving provides: 3 Protein Exchanges; 1½ Vegetable Exchanges; ½ Fat Exchange; 15 calories Optional Exchange
Per serving: 289 calories; 18 g protein; 3 g fat; 50 g carbohydrate; 111 mg calcium; 1,028 mg sodium; 0 mg cholesterol

SERVING SUGGESTIONS:

1. Serve each portion topped with ½ cup hot cooked long-grain rice. Add 1 Bread Exchange to Exchange Information.

Per serving: 401 calories; 20 g protein; 3 g fat; 75 g carbohydrate; 121 mg calcium; 1,028 mg sodium; 0 mg cholesterol

2. Serve each portion topped with 1 ounce shredded Cheddar or Monterey Jack cheese and 2 tablespoons diced red onion. Increase Protein Exchange to 4 Exchanges and Vegetable Exchange to 1¾ Exchanges.

Per serving with Cheddar: 410 calories; 25 g protein; 13 g fat; 52 g carbohydrate; 320 mg calcium; 1,204 mg sodium; 30 mg cholesterol
With Monterey Jack: 402 calories; 25 g protein; 12 g fat; 52 g carbohydrate; 327 mg calcium; 1,180 mg sodium; 25 mg cholesterol

Carol R. Hogan
Niota, Illinois

Versatile Fresh Vegetables and Cheese ◑

Nan is a receptionist and weigher for Weight Watchers. The mother of two young children, she enjoys doing needlework in her spare time. Nan created this dish one evening when she needed to fix a fast and tasty meal.

¾ cup *each* broccoli florets
   and cauliflower florets
¼ cup sliced carrot
½ ounce diced cooked ham
⅛ teaspoon *each* garlic
   powder, onion powder,
   basil leaves, and oregano
   leaves
Dash ground pepper,
   or to taste
2 ounces shredded Muenster
   cheese

In 1½-quart microwave-safe casserole combine all ingredients except cheese, mixing well. Cover casserole and microwave on High until vegetables are tender-crisp, about 3 minutes.* Sprinkle cheese evenly over vegetable mixture, cover casserole, and microwave on High until cheese is melted, 30 to 40 seconds longer.

MAKES 1 SERVING

*Cooking time may be different in your microwave oven. To help ensure good results, check the instructions accompanying your unit regarding length of time to cook broccoli and cauliflower.

Each serving provides: 2½ Protein Exchanges; 3½ Vegetable Exchanges
Per serving: 300 calories; 22 g protein; 18 g fat; 15 g carbohydrate; 488 mg calcium; 578 mg sodium; 62 mg cholesterol

VARIATION:

Substitute Colby, Cheddar, or Monterey Jack cheese for the Muenster cheese.

Per serving with Colby cheese: 314 calories; 22 g protein; 20 g fat; 16 g carbohydrate; 470 mg calcium; 564 mg sodium; 61 mg cholesterol
With Cheddar cheese: 319 calories; 23 g protein; 20 g fat; 15 g carbohydrate; 490 mg calcium; 573 mg sodium; 67 mg cholesterol
With Monterey Jack cheese: 302 calories; 23 g protein; 18 g fat; 15 g carbohydrate; 505 mg calcium; 526 mg sodium; 57 mg cholesterol

*Nan Gminski Cornell
Buda, Texas*

Cheese Fondue ◑

This delicious and filling fondue-and-dippers recipe is a meal in itself. Christine developed the recipe when her daughter, Sarah, expressed an interest in cooking, and it's become a family favorite.

9 ounces pasteurized process cheese spread, cut into 1-inch cubes
¼ cup skim milk
1 cup cottage cheese
4 ounces Italian bread, toasted and cut into 1-inch cubes
18 cherry tomatoes
1 cup *each* Chinese pea pods, green beans, and diagonally sliced carrots
½ cup *each* cauliflower florets and sliced yellow squash, blanched

In 1-quart microwave-safe casserole combine cheese cubes and milk; cover with plastic wrap and microwave on High, stirring once during cooking, until cheese is melted, 2 to 4 minutes.* Let casserole stand, covered, for 1 minute.

In blender container process cottage cheese until smooth; stir into cheese-milk mixture and pour into small fondue pot or divide into 4 small bowls. On serving platter or in small bowls arrange bread cubes and vegetables. Using fondue forks or tooth picks, dip into cheese mixture.

MAKES 4 SERVINGS

*Cooking time may be different in your microwave oven. To help ensure good results, be sure to check for doneness while cooking.

Each serving provides: 3 Protein Exchanges; 1 Bread Exchange; 2¾ Vegetable Exchanges; 5 calories Optional Exchange
Per serving: 379 calories; 24 g protein; 16 g fat; 35 g carbohydrate; 498 mg calcium; 1,374 mg sodium; 52 mg cholesterol

VARIATION:

Serve with 4 ounces frankfurters, heated and cut into 1-inch pieces. Increase Protein Exchange to 4 Exchanges.

Per serving: 470 calories; 27 g protein; 25 g fat; 35 g carbohydrate; 502 mg calcium; 1,692 mg sodium; 67 mg cholesterol

NOTE: In addition to the vegetables used above, whole small mushrooms, blanched broccoli florets, and celery sticks make for tasty dipping.

Christine L. Dominiak
White Bear Lake, Minnesota

Today's Catch
Seafood

Clam Spread

Clams are a favorite of Sharon's, and here she combines them with cheese into a rich-tasting spread. Try it on crackers, slices of jicama, or as a sandwich spread.

1 cup part-skim ricotta cheese
2 tablespoons reduced-calorie mayonnaise
4 ounces drained canned minced clams
¼ cup chopped scallions (green onions)
1 teaspoon Dijon-style mustard
½ teaspoon Worcestershire sauce
¼ teaspoon salt
Dash pepper

In blender container combine cheese and mayonnaise and process until smooth and creamy, scraping down sides of container as necessary. Transfer to small mixing bowl; add remaining ingredients and mix until thoroughly combined. Cover bowl with plastic wrap and refrigerate to allow flavors to blend, at least 3 hours.

MAKES 4 SERVINGS

Each serving provides: 2 Protein Exchanges; ⅛ Vegetable Exchange; ½ Fat Exchange; 10 calories Optional Exchange
Per serving: 137 calories; 12 g protein; 8 g fat; 5 g carbohydrate; 188 mg calcium; 346 mg sodium; 39 mg cholesterol

Sharon Vircks
Auburn, Washington

Linguine with Creamy Clam Sauce ◑

Mary's pasta-loving family finds this dish a winner. The ricotta cheese makes the sauce in this hearty entrée creamy while the white wine gives it a touch of elegance.

**3 ounces drained canned
   chopped clams (reserve
   ½ cup clam juice)
1 cup part-skim ricotta cheese
1 teaspoon olive oil
½ cup chopped onion
1 garlic clove, minced
½ cup dry white table wine
½ teaspoon *each* salt and
   basil leaves
Dash pepper
1 cup cooked linguine (hot)**

Set aside chopped clams. In blender container combine clam juice and ricotta cheese and process until smooth; set aside.

In 10-inch skillet heat oil over medium heat; add onion and garlic and sauté, stirring occasionally, until onion is softened, 1 to 2 minutes. Add ricotta cheese mixture and wine to skillet; stir to combine. Reduce heat to low and let simmer 5 to 7 minutes, stirring frequently; add reserved clams, salt, basil, and pepper and let simmer until clams are heated through, about 1 minute longer. Serve clam sauce over hot linguine.

MAKES 2 SERVINGS

Each serving provides: 3½ Protein Exchanges; 1 Bread Exchange; ½ Vegetable Exchange; ½ Fat Exchange; 70 calories Optional Exchange
Per serving: 387 calories; 25 g protein; 13 g fat; 31 g carbohydrate; 393 mg calcium; 996 mg sodium; 70 mg cholesterol

*Mary M. Kingsford-Smith
Mukilteo, Washington*

Seafood-Linguine Mornay ◖

Jeanne's delectable seafood-and-pasta dish is elegant enough for a dinner party. When she's not busy caring for her four children, Jeanne likes to crochet, knit, and do calligraphy.

2 tablespoons margarine, divided
1 cup broccoli florets
½ cup *each* sliced mushrooms and diced onion
2 tablespoons all-purpose flour
2 cups skim milk
2 ounces *each* Swiss cheese, shredded, and grated Parmesan cheese
4 ounces *each* cooked fresh or thawed and drained frozen crabmeat and cooked shelled and deveined shrimp
2 cups cooked linguine
½ teaspoon salt
Dash white pepper, or to taste

In 10-inch nonstick skillet heat 1 tablespoon margarine until bubbly and hot; add broccoli, mushrooms, and onion and cook, stirring quickly and frequently, until vegetables are tender-crisp. Using a slotted spoon remove vegetables from skillet and set aside. In same skillet heat remaining tablespoon margarine until bubbly and hot. Sprinkle margarine with flour and stir quickly to combine; cook, stirring constantly, for 1 minute. Gradually stir in milk; cook over medium heat, stirring constantly, until mixture is smooth and thickened. Add cheese and cook, stirring frequently, until melted. Return sautéed vegetables to skillet; add crabmeat, shrimp, and linguine and toss to combine. Reduce heat to low and cook until thoroughly heated. Sprinkle with salt and pepper and stir to combine.

MAKES 4 SERVINGS

Each serving provides: 3 Protein Exchanges; 1 Bread Exchange; 1 Vegetable Exchange; 1½ Fat Exchanges; ½ Milk Exchange; 15 calories Optional Exchange

Per serving: 382 calories; 30 g protein; 15 g fat; 30 g carbohydrate; 556 mg calcium; 813 mg sodium; 98 mg cholesterol

Jeanne Waudé
Kirkland, Washington

Crustless Crab Quiche

A busy grandmother, Edith does volunteer work in a hospital, works as a Weight Watchers receptionist, and sews her own clothes. She developed her quiche to fit the Food Plan, and serves it once or twice a month.

4 ounces thawed and
    thoroughly drained frozen
    crabmeat, flaked
4 ounces Cheddar cheese,
    shredded
¼ cup chopped scallions
    (green onions)
4 eggs
1 cup evaporated skimmed
    milk
½ teaspoon *each* salt and
    powdered mustard
⅛ teaspoon pepper
Dash paprika

Preheat oven to 400°F. Spray 8-inch glass pie plate with nonstick cooking spray; set aside.

In medium bowl combine crabmeat, cheese, and scallions; using back of a spoon, press crabmeat mixture over bottom and up sides of sprayed pie plate.

Using a wire whisk, in medium mixing bowl beat together eggs, milk, salt, mustard, and pepper; pour over crabmeat mixture. Sprinkle with paprika and bake until set, about 30 minutes. Remove from oven and let stand for 5 minutes before serving.

MAKES 4 SERVINGS

Each serving provides: 3 Protein Exchanges; ⅛ Vegetable Exchange; ½ Milk Exchange
Per serving: 272 calories; 23 g protein; 16 g fat; 9 g carbohydrate; 436 mg calcium; 651 mg sodium; 335 mg cholesterol

VARIATION:

Shelled and deveined cooked shrimp may be substituted for the crabmeat.

Per serving: 279 calories; 25 g protein; 15 g fat; 9 g carbohydrate; 456 mg calcium; 632 mg sodium; 349 mg cholesterol

Edith Purser
Toronto, Ontario, Canada

Fusilli with Pepper and Shrimp ◑

This is an updated version of a classic Italian pasta-and-shrimp dish. One-half cup zucchini or broccoli may be substituted for the bell pepper.

1 teaspoon *each* olive oil and margarine
¼ cup diced onion
1 garlic clove, minced
½ medium yellow *or* red bell pepper, seeded and thinly sliced
½ cup sliced mushrooms
1 cup drained canned Italian tomatoes, seeded and chopped
2 tablespoons dry vermouth
1 tablespoon chopped fresh basil *or* 1 teaspoon dried
5 ounces shelled and deveined small shrimp
½ ounce pignolias (pine nuts), lightly toasted
2 tablespoons half-and-half (blend of milk and cream)
Dash *each* salt and freshly ground pepper
2 cups cooked fusilli *or* similar macaroni (hot)

In 9- or 10-inch skillet combine oil and margarine and heat over medium heat until margarine is bubbly and hot; add onion and garlic and sauté for 1 minute *(do not brown garlic)*. Reduce heat to low; add bell pepper and mushrooms and sauté until vegetables are soft, 3 to 4 minutes longer. Add tomatoes, vermouth, and basil to skillet and, stirring occasionally, bring mixture to a boil; stir in shrimp and pignolias and cook over medium-high heat until shrimp turn pink, 3 to 5 minutes. Remove skillet from heat and add half-and-half, salt, and pepper; stir to blend thoroughly. Add fusilli to mixture and, using 2 forks, toss to thoroughly coat with sauce.

MAKES 2 SERVINGS

Each serving provides: 2 Protein Exchanges; 2 Bread Exchanges; 2¼ Vegetable Exchanges; 1 Fat Exchange; 80 calories Optional Exchange

Per serving with bell pepper: 372 calories; 22 g protein; 11 g fat; 44 g carbohydrate; 133 mg calcium; 394 mg sodium; 112 mg cholesterol

With zucchini: 372 calories; 22 g protein; 11 g fat; 44 g carbohydrate; 137 mg calcium; 394 mg sodium; 112 mg cholesterol

With broccoli: 374 calories; 22 g protein; 11 g fat; 45 g carbohydrate; 142 mg calcium; 399 mg sodium; 112 mg cholesterol

Weight Watchers Kitchens

Shrimp Creole

Barbara regards her 46-pound weight loss as one of the best things she ever did for herself. She developed her spicy Louisiana-style seafood dish from what was originally a tomato sauce.

2 teaspoons vegetable oil
½ cup sliced onion
¼ cup *each* sliced celery and red *or* green bell pepper
1 small garlic clove, minced
4 cups canned whole tomatoes (with liquid); drain and chop tomatoes, reserving liquid
1 tablespoon *each* tomato paste and Worcestershire sauce
2 teaspoons chili powder
1 teaspoon salt
¼ to ½ teaspoon crushed red pepper
¼ teaspoon oregano leaves
1 bay leaf
15 ounces shelled and deveined shrimp
¼ cup shredded fresh Italian (flat-leaf) parsley, divided
2 cups cooked long-grain rice (hot)

In 4-quart saucepan heat oil; add onion, celery, bell pepper, and garlic and cook, stirring frequently, until vegetables are tender. Stir in reserved tomato liquid along with remaining ingredients except shrimp, parsley, and rice; bring mixture to a boil. Reduce heat to low and let simmer 30 to 35 minutes. Stir in shrimp and 2 tablespoons parsley and continue cooking until shrimp turn pink, 5 to 8 minutes. Remove and discard bay leaf. Arrange rice on serving platter and top with shrimp mixture; garnish with remaining 2 tablespoons parsley.

MAKES 4 SERVINGS

Each serving provides: 3 Protein Exchanges; 1 Bread Exchange; 2½ Vegetable Exchanges; ½ Fat Exchange
Per serving: 301 calories; 24 g protein; 4 g fat; 42 g carbohydrate; 166 mg calcium; 1,185 mg sodium; 159 mg cholesterol

SERVING SUGGESTION:

For an attractive presentation, reserve 1 cooked shelled and deveined shrimp (tail left on) and garnish platter with shrimp and 2 bay leaves (remove and discard bay leaves before serving).

Barbara Albers
Champaign, Illinois

Szechuan Shrimp ◑

Szechuan Chinese cooking is known for its pungent flavor. You can make this dish fiery by substituting chili oil for the sesame oil.

1½ teaspoons peanut oil
½ cup *each* diced red bell pepper (1-inch dice), diced green bell pepper (1-inch dice), and chopped leeks
1 garlic clove, minced
½ teaspoon *each* minced pared ginger root and Chinese sesame oil
10 ounces shelled and deveined large shrimp, cut lengthwise into halves
¼ cup canned ready-to-serve chicken broth
1 tablespoon *each* dry sherry and ketchup
¾ teaspoon cornstarch
¼ teaspoon granulated sugar

In 10-inch skillet or a wok heat peanut oil; add bell peppers, leeks, garlic, and ginger and sauté until vegetables are tender-crisp, about 2 minutes. Remove to plate and set aside.

In same skillet (or wok) heat sesame oil; add shrimp and sauté until shrimp turn pink. Return sautéed vegetables to skillet (or wok) and stir to combine.

In small bowl thoroughly combine broth, sherry, ketchup, cornstarch, and sugar, stirring to dissolve cornstarch; pour over shrimp and vegetables and, stirring constantly, bring to a boil. Cook over high heat, stirring constantly, until mixture thickens.

MAKES 2 SERVINGS

Each serving provides: 4 Protein Exchanges; 1½ Vegetable Exchanges; 1 Fat Exchange; 25 calories Optional Exchange
Per serving: 228 calories; 27 g protein; 6 g fat; 13 g carbohydrate; 114 mg calcium; 429 mg sodium; 213 mg cholesterol

Weight Watchers Kitchens

Chinese Scallops ❶

Patricia adapted a recipe given to her by a Chinese friend. This tasty dish takes only minutes to prepare and is festive enough for parties. A biochemist, university professor, and mother of two, Patricia enjoys cooking, reading, swimming, and stained-glass work.

2 teaspoons peanut *or* vegetable oil
3 thin slices pared ginger root
1 large garlic clove, crushed or minced
3 cups sliced mushrooms
2 packets instant chicken broth and seasoning mix, dissolved in 1¼ cups hot water
1 pound 3 ounces bay scallops (or sea scallops, cut into 1-inch pieces)
3 cups shredded spinach leaves *or* Swiss chard
¼ cup water
2 tablespoons cornstarch
1 tablespoon reduced-sodium soy sauce
1 egg, beaten in heatproof cup
6 medium scallions (green onions), thinly sliced

In 12-inch skillet or a wok heat oil; add ginger and garlic and cook, stirring quickly and frequently, until lightly browned *(be careful not to burn)*. Add mushrooms and continue to stir-fry for 2 to 3 minutes. Gradually stir in dissolved broth mix and, stirring frequently, bring to a boil. Reduce heat; add scallops and spinach (or chard) and stir to combine. Cover and let steam 2 to 3 minutes. In small bowl combine water, cornstarch, and soy sauce, stirring to dissolve cornstarch; add to scallop mixture and stir to combine. Remove ½ cup broth from skillet (or wok) and stir into beaten egg. Slowly pour egg mixture into scallop mixture, stirring rapidly to prevent lumping; cook, stirring constantly, until mixture thickens *(do not boil)*. Add scallions to scallop mixture and stir to combine.

MAKES 4 SERVINGS

Each serving provides: 4 Protein Exchanges; 3⅛ Vegetable Exchanges; ½ Fat Exchange; 20 calories Optional Exchange
Per serving with spinach: 201 calories; 26 g protein; 4 g fat; 15 g carbohydrate; 102 mg calcium; 965 mg sodium; 116 mg cholesterol
With Swiss chard: 197 calories; 25 g protein; 4 g fat; 14 g carbohydrate; 74 mg calcium; 990 mg sodium; 116 mg cholesterol

Patricia Eagon Stafford
Carnegie, Pennsylvania

Coquilles St. Jacques ◐

Diane has adapted this from the classic seafood dish that's served in the finest French restaurants. The creamy mushroom-wine sauce is also excellent served over your favorite fish fillet.

1 tablespoon plus 1 teaspoon reduced-calorie margarine (tub), divided
1 tablespoon plus 1½ teaspoons all-purpose flour
½ cup *each* skim milk and dry white table wine
¼ teaspoon *each* garlic salt and onion salt
Dash pepper, or to taste
4 cups sliced mushrooms
10 ounces bay scallops (or sea scallops, cut into quarters)

In small saucepan heat 1 tablespoon margarine over medium heat until bubbly and hot; add flour and stir quickly to combine. Gradually stir in milk and wine; add garlic salt, onion salt, and pepper and cook, stirring constantly, until mixture is smooth. Reduce heat to low and let simmer until sauce thickens, 5 to 7 minutes. Remove pan from heat and set aside.

In 10-inch nonstick skillet heat remaining teaspoon margarine over medium heat until bubbly and hot; add mushrooms and sauté, stirring often, until mushrooms are tender, 2 to 3 minutes. Using slotted spoon, remove mushrooms from skillet and set aside; add scallops to skillet and sauté until opaque, 3 to 4 minutes. Add reserved sauce and mushrooms to skillet and stir to combine; cook, stirring frequently, until mixture is heated through, 1 to 2 minutes longer. Serve in scallop shells.

MAKES 2 SERVINGS

Each serving provides: 4 Protein Exchanges; 4 Vegetable Exchanges; 1 Fat Exchange; ¼ Milk Exchange; 85 calories Optional Exchange
Per serving: 277 calories; 27 g protein; 5 g fat; 21 g carbohydrate; 126 mg calcium; 909 mg sodium; 51 mg cholesterol

Diane E. Miller
Reedsport, Oregon

Scallop Sauté over Rice ◐

Fresh bay scallops are the basis of Jean's rich-tasting skillet dinner. It's easy to make and is excellent for special occasions. Jean, who makes and sells silver jewelry, also enjoys drawing and gardening.

2 teaspoons margarine
1 cup sliced mushrooms
4 medium scallions (green onions), cut into 1-inch pieces
2 garlic cloves, minced
8 ounces bay scallops (or sea scallops, cut into 1-inch pieces)
2 tablespoons dry sherry
1 tablespoon plus 1 teaspoon grated Parmesan cheese
1 teaspoon lemon juice
¼ teaspoon salt
⅛ teaspoon pepper
1 ounce provolone cheese, shredded
1 cup cooked long-grain rice (hot)

In 10-inch skillet heat margarine until bubbly and hot; add mushrooms, scallions, and garlic and sauté, stirring constantly, for 3 minutes. Add scallops and sauté for 2 minutes; stir in sherry, Parmesan cheese, lemon juice, salt, and pepper and bring mixture to a boil. Sprinkle with provolone cheese, cover, and cook until cheese is melted, about 1 minute. Serve over rice.

MAKES 2 SERVINGS

Each serving provides: 3½ Protein Exchanges; 1 Bread Exchange; 1¼ Vegetable Exchanges; 1 Fat Exchange; 35 calories Optional Exchange
Per serving: 341 calories; 26 g protein; 9 g fat; 34 g carbohydrate; 214 mg calcium; 794 mg sodium; 52 mg cholesterol

Jean Westgate
Everson, Washington

Au Gratin Fish Supreme ◐

Edith is a Weight Watchers leader whose hobbies are cooking and traveling. She's also the mother of four sons and two daughters. Try her fast-and-delicious fish dish—it's a great way to use up leftover cooked fish!

1 tablespoon plus 1 teaspoon reduced-calorie margarine (tub)
1 cup sliced mushrooms
¼ cup diced onion
1 tablespoon plus 1 teaspoon all-purpose flour
½ teaspoon salt
Dash pepper
1 cup skim milk
1 package (9 ounces) frozen French-style green beans, cooked according to package directions (about 2 cups)
4 ounces cooked cod, haddock, flounder, or scrod fillets
1 English muffin (2 ounces), split in half and toasted
2 ounces Cheddar cheese, shredded

In 10-inch nonstick skillet heat margarine until bubbly and hot; add mushrooms and onion and sauté until onion is translucent. Sprinkle vegetables with flour, salt, and pepper and stir quickly to combine; cook, stirring constantly, for 1 minute. Continuing to stir, gradually add milk and bring just to a boil. Reduce heat and let simmer until mixture is smooth and thickened, stirring frequently. Stir in green beans and fish and cook until fish is heated through.

Set each muffin half on a flameproof plate; top each half with half of fish mixture and 1 ounce cheese. Broil until cheese is melted and lightly browned, about 1 minute.

MAKES 2 SERVINGS

Each serving provides: 3 Protein Exchanges; 1 Bread Exchange; 3¼ Vegetable Exchanges; 1 Fat Exchange; ½ Milk Exchange; 20 calories Optional Exchange

Per serving with cod or scrod: 392 calories; 32 g protein; 15 g fat; 34 g carbohydrate; 426 mg calcium; 1,077 mg sodium; 75 mg cholesterol

With haddock: 393 calories; 32 g protein; 15 g fat; 34 g carbohydrate; 437 mg calcium; 1,070 mg sodium; 83 mg cholesterol

With flounder: 393 calories; 31 g protein; 15 g fat; 34 g carbohydrate; 428 mg calcium; 1,084 mg sodium; 75 mg cholesterol

Edith M. Weisenbeck
Durand, Wisconsin

Cod with Dill, Green Onion, and Soy Sauce ☾◐

Patricia wanted an alternative to the deep-fried fish she loved, so she created this delicacy, which her whole family enjoys. Musicians by avocation, Patricia and her husband have their own band and have cut several records.

1 cod fillet (10 ounces)
3 tablespoons chopped fresh dill
2 tablespoons chopped scallions (green onions)
¼ cup reduced-sodium soy sauce
½ teaspoon *each* Worcestershire sauce and garlic powder
Dash pepper, or to taste

Preheat oven to 350°F. Spray 14-inch-long sheet of foil with nonstick cooking spray; set fillet on center of sheet. Sprinkle surface of fish with dill and scallions and set aside. In small bowl or measuring cup combine remaining ingredients; pour mixture over cod. Fold foil over fillet to enclose, crimping edges to seal. Place foil packet on rack in oven and bake 20 to 25 minutes (until fish flakes easily when tested with a fork). Carefully unwrap foil, cut fillet in half, and transfer to serving platter.

MAKES 2 SERVINGS

Each serving provides: 4 Protein Exchanges; ⅛ Vegetable Exchange
Per serving: 139 calories; 27 g protein; 0.5 g fat; 4 g carbohydrate; 39 mg calcium; 1,329 mg sodium; 71 mg cholesterol

VARIATION:

Omit Worcestershire sauce and add 2 tablespoons seeded and chopped, drained, canned Italian tomatoes to soy sauce. Increase Vegetable Exchange to ¼ Exchange.

Per serving: 141 calories; 28 g protein; 0.5 g fat; 4 g carbohydrate; 43 mg calcium; 1,340 mg sodium; 71 mg cholesterol

Patricia Anne Krupa
Lake Audy, Manitoba, Canada

Fish Fillets Amandine ◐

A classic fish entrée using sliced or slivered almonds. For an elegant meal, serve with sautéed new potatoes, steamed asparagus, and white wine.

1 tablespoon margarine, divided
½ ounce sliced *or* slivered almonds
2 teaspoons all-purpose flour
⅛ teaspoon salt
Dash pepper
2 cod, flounder, *or* haddock fillets (5 ounces each)*
½ to 1 teaspoon fresh lemon juice
2 *each* lemon wedges and parsley sprigs

In 8- or 9-inch skillet heat 1 teaspoon margarine until bubbly and hot; add almonds and sauté until golden. Remove almonds from skillet and set aside.

In small bowl combine flour, salt, and pepper; sprinkle both sides of each fillet with an equal amount of seasoned flour. In same skillet heat remaining 2 teaspoons margarine over medium heat until bubbly and hot; add fish and cook until golden brown on bottom. Carefully turn fillets over and cook until other side is browned and fish flakes easily when tested with a fork; remove to a serving platter. Reduce heat to low; add lemon juice and sautéed almonds to skillet and cook over low heat, stirring, until heated. Top fillets with almond mixture; garnish with lemon wedges and parsley.

MAKES 2 SERVINGS

*Any firm fish fillet may be substituted.

Each serving provides: 4 Protein Exchanges; 1½ Fat Exchanges; 55 calories Optional Exchange
Per serving with cod: 213 calories; 27 g protein; 10 g fat; 4 g carbohydrate; 37 mg calcium; 305 mg sodium; 71 mg cholesterol
With flounder: 215 calories; 25 g protein; 11 g fat; 4 g carbohydrate; 40 mg calcium; 317 mg sodium; 71 mg cholesterol
With haddock: 215 calories; 28 g protein; 10 g fat; 4 g carbohydrate; 55 mg calcium; 293 mg sodium; 85 mg cholesterol

Weight Watchers Kitchens

❖❖❖

Northwest Cioppino

This San Francisco specialty makes good use of seafood, which is plentiful in Mary's area. In developing the recipe, she tried to duplicate the flavors of the original. Mary is a housewife, mother, and part-time student who enjoys writing, reading, hiking, and playing piano.

2 teaspoons olive *or* vegetable oil
1 cup *each* thinly sliced onions and green bell peppers
½ cup *each* thinly sliced carrot and celery
1 small garlic clove, minced
3½ cups canned crushed tomatoes
1 cup *each* tomato sauce and water
¼ cup dry white table wine
2 packets instant chicken broth and seasoning mix
1 bay leaf
½ teaspoon oregano leaves
⅛ teaspoon *each* salt and pepper
Dash ground red pepper *or* hot sauce
15 ounces fish fillets,* cut into 1-inch pieces

In 3½- or 4-quart saucepan heat oil; add onions, green peppers, carrot, celery, and garlic and sauté, stirring frequently, until vegetables are tender, about 2 minutes. Add remaining ingredients except fish and bring to a boil. Reduce heat and let simmer until flavors are blended, about 20 minutes; stir in fish and cook until fish flakes easily when tested with fork, 7 to 10 minutes. Remove bay leaf before serving.

MAKES 4 SERVINGS

*Cod, flounder, grouper, halibut, scrod, or snapper are equally delicious in this dish.

Each serving provides: 3 Protein Exchanges; 4¼ Vegetable Exchanges; ½ Fat Exchange; 20 calories Optional Exchange
Per serving: 212 calories; 22 g protein; 4 g fat; 21 g carbohydrate; 104 mg calcium; 1,300 mg sodium; 53 mg cholesterol

SERVING SUGGESTION:

Serve each portion with 2 ounces French bread. Add 2 Bread Exchanges to Exchange Information.

Per serving: 376 calories; 27 g protein; 6 g fat; 53 g carbohydrate; 129 mg calcium; 1,629 mg sodium; 55 mg cholesterol

Mary M. Kingsford-Smith
Mukilteo, Washington

Parmesan Fish Sauté ⓒ ⓞ

Mary loves to cook meals for her husband that fit the Food Plan, and she especially likes the Weight Watchers cookbooks. Mary's home sewing business keeps her busy, too.

¼ cup buttermilk
1 ounce grated Parmesan
   cheese
2 teaspoons all-purpose flour
¼ teaspoon salt
Dash *each* onion powder,
   garlic powder, and pepper
2¼ ounces (⅓ cup plus
   2 teaspoons) uncooked
   yellow cornmeal
9 ounces haddock, flounder,
   or sole fillets
1 tablespoon plus 1 teaspoon
   vegetable oil

In small bowl combine buttermilk and cheese; set aside. In separate small bowl combine flour and seasonings; set aside. Onto sheet of wax paper or a paper plate spoon cornmeal; set aside.

Sprinkle flour mixture over fish, then dip fish into buttermilk mixture, coating both sides and using entire mixture. Dip fillets into cornmeal, turning to coat both sides and pressing cornmeal to make sure it adheres.

In 12-inch skillet heat oil; add fish and cook until golden brown on bottom, about 3 minutes. Carefully turn fillets over and cook until other side is browned and fish flakes easily when tested with a fork.

MAKES 2 SERVINGS

Each serving provides: 4 Protein Exchanges; 1½ Bread Exchanges; 2 Fat
   Exchanges; 25 calories Optional Exchange
Per serving with haddock: 384 calories; 33 g protein; 14 g fat; 29 g
   carbohydrate; 265 mg calcium; 644 mg sodium; 89 mg cholesterol
With flounder or sole: 384 calories; 31 g protein; 15 g fat; 29 g carbohydrate;
   251 mg calcium; 666 mg sodium; 76 mg cholesterol

Mary E. Burke
Champlin, Minnesota

Salmon-Dill Loaf

Warm or chilled, Dinah's delicious salmon loaf is sure to please—and it's a nice change from meat loaf. Dinah finds cooking a relaxing pastime, and she enjoys painting as well.

15 ounces skinned drained canned salmon
6 ounces drained canned water chestnuts, diced
1 egg, beaten
½ cup *each* diced celery and onion *or* scallions (green onions)
⅓ cup plus 2 teaspoons ketchup
1 teaspoon chopped fresh dill *or* ¼ teaspoon dried
¼ teaspoon *each* pepper and Worcestershire sauce
Dash hot sauce (optional)
4 lemon *or* lime wedges

Preheat oven to 350°F. In large bowl combine all ingredients except lemon (or lime) wedges. Spray baking sheet with nonstick cooking spray; turn salmon mixture out onto sheet and shape into loaf. Bake until top of loaf is lightly browned, 35 to 45 minutes. Serve warm or let cool, then cover and refrigerate until chilled. Slice loaf and serve with lemon or lime wedges.

MAKES 4 SERVINGS

Each serving provides: 4 Protein Exchanges; ½ Bread Exchange; ½ Vegetable Exchange; 25 calories Optional Exchange
Per serving: 235 calories; 25 g protein; 8 g fat; 16 g carbohydrate; 235 mg calcium; 717 mg sodium; 106 mg cholesterol

Dinah S. Riddle
Los Angeles, California

Salmon Pie in Rice Crust

A flavorful dish, Marjorie's pie would make a wonderful entrée for family or guests. Marjorie reached her goal weight while following the Weight Watchers program and enjoys cooking, reading, roller skating, and doing cross-stitch.

4 eggs
2 cups cooked long-grain rice
1 ounce Cheddar cheese, shredded
½ teaspoon salt
⅛ teaspoon white pepper
½ cup finely chopped celery
¼ cup *each* finely chopped onion and green bell pepper
1 cup tomato sauce
8 ounces skinned drained canned salmon, flaked
3 ounces Swiss cheese, shredded
1 cup skim milk

Preheat oven to 425°F. In medium bowl beat 1 egg; add rice, Cheddar cheese, salt, and pepper, mixing well. Spray 8 x 8 x 2-inch baking pan with nonstick cooking spray and, using back of a spoon, press mixture firmly over bottom and up sides of pan. Bake until lightly browned, 15 to 20 minutes. Remove from oven and set aside.

Reduce oven temperature to 350°F. Spray 8-inch nonstick skillet with nonstick cooking spray and heat over medium heat; add celery, onion, and bell pepper and cook until softened, 1 to 2 minutes. Stir in tomato sauce. Reduce heat; let simmer 2 to 3 minutes. Transfer to medium mixing bowl; add salmon and Swiss cheese, mixing well.

Using wire whisk, in small bowl beat together milk and remaining 3 eggs; add to salmon mixture and stir until thoroughly combined. Pour salmon mixture into prepared crust and bake in middle of center oven rack for 40 to 45 minutes (until pie is lightly browned and a knife, inserted in center, comes out clean). Remove from oven and let stand 5 to 10 minutes before serving.

MAKES 4 SERVINGS

Each serving provides: 4 Protein Exchanges; 1 Bread Exchange; 1½ Vegetable Exchanges; ¼ Milk Exchange
Per serving: 427 calories; 31 g protein; 17 g fat; 35 g carbohydrate; 499 mg calcium; 1,076 mg sodium; 322 mg cholesterol

Marjorie L. Jones
La Fontaine, Indiana

Texas Tuna Burgers ⊙⊙

Tired of the same old hamburgers? Try Cathy's tuna burgers for dinner in a jiffy — or double the recipe and cook for a crowd. In her spare time, Cathy enjoys flying, swimming, and playing tennis.

11 ounces drained canned tuna, flaked
²⁄₃ cup instant nonfat dry milk powder
12 saltines, made into crumbs
½ cup *each* chopped onion and drained canned mild green chili peppers, chopped
1 egg, beaten
1 tablespoon plus 1 teaspoon vegetable oil
2 cups canned crushed tomatoes
1 teaspoon chili powder
2 ounces Monterey Jack cheese, shredded

In medium mixing bowl combine tuna, milk powder, cracker crumbs, onion, chili peppers, and egg; mix well and form into 8 equal burgers.

In 12-inch nonstick skillet heat oil over medium heat; add tuna burgers and cook, turning once, until lightly browned, 2 to 4 minutes on each side. In measuring cup or small bowl combine tomatoes and chili powder and pour over burgers. Cover pan, reduce heat to low, and let simmer until sauce is thoroughly heated, about 5 minutes. Transfer burgers and sauce to flame-proof serving platter and sprinkle with cheese. Broil until cheese is melted and lightly browned, 1 to 2 minutes.

MAKES 4 SERVINGS

Each serving provides: 3½ Protein Exchanges; ½ Bread Exchange; 1½ Vegetable Exchanges; 1 Fat Exchange; ½ Milk Exchange
Per serving: 391 calories; 31 g protein; 21 g fat; 20 g carbohydrate; 302 mg calcium; 826 mg sodium; 103 mg cholesterol

Cathy McKinley
Spokane, Washington

Tuna Cakes ☾◐

Linda likes salmon cakes but she wanted to avoid the bones usually found in canned salmon, so she substituted tuna. A busy mother of two young daughters, Linda enjoys cooking, sewing, and needlework.

6 ounces drained canned tuna, flaked
12 saltines, made into crumbs
1 egg, beaten
¼ cup skim milk
1 tablespoon minced onion
1 teaspoon chopped fresh parsley
¼ teaspoon Worcestershire sauce
Dash pepper
1 teaspoon margarine

In medium bowl combine all ingredients except margarine and shape into 6 equal patties. In 10-inch nonstick skillet heat margarine until bubbly and hot; add patties and cook over medium heat, turning once, until browned on both sides.

MAKES 2 SERVINGS, 3 CAKES EACH

Each serving provides: 3½ Protein Exchanges; 1 Bread Exchange; ½ Fat Exchange; 10 calories Optional Exchange
Per serving: 322 calories; 27 g protein; 17 g fat; 15 g carbohydrate; 67 mg calcium; 676 mg sodium; 160 mg cholesterol

Linda S. Jones
Henderson, Texas

Birds of a Feather
Poultry

Almond-Crumb Chicken ◐

Almonds add a nutty goodness to ordinary crumb-coated chicken. We found this easy-to-make, delicious dish to be very special. You'll be "nuts" about it too.

1 ounce blanched almonds, ground
1 tablespoon plain dried bread crumbs
1½ teaspoons grated Parmesan cheese
⅛ teaspoon *each* salt and basil leaves
2 chicken cutlets (4 ounces each), pounded to ⅛-inch thickness
1 tablespoon *each* skim milk and vegetable oil
2 lemon wedges

On sheet of wax paper or a paper plate combine ground almonds, bread crumbs, cheese, salt, and basil. Dip 1 chicken cutlet into milk, then into crumb mixture, coating both sides evenly; repeat procedure with remaining cutlet, being sure to use all of milk and crumb mixture.

In 12-inch skillet heat oil; add chicken and coat, turning once, until browned on both sides, 3 to 4 minutes on each side. Serve with lemon wedges.

MAKES 2 SERVINGS, 1 CUTLET EACH

Each serving provides: 3 Protein Exchanges; 1½ Fat Exchanges; 110 calories Optional Exchange
Per serving: 289 calories; 30 g protein; 16 g fat; 5 g carbohydrate; 81 mg calcium; 264 mg sodium; 67 mg cholesterol

Weight Watchers Kitchens

Cashew Chicken

You'll find dishes similar to this one on the menu of most Oriental restaurants.

10 ounces skinned and boned chicken breasts, cubed
1½ teaspoons cornstarch
1 tablespoon dry sherry
1½ teaspoons reduced-sodium soy sauce
1 tablespoon peanut *or* vegetable oil, divided
½ cup sliced onions
1 ounce shelled roasted cashews
¼ cup *each* red bell pepper strips and sliced mushrooms
½ small garlic clove, minced
3 ounces drained canned water chestnuts, whole or sliced (reserve ¼ cup liquid)
1½ teaspoons hoisin sauce
1 tablespoon thinly sliced scallion (green onion)

In 1-quart bowl (not aluminum*) sprinkle chicken with cornstarch, tossing to coat; add sherry and soy sauce and stir to combine. Let mixture marinate for 15 minutes.

In 8- or 9-inch nonstick skillet heat 1½ teaspoons oil; using a slotted spoon, transfer several chicken cubes to skillet, allowing marinade that adheres to chicken to drip into bowl. Cook chicken, stirring quickly and frequently, until browned. Remove from skillet and repeat with remaining chicken, reserving marinade left in bowl.

In same skillet heat remaining oil; add onion and cashews and stir-fry until onion is translucent. Add pepper, mushrooms, and garlic; stir-fry 1 minute. Return chicken to skillet; add water chestnuts, reserved liquid, hoisin sauce, and reserved marinade and stir until combined. Cover and cook until chicken is cooked through and sauce thickens, 1 to 2 minutes. Serve sprinkled with scallion.

MAKES 2 SERVINGS

*It is best to marinate in glass or stainless-steel containers; ingredients such as sherry and soy sauce may react with aluminum, causing color and flavor changes in foods.

Each serving provides: 4 Protein Exchanges; ½ Bread Exchange; 1 Vegetable Exchange; 1½ Fat Exchanges; 110 calories Optional Exchange
Per serving: 375 calories; 37 g protein; 16 g fat; 19 g carbohydrate; 33 mg calcium; 460 mg sodium; 82 mg cholesterol

Weight Watchers Kitchens

Chicken and Sprouts ●◐

Carol loves to cook and play tennis. She enjoys adapting recipes to fit the Food Plan, and thinks stir-frying is the best way to cook vegetables.

2 teaspoons vegetable oil, divided
1 cup bean sprouts, rinsed and dried thoroughly
5 ounces skinned and boned chicken breast, cut into 1-inch pieces
¼ teaspoon minced pared ginger root
¼ cup chopped scallions (green onions)
1 tablespoon reduced-sodium soy sauce
2½ teaspoons honey

In wok or 8-inch nonstick skillet heat 1 teaspoon oil over high heat; add sprouts and cook, stirring quickly and frequently, until lightly browned and tender, 1 to 2 minutes. Transfer sprouts to plate and keep warm.

To same wok (or skillet) add remaining teaspoon oil and heat for 30 seconds to 1 minute; add chicken and ginger and stir-fry for 2 minutes. Add scallions and continue stir-frying until chicken is tender and browned on all sides, 2 to 3 minutes longer. Add soy sauce and honey and mix well; cook, stirring constantly, for 1 minute longer. Top warm sprouts with chicken mixture.

MAKES 1 SERVING

Each serving provides: 4 Protein Exchanges; 2½ Vegetable Exchanges; 2 Fat Exchanges; 50 calories Optional Exchange
Per serving: 338 calories; 37 g protein; 11 g fat; 23 g carbohydrate; 45 mg calcium; 707 mg sodium; 82 mg cholesterol

Carol Funk
Mountainside, New Jersey

Chicken Enchiladas

When not busy with law school, Sherri enjoys the great outdoors. She once worked as a disc jockey for a Santa Fe radio station, and hopes to settle out west.

½ cup chopped onion
2 garlic cloves, minced
1½ cups canned Italian
   tomatoes (with liquid);
   drain, seed, and chop
   tomatoes, reserving liquid
½ cup sliced mushrooms
1 teaspoon *each* seeded and
   minced jalapeño *or* serrano
   pepper and salt
⅛ teaspoon pepper
8 ounces skinned and boned
   cooked chicken (preferably
   breasts), chopped
4 corn tortillas (6-inch
   diameter each)
4 ounces sharp Cheddar
   cheese, shredded, divided
8 pitted black olives, sliced
½ cup plain low-fat yogurt

Spray 10-inch nonstick skillet with nonstick cooking spray and set over medium heat; add onion and garlic and cook, stirring constantly, about 1 minute. Add tomatoes and reserved liquid, the mushrooms, pepper, and seasonings and cook, stirring occasionally, until sauce is thickened, 5 to 8 minutes. Transfer half of sauce to medium heatproof mixing bowl, reserving remaining sauce; add chicken to bowl and mix thoroughly. Set aside. Preheat oven to 375°F. Set 8-inch nonstick skillet over medium heat; add 1 tortilla and heat, turning once, just until tortilla becomes flexible, about 1 minute (*do not overcook*). Carefully remove tortilla from pan and lay flat; spread ½ ounce cheese along center, top with ¼ of chicken mixture, and roll to enclose. Set seam-side down in 8 x 8 x 2-inch baking dish; repeat procedure 3 more times. Pour reserved sauce over enchiladas, top with remaining cheese, and bake until cheese is lightly browned, 15 to 20 minutes. Top with olives; serve with yogurt.

MAKES 4 SERVINGS

Each serving provides: 3 Protein Exchanges; 1 Bread Exchange; 1¼ Vegetable Exchanges; ¼ Milk Exchange; 10 calories Optional Exchange
Per serving: 311 calories; 29 g protein; 14 g fat; 18 g carbohydrate; 348 mg calcium; 1,011 mg sodium; 80 mg cholesterol

Sherri Rosenberg
Glen Head, New York

Chicken in Cheddar-Wine Sauce

French cuisine on a weight-loss program? But of course, says Dorothy, who was inspired to create this recipe by watching French chefs. Dorothy serves this dish several times a month for both family and company dinners. Magnifique!

½ cup skim milk
1 tablespoon plus 1 teaspoon all-purpose flour
2 ounces Cheddar cheese, shredded, divided
8 ounces skinned and boned chicken breasts
1 cup canned ready-to-serve chicken broth
1 medium carrot (3 to 4 ounces), pared and cut into long thin strips
1 large celery rib (about 8 inches long), cut into long thin strips
1 medium turnip (about 2 ounces), cut into long thin strips
1 small onion (about 2 ounces), cut into long thin strips
½ cup dry white table wine
⅛ teaspoon salt
Dash white pepper, or to taste

In 1-quart saucepan combine milk and flour, stirring to dissolve flour; cook over medium heat, stirring occasionally, until smooth and thick. Add 1 ounce cheese, reserving remaining cheese, and stir until melted. Reduce heat to lowest possible setting and keep sauce warm.

Spray 10-inch skillet with nonstick cooking spray and set over medium heat; add chicken and cook, turning once, until lightly browned on both sides and cooked through, 2 to 3 minutes per side. Remove chicken from skillet and keep warm. To same skillet add remaining ingredients except reserved cheese and bring to a boil; reduce heat to low and cook until vegetables are tender and liquid is reduced by half, 4 to 6 minutes.

Using slotted spoon, transfer vegetables to flameproof serving platter, reserving pan liquid; top vegetables with chicken. Add pan liquid to cheese sauce and stir until thoroughly combined; pour sauce evenly over chicken and vegetables and sprinkle with remaining ounce cheese. Broil until cheese is melted and lightly browned, 1 to 2 minutes.

MAKES 2 SERVINGS

Each serving provides: 4 Protein Exchanges; 2½ Vegetable Exchanges; ¼ Milk Exchange; 100 calories Optional Exchange
Per serving: 382 calories; 38 g protein; 11 g fat; 19 g carbohydrate; 337 mg calcium; 1,012 mg sodium; 97 mg cholesterol

Dorothy M. Collier
Indianapolis, Indiana

❖❖

Chicken Scarpariello ◑

Arlene is a school administrator who loves to travel in her spare time. Her Italian skillet dinner has been enjoyed by family and guests.

10 ounces skinned and boned chicken breasts, cut into 1 x 3-inch strips
3 tablespoons all-purpose flour
2 teaspoons *each* vegetable oil and margarine
2 tablespoons minced shallots *or onion*
2 garlic cloves, minced
1 cup water
½ cup dry white table wine
1 packet instant chicken broth and seasoning mix
½ teaspoon ground rosemary leaves
¼ teaspoon salt
Dash pepper
1 tablespoon chopped chives

On sheet of wax paper or a paper plate dredge chicken in flour. In 10-inch nonstick skillet combine oil and margarine and heat over medium-high heat until margarine is bubbly and hot; add chicken and cook, turning occasionally, until lightly browned on all sides, 3 to 4 minutes. Using tongs or slotted spoon, remove chicken from skillet and set aside.

To same skillet add shallots (or onion) and garlic and sauté until softened, about 1 minute; add water, wine, broth mix, and seasonings and, using a wooden spoon, stir well. Cook, stirring frequently, until liquid is reduced by half, 3 to 4 minutes; return chicken to skillet and cook until sauce is thick and chicken is heated through, 1 to 2 minutes. Serve sprinkled with chives.

MAKES 2 SERVINGS

Each serving provides: 4 Protein Exchanges; ½ Bread Exchange; ⅛ Vegetable Exchange; 2 Fat Exchanges; 65 calories Optional Exchange
Per serving: 340 calories; 35 g protein; 10 g fat; 15 g carbohydrate; 40 mg calcium; 829 mg sodium; 82 mg cholesterol

SERVING SUGGESTION:

Serve each portion over ½ cup cooked spaghetti or long-grain rice. Add 1 Bread Exchange to Exchange Information.

Per serving with spaghetti: 418 calories; 37 g protein; 11 g fat; 31 g carbohydrate; 46 mg calcium; 829 mg sodium; 82 mg cholesterol
With rice: 452 calories; 37 g protein; 10 g fat; 40 g carbohydrate; 50 mg calcium; 829 mg sodium; 82 mg cholesterol

Arlene R. Delloro
Pomona, New York

Chicken-Vegetable Stir-Fry ◐

This colorful Chinese-style dish is a big hit in the Hogan household. Brenda, a homemaker who enjoys sewing and cooking, makes it often for herself and her husband.

1 tablespoon vegetable oil, divided
10 ounces skinned and boned chicken breasts, cut into 2 x ¼-inch strips
¾ cup sliced celery
½ cup *each* thinly sliced carrot and chopped broccoli
1 garlic clove, minced
½ teaspoon minced pared ginger root
¾ cup sliced mushrooms
½ cup sliced scallions (green onions), 1-inch-long pieces
¾ cup chopped Chinese cabbage
½ cup bean sprouts
3 ounces drained canned water chestnuts
½ cup canned ready-to-serve chicken broth
1 tablespoon cornstarch
2 tablespoons reduced-sodium soy sauce

In wok or 10-inch skillet heat 1½ teaspoons oil over high heat; add chicken and cook, stirring quickly and frequently, until lightly browned on all sides, 2 to 3 minutes. Remove from pan and set aside. To same pan add remaining 1½ teaspoons oil and heat; add celery, carrot, broccoli, garlic, and ginger and stir-fry until vegetables are tender-crisp, 2 to 3 minutes. Add mushrooms and scallions and continue to stir-fry for 1 to 2 minutes; add cabbage, bean sprouts, and water chestnuts and stir-fry for 1 to 2 minutes longer. Combine broth and cornstarch, stirring to dissolve cornstarch; add to vegetable mixture along with soy sauce and cook, stirring constantly, until sauce is thickened, 2 to 3 minutes. Return chicken to pan and cook until chicken is heated through, about 1 minute longer.

MAKES 2 SERVINGS

Each serving provides: 4 Protein Exchanges; ½ Bread Exchange; 4¼ Vegetable Exchanges; 1½ Fat Exchanges; 25 calories Optional Exchange
Per serving: 329 calories; 38 g protein; 9 g fat; 23 g carbohydrate; 98 mg calcium; 1,033 mg sodium; 82 mg cholesterol

Brenda Hogan
Lufkin, Texas

Chicken-Zucchini-Pineapple Stir-Fry

Pamela is a busy secretary who likes cooking and entertaining. Her love of fruit makes this stir-fry especially appealing to her.

2 tablespoons plus 2
  teaspoons pineapple juice
  (no sugar added)
½ cup canned ready-to-serve
  chicken broth
1 tablespoon reduced-sodium
  soy sauce
⅛ teaspoon garlic powder,
  or to taste
5 ounces skinned and boned
  chicken breast, cut into
  3 x ½-inch strips
1 teaspoon vegetable oil
2 medium celery ribs (each
  about 6 inches long), sliced
  diagonally
½ cup *each* diced zucchini,
  drained canned pineapple
  chunks (no sugar added),
  and sliced fresh *or* drained
  canned mushrooms
¼ cup diagonally sliced
  scallions (green onions)
1 teaspoon cornstarch

In small glass or stainless-steel bowl (not aluminum*) combine first 4 ingredients; add chicken, stirring to coat thoroughly. Cover with plastic wrap and refrigerate for at least 30 minutes.

Using slotted spoon, remove chicken from marinade, reserving marinade; using paper towels, pat chicken dry. In wok or 10-inch skillet heat oil over high heat; add chicken and cook, stirring quickly and frequently until lightly browned, 2 to 3 minutes. Transfer chicken to plate and keep warm. To same pan add celery and zucchini and stir-fry for 1 to 2 minutes; add pineapple, mushrooms, and scallions and stir-fry for 1 minute longer. Dissolve cornstarch in reserved marinade and add to pan along with chicken; cook, stirring constantly, until sauce is thickened, 2 to 3 minutes.

MAKES 1 SERVING

*It's best to marinate in glass or stainless-steel containers; acidic ingredients such as pineapple juice may react with aluminum, causing color and flavor changes in foods.

Each serving provides: 4 Protein Exchanges; 3½ Vegetable Exchanges; 1 Fat Exchange; 1½ Fruit Exchanges; 30 calories Optional Exchange
Per serving with fresh mushrooms: 361 calories; 38 g protein; 7 g fat; 36 g carbohydrate; 90 mg calcium; 1,294 mg sodium; 82 mg cholesterol
With canned mushrooms: 371 calories; 39 g protein; 7 g fat; 34 g carbohydrate; 92 mg calcium; 1,605 mg sodium; 82 mg cholesterol

Pamela J. Spellman
Indianapolis, Indiana

Easy Chicken and Broccoli ◑

Inspired by Chinese restaurants in her area that serve this dish, Deborah experimented until she found the perfect combination of flavors. Her easy-to-prepare skillet dinner is delicious over hot cooked rice. Deborah's job and two school-age children keep her very busy.

1 teaspoon margarine
10 ounces skinned and boned chicken breasts, cut into 3 x 1-inch strips
4 broccoli spears, blanched and cut into 1-inch pieces
1 garlic clove, minced
½ teaspoon minced pared ginger root
¾ cup canned ready-to-serve chicken broth
2 tablespoons oyster sauce
2 teaspoons cornstarch
Dash pepper, or to taste

In 10-inch nonstick skillet heat margarine over medium-high heat until bubbly and hot; add chicken and cook, turning when necessary, until lightly browned on all sides, 3 to 4 minutes. Remove from skillet and set aside.

To same skillet add broccoli, garlic, and ginger and sauté for 1 minute. In 2-cup measure or small mixing bowl combine broth, oyster sauce, and cornstarch, stirring to dissolve cornstarch; add to broccoli mixture and return chicken to skillet. Reduce heat to low, add pepper, and cook, stirring occasionally, until sauce is thickened, 5 to 10 minutes.

MAKES 2 SERVINGS

Each serving provides: 4 Protein Exchanges; 1 Vegetable Exchange; ½ Fat Exchange; 55 calories Optional Exchange
Per serving: 237 calories; 38 g protein; 4 g fat; 10 g carbohydrate; 100 mg calcium; 1,242 mg sodium; 82 mg cholesterol

Deborah Brooks
Mt. Marion, New York

❖❖❖❖❖❖❖❖❖❖❖❖❖❖❖❖❖❖❖❖❖❖❖❖❖❖❖❖❖❖❖❖❖❖❖❖❖❖❖

Easy But Elegant Chicken Supreme ◐

Linda created this adaptation of a restaurant dish so she could entertain and remain on the Food Plan. It worked! Linda stays active by walking, biking, and playing tennis. P.S. Her guests love this dish.

⅓ cup plus 2 teaspoons plain dried bread crumbs
2 tablespoons plus 1 teaspoon flour, divided
9 ounces skinned and boned chicken breasts
1 egg, lightly beaten
2 teaspoons *each* margarine and vegetable oil
½ cup sliced mushrooms
¼ cup *each* canned ready-to-serve chicken broth and dry white table wine
2 slices provolone cheese (½ ounce each), cut into strips
Italian (flat-leaf) parsley sprigs

In shallow bowl or on a paper plate combine bread crumbs and 2 tablespoons flour; dip chicken into egg, making sure all sides are coated, then dredge in crumb mixture. Repeat procedure, being sure to use all of egg and crumbs; set aside.

In 10-inch nonstick skillet combine margarine and oil; heat over medium heat until margarine is bubbly and hot. Add chicken and cook, turning once, until both sides are lightly browned and chicken is cooked through, 2 to 3 minutes on each side; transfer to plate and keep warm. To same skillet add mushrooms and sauté until lightly browned, 1 to 2 minutes; sprinkle with remaining teaspoon flour and stir quickly to combine. Add broth and wine and cook, stirring constantly, until mixture thickens, about 1 minute. Return chicken to skillet and top evenly with cheese; cover and cook until cheese is melted, 2 to 3 minutes. Serve garnished with parsley.

MAKES 2 SERVINGS

Each serving provides: 4½ Protein Exchanges; 1 Bread Exchange; ½ Vegetable Exchange; 2 Fat Exchanges; 70 calories Optional Exchange
Per serving: 443 calories; 40 g protein; 18 g fat; 23 g carbohydrate; 165 mg calcium; 561 mg sodium; 222 mg cholesterol

Linda Lyons
Sarasota, Florida

Oriental Pepper-Chicken Stir-Fry

After a bit of experimenting, Jackie stirred up a dish that's as pretty as it is flavorful. Red bell pepper is the secret. Jackie, who loves to cook and entertain in her spare time, says this stir-fry is one of her favorites.

1 cup canned ready-to-serve chicken broth, divided
1 tablespoon plus 1 teaspoon reduced-sodium soy sauce
2 teaspoons Chinese sesame oil, divided
½ teaspoon garlic powder
¼ teaspoon ground ginger
10 ounces skinned and boned chicken breasts, cut into 1-inch pieces
½ cup *each* diagonally sliced celery, thinly sliced green bell pepper, thinly sliced red bell pepper, and thinly sliced onion
1 cup sliced mushrooms
3 ounces drained canned water chestnuts
1 teaspoon cornstarch

In medium mixing bowl combine ½ cup broth with the soy sauce, 1 teaspoon oil, and the garlic powder and ginger, mixing well; add chicken and stir to coat thoroughly. Cover with plastic wrap and refrigerate for at least 30 minutes.

In 12-inch nonstick skillet or a wok heat remaining teaspoon oil over high heat; using slotted spoon, transfer chicken to skillet, reserving marinade, and cook, stirring quickly and frequently, until lightly browned, 2 to 3 minutes. Transfer chicken to plate and keep warm. To same skillet add celery, peppers, and onion and stir-fry for 1 minute; add mushrooms and water chestnuts and stir-fry for 1 minute longer. Add cornstarch and remaining ½ cup chicken broth to reserved marinade, stirring to dissolve cornstarch; pour into skillet, add cooked chicken, and cook, stirring occasionally, until sauce is thickened and vegetables are tender-crisp, 3 to 5 minutes longer.

MAKES 2 SERVINGS

Each serving provides: 4 Protein Exchanges; ½ Bread Exchange; 3 Vegetable Exchanges; 1 Fat Exchange; 25 calories Optional Exchange
Per serving: 292 calories; 37 g protein; 7 g fat; 18 g carbohydrate; 48 mg calcium; 1,070 mg sodium; 82 mg cholesterol

Jackie L. Jones
Provo, Utah

Good

Chinese Sesame Chicken (Turkey)

Jan is a Weight Watchers leader and an avid aerobics fan. She adapted a family recipe to fit the Food Plan and it's become a big hit with her husband and two teenage sons. Jan suggests that you toast the sesame seeds at 350°F. for about 10 minutes.

3 pounds chicken parts, skinned
½ cup plus 1 tablespoon water, divided
⅓ cup apple juice (no sugar added)
2 tablespoons *each* reduced-sodium soy sauce and sliced scallion (green onion)
1 tablespoon *each* ketchup and firmly packed dark brown sugar
2 garlic cloves, minced
Dash ground red pepper, or to taste
1 teaspoon cornstarch
2 teaspoons sesame seed, toasted

Spray 5-quart saucepot or Dutch oven with nonstick cooking spray and set over medium heat; add chicken parts and cook, turning when necessary, until chicken is browned on all sides, 4 to 6 minutes. Transfer chicken to platter and set aside.

In 2-cup measure or small mixing bowl combine ½ cup water with the juice, soy sauce, scallion, ketchup, sugar, garlic, and red pepper, mixing well; pour into pot and cook over medium heat for 1 to 2 minutes, stirring constantly to scrape up any browned particles from bottom of pan. Reduce heat to low and return chicken to pot; cover and cook until chicken is tender, 20 to 25 minutes. Transfer chicken to platter and keep warm, reserving liquid in pot.

Dissolve cornstarch in remaining tablespoon water and add to liquid in pot; cook, stirring frequently, until sauce is thickened, 3 to 4 minutes. Pour sauce evenly over chicken and sprinkle with toasted sesame seed.

MAKES 4 SERVINGS

Each serving provides: 4 Protein Exchanges; 45 calories Optional Exchange
Per serving: 260 calories; 34 g protein; 9 g fat; 9 g carbohydrate; 29 mg calcium; 448 mg sodium; 101 mg cholesterol

Jan Kiser
Napa, California

Chicken Bengali ◑

Lynn ate a dish similar to this one in an Indian restaurant in England and decided to adapt the recipe to the Food Plan. Lynn is a medical technologist who plays volleyball for fun.

1 tablespoon plus 1 teaspoon margarine
1½ teaspoons *each* all-purpose flour and Worcestershire sauce
1 teaspoon powdered mustard
½ teaspoon curry powder
1½ pounds chicken thighs, skinned

Preheat oven to 375°F. In small saucepan heat margarine over medium heat until bubbly and hot; add remaining ingredients except chicken and cook, stirring constantly, until mixture is thick and smooth.

Spray 9 x 9 x 2-inch baking dish with nonstick cooking spray; arrange chicken in a single layer in dish. Using pastry brush, brush chicken evenly with curry mixture; bake until chicken is browned and cooked through, 35 to 40 minutes, basting with pan juices every 20 minutes.

MAKES 4 SERVINGS

Each serving provides: 4 Protein Exchanges; 1 Fat Exchange; 5 calories Optional Exchange
Per serving: 279 calories; 30 g protein; 16 g fat; 1 g carbohydrate; 18 mg calcium; 165 mg sodium; 108 mg cholesterol

Lynn Woodward
Vestal, New York

Chicken, Cheese, 'n' Biscuits ⓒ

Lois is a farm wife and a Weight Watchers leader who is always looking for simple, down-to-earth recipes that farm families will enjoy. This hearty casserole fills the bill.

1 tablespoon plus 1 teaspoon
   margarine
2 tablespoons plus 2 tea-
   spoons all-purpose flour
½ teaspoon powdered
   mustard
¼ teaspoon rubbed sage
1½ cups skim milk
1 packet instant chicken
   broth and seasoning mix
Dash white pepper, or to taste
4 ounces Cheddar cheese,
   shredded
8 ounces skinned and boned
   cooked chicken, diced
1 cup *each* sliced carrots,
   stemmed sliced mushrooms,
   and sliced green beans
   (tender-crisp)
4 ready-to-bake refrigerated
   buttermilk flaky biscuits
   (1 ounce each)*

In 3-quart saucepan heat margarine over medium heat until bubbly and hot; add flour, mustard, and sage and stir quickly to combine thoroughly. Stirring constantly, gradually add milk; continue to stir and cook until smooth. Add broth mix and pepper and mix well. Reduce heat to low and cook, stirring occasionally, until mixture is thick, 5 to 10 minutes; add cheese and cook, stirring, until melted. Add chicken and vegetables and continue cooking until chicken and vegetables are heated through, 3 to 5 minutes longer.

Preheat oven to 400°F. Spray 1½-quart casserole with nonstick cooking spray and pour chicken mixture into casserole. Carefully separate each biscuit into 2 layers of dough, making eight circles; arrange biscuits over chicken mixture in an even layer, overlapping circles slightly, and bake until biscuits are golden, 7 to 10 minutes.

MAKES 4 SERVINGS

*Keep biscuits refrigerated until ready to use. Separate dough into layers as soon as biscuits are removed from refrigerator; they will be difficult to work with if allowed to come to room temperature.

Each serving provides: 3 Protein Exchanges; 1 Bread Exchange; 1½ Vegetable Exchanges; 1 Fat Exchange; ¼ Milk Exchange; 35 calories Optional Exchange
Per serving: 428 calories; 30 g protein; 21 g fat; 29 g carbohydrate; 357 mg calcium; 846 mg sodium; 82 mg cholesterol

Lois Ballard
Ogema, Minnesota

Chicken Breasts Florentine

This delicious entrée is one of Melody's specialties. She frequently prepares it for company dinners and has also served it at brunches at the school where she teaches. In her spare time, Melody enjoys doing cross-stitch and photography.

½ cup diced onion
1 garlic clove, minced
½ cup *each* chopped
  mushrooms, well-drained
  cooked chopped spinach,
  and part-skim ricotta
  cheese
½ teaspoon salt, divided
¼ teaspoon oregano leaves
¼ teaspoon pepper, divided
4 skinned and boned chicken
  breasts (4 ounces each),
  pounded to ¼-inch
  thickness
1 tablespoon plus 1 teaspoon
  each reduced-calorie
  margarine (tub) and plain
  dried bread crumbs
2 tablespoons plus 2 tea-
  spoons dry white table wine

Spray 10-inch skillet with nonstick cooking spray and heat; add onion and garlic and cook, stirring constantly, until softened. Add mushrooms and sauté until browned, about 5 minutes; remove from heat and stir in spinach, cheese, ¼ teaspoon salt, the oregano, and ⅛ teaspoon pepper. Sprinkle chicken breasts evenly with remaining ¼ teaspoon salt and ⅛ teaspoon pepper. Spread ¼ of spinach mixture over each breast, leaving ½-inch border on all sides; carefully roll chicken breasts crosswise to enclose filling and secure each with small skewers. Spray 11 x 7 x 2-inch baking dish with nonstick cooking spray and transfer chicken rolls to dish.

Preheat oven to 350°F. In small skillet melt margarine; stir in bread crumbs, then sprinkle mixture evenly over chicken rolls. Add wine to baking dish, cover with foil, and bake for 20 minutes; remove foil and bake until crumbs are lightly browned, 8 to 10 minutes longer.

MAKES 4 SERVINGS

Each serving provides: 3½ Protein Exchanges; ¾ Vegetable Exchange; ½ Fat Exchange; 20 calories Optional Exchange
Per serving: 216 calories; 31 g protein; 6 g fat; 7 g carbohydrate; 141 mg calcium; 458 mg sodium; 75 mg cholesterol

Melody D. Foltz
Gladstone, Missouri

Chicken 'n' Kraut ◐◑

A teacher who also loves to travel, Judy discovered this dish while vacationing at Hilton Head Island, South Carolina. She adapted it to fit the Food Plan and prepares it often, just for herself.

4 ounces skinned and boned chicken breast
Dash *each* salt and pepper
½ cup rinsed and drained sauerkraut*
1 slice provolone cheese (1 ounce)
1 tablespoon reduced-calorie Russian dressing (30 calories per tablespoon)

Preheat oven to 350° F. Spray individual baking dish with nonstick cooking spray and set chicken in bottom of dish; sprinkle with salt and pepper. Spread sauerkraut over chicken and top with cheese; spread dressing evenly over cheese, cover dish with aluminum foil, and bake until cheese is melted and chicken is tender, 15 to 20 minutes.

MAKES 1 SERVING

*Use the sauerkraut that is packaged in plastic bags and stored in the refrigerator section of the supermarket; it is usually crisper and less salty than the canned.

Each serving provides: 4 Protein Exchanges; 1 Vegetable Exchange; 30 calories Optional Exchange
Per serving: 278 calories; 35 g protein; 11 g fat; 10 g carbohydrate; 277 mg calcium; 1,218 mg sodium; 85 mg cholesterol

Judy Taylor
Pitman, New Jersey

Oven-Barbecued Chicken ☻

Dorace's kids loved this chicken when they were growing up, and your family's sure to love it, too. Dorace still serves this when her children and grandchildren come south for a visit.

1½ cups tomato juice
¾ cups distilled white vinegar
1 tablespoon plus 1½ teaspoons Worcestershire sauce
1 tablespoon firmly packed dark brown sugar
1 bay leaf
½ teaspoon salt
¼ teaspoon *each* ground red pepper and powdered mustard
Dash pepper, or to taste
3 pounds chicken parts, skinned
1 cup thinly sliced onions

Preheat oven to 350°F. In 1-quart saucepan combine all ingredients except chicken and onions; cook over medium heat, stirring frequently, until flavors are blended, 5 to 10 minutes.

In 13 x 9 x 2-inch baking dish arrange chicken parts in an even layer; top with onion slices, then tomato juice mixture. Bake, basting chicken frequently, until chicken is cooked through, 50 minutes to 1 hour. Remove and discard bay leaf before serving.

MAKES 4 SERVINGS

Each serving provides: 4 Protein Exchanges; ½ Vegetable Exchange; 35 calories Optional Exchange
Per serving: 269 calories; 34 g protein; 9 g fat; 14 g carbohydrate; 42 mg calcium; 509 mg sodium; 101 mg cholesterol

Dorace M. Belknap
New Port Richey, Florida

Teriyaki-Sesame Chicken

Sandra, a registered nurse and mother of two, lost 28 pounds on the Weight Watchers program. She taught herself international cooking and likes to adapt recipes to fit the Food Plan. This one is a family favorite.

½ cup orange juice (no sugar added)
2 tablespoons teriyaki sauce
¼ teaspoon *each* garlic powder and ground ginger
2 pounds chicken breasts, skinned
⅓ cup plus 2 teaspoons plain dried bread crumbs
1 tablespoon sesame seed

In large glass or stainless-steel mixing bowl (not aluminum*) combine juice, teriyaki sauce, garlic powder, and ginger; add chicken breasts and turn to coat with marinade. Cover bowl with plastic wrap and refrigerate for at least 2 hours.

Preheat oven to 350°F. In shallow bowl or on paper plate combine bread crumbs and sesame seed; remove chicken breasts from marinade, reserving marinade, and coat skin-side of each with an equal amount of crumb mixture. Spray 13 x 9 x 2-inch flameproof baking dish with nonstick cooking spray; transfer chicken to sprayed dish, bone-side down, and pour reserved marinade into dish. Bake until chicken is cooked through, 40 to 45 minutes. Turn oven control to broil and broil until chicken is crisped and lightly browned, 3 to 5 minutes. Transfer chicken to serving platter and drizzle with pan juices.

MAKES 4 SERVINGS

*It's best to marinate in glass or stainless-steel containers; acidic ingredients such as orange juice may react with aluminum, causing color and flavor changes in foods.

Each serving provides: 4 Protein Exchanges; ½ Bread Exchange; 30 calories Optional Exchange
Per serving: 260 calories; 37 g protein; 6 g fat; 13 g carbohydrate; 53 mg calcium; 453 mg sodium; 97 mg cholesterol

Sandra R. Parkington
Silver Spring, Maryland

Orange-Glazed Chicken Tidbits ☻

A receptionist at a medical center, Diane lives on a farm with her husband and two daughters. Her leisure-time activities are handicrafts and traveling.

¼ cup reduced-calorie orange
  spread (16 calories per
  2 teaspoons)
2 tablespoons soy sauce*
½ teaspoon ground ginger
⅛ teaspoon garlic powder
15 ounces skinned and boned
  chicken breasts, cut into
  1-inch pieces

In medium mixing bowl combine orange spread, soy sauce, ginger, and garlic powder, mixing well; add chicken pieces and toss to coat. Cover with plastic wrap and refrigerate for 30 minutes, tossing chicken again after 15 minutes. Transfer chicken pieces to rack in broiling pan and broil for 5 minutes; turn chicken over, brush with any remaining marinade, and broil until done, about 3 minutes longer.

MAKES 4 SERVINGS

Each serving provides: 3 Protein Exchanges; 24 calories Optional Exchange
Per serving: 143 calories; 25 g protein; 1 g fat; 7 g carbohydrate; 35 mg
    calcium; 733 mg sodium; 62 mg cholesterol

*Reduced-sodium soy sauce may be substituted. Reduce calories to 142, carbohydrate to 6 g, calcium to 28 mg, and sodium to 373 mg.

Diane Papke
Miles, Iowa

❖❖

Eggplant-Turkey Italiano ☉

Turkey and vegetables are the basis for this tasty and filling dish. Frances used to make it with ground beef until she joined Weight Watchers.

1 medium eggplant (1 to 1¼ pounds), pared and cubed
1 quart water
2 teaspoons salt, divided
10 ounces ground turkey
1 cup *each* diced onions and green bell pepper
1 teaspoon oregano leaves
1 small garlic clove, minced, or ¼ to ½ teaspoon garlic powder
½ teaspoon pepper
Dash ground red pepper
1 cup tomato sauce
2 tablespoons chopped fresh parsley *or* 1 tablespoon dried
1 tablespoon grated Parmesan cheese

In 4-quart saucepan combine eggplant, water, and 1 teaspoon salt and bring to a boil. Reduce heat and cook for 5 minutes; drain and set aside.

Spray 12-inch nonstick skillet with nonstick cooking spray and heat over medium heat; add turkey and, using back of a wooden spoon to crumble meat, cook, stirring occasionally, until turkey is lightly browned, 3 to 4 minutes. Stir in onions, bell pepper, and seasonings and cook, stirring frequently, until vegetables are tender, about 4 minutes; add eggplant, tomato sauce, and parsley and stir to combine. Cover and let simmer until flavors are blended, 30 to 35 minutes. Serve sprinkled with cheese.

MAKES 4 SERVINGS, ABOUT 1½ CUPS EACH

Each serving provides: 2 Protein Exchanges; 3½ Vegetable Exchanges; 10 calories Optional Exchange
Per serving: 189 calories; 16 g protein; 8 g fat; 16 g carbohydrate; 113 mg calcium; 1,289 mg sodium; 48 mg cholesterol

VARIATION:

Parmesan cheese may be omitted. Omit Optional Exchange from Exchange Information.

Per serving: 183 calories; 15 g protein; 8 g fat; 16 g carbohydrate; 96 mg calcium; 1,265 mg sodium; 48 mg cholesterol

Frances Schlotzhauer
Holden, Missouri

Sloppy Joes ◑◑

Priscilla is a grandmother who has lost 74 pounds on the Weight Watchers program. A writer, she has completed a historical novel based on four generations of her own family, and has written over 900 poems as well, some of which have been published. Her adaptation of this family recipe is sure to please everyone in your family.

1 teaspoon vegetable oil
1 cup chopped celery
²⁄₃ cup *each* chopped onions
   and green bell pepper
5 ounces ground turkey
4 ounces drained canned red
   kidney beans, rinsed
½ cup tomato puree
1 tablespoon firmly packed
   brown sugar
2 hamburger buns (2 ounces
   each), cut into halves and
   toasted

In 8-inch nonstick skillet heat oil over medium-high heat; add celery, onions, and pepper and sauté, stirring occasionally, until onions are translucent. Add turkey and, using back of a wooden spoon to crumble meat, cook, stirring occasionally, for 2 minutes; stir in remaining ingredients except buns and bring to a boil. Reduce heat and let simmer, stirring occasionally, until turkey is cooked through and flavors are blended, 12 to 15 minutes.

To serve, onto bottom half of each bun spoon half of turkey mixture; top each with a remaining bun half and serve immediately.

MAKES 2 SERVINGS

Each serving provides: 3 Protein Exchanges; 2 Bread Exchanges; 3¼ Vegetable Exchanges; ½ Fat Exchange; 30 calories Optional Exchange
Per serving: 469 calories; 26 g protein; 14 g fat; 62 g carbohydrate; 131 mg calcium; 850 mg sodium (estimated); 56 mg cholesterol

Priscilla A. C. Osgood
Bangor, Maine

❖❖❖

Stuffed Pitas ☾◑

Hazel is a Weight Watchers leader. These pita pockets are a favorite of hers.

1 tablespoon plus 1 teaspoon reduced-calorie margarine (tub)

10 ounces turkey sausage, cut into ¼-inch pieces

½ cup *each* diced onion and green bell pepper

1 cup drained and rinsed sauerkraut*

1½ teaspoons horseradish mustard *or* ¾ teaspoon *each* prepared horseradish and prepared mustard

4 pita breads (1 ounce each), each cut horizontally to form pocket

In 9-inch skillet heat margarine until bubbly and hot; add turkey sausage and sauté for 2 minutes. Add onion and bell pepper and sauté until tender-crisp, about 2 minutes; add sauerkraut and horseradish mustard (or horseradish and mustard) and cook over medium heat, stirring frequently, until thoroughly heated, about 4 minutes. Let cool slightly, then fill each pita pocket with ¼ of sausage mixture.

MAKES 4 SERVINGS

*Use sauerkraut that is packaged in plastic bags and stored in the refrigerator section of the supermarket; it is usually crisper and less salty than the canned.

Each serving provides: 2 Protein Exchanges; 1 Bread Exchange; 1 Vegetable Exchange; ½ Fat Exchange
Per serving: 231 calories; 13 g protein; 9 g fat; 24 g carbohydrate; 43 mg calcium; 1,123 mg sodium; 45 mg cholesterol

VARIATION:

Substitute 8 ounces turkey frankfurters for the sausage.

Per serving: 254 calories; 10 g protein; 13 g fat; 25 g carbohydrate; 109 mg calcium; 1,079 mg sodium; 49 mg cholesterol

Hazel Hamilton
Peoria, Illinois

Smoky Po ◐◑

Debra experimented for a while to come up with a dish similar to the one her father used to make. Now her variation has become a family favorite. Debra, who loves to cook, has lost over 100 pounds on the Program.

1 medium green bell pepper,
    seeded and cut into 1-inch
    pieces
1 cup diced onions
¼ cup water
12 ounces peeled cooked
    potatoes, diced
12 ounces precooked smoked
    turkey sausage, sliced

In 10-inch nonstick skillet combine bell pepper, onions, and water; cover and cook over medium heat until vegetables are tender-crisp, 3 to 4 minutes. Add potatoes and sausage to vegetables and cook uncovered, stirring occasionally, until mixture is heated through, 2 to 3 minutes.

MAKES 4 SERVINGS

Each serving provides: 3 Protein Exchanges; 1 Bread Exchange; 1 Vegetable
    Exchange
Per serving: 257 calories; 16 g protein; 12 g fat; 22 g carbohydrate; 33 mg
    calcium; 672 mg sodium; 58 mg cholesterol

VARIATION:

Substitute precooked smoked beef sausage or kielbasa for the turkey sausage.

Per serving with beef sausage: 373 calories; 13 g protein; 25 g fat; 24 g
    carbohydrate; 18 mg calcium; 842 mg sodium; 25 mg cholesterol
With kielbasa: 369 calories; 14 g protein; 25 g fat; 22 g carbohydrate; 28
    mg calcium; 751 mg sodium; 60 mg cholesterol

Debra Jo Riley
Fort Mill, South Carolina

Turkey and Vegetables ◉◑

An artist and grandmother of eight, Jewell created this recipe by combining foods that suit her taste. To vary her creation she recommends adding herbs such as marjoram or oregano, or substituting beef broth for the chicken broth.

1 cup *each* shredded green
   cabbage and cauliflower
   florets
¾ cup julienne-cut carrots
½ cup canned ready-to-serve
   chicken broth
4 ounces precooked smoked
   turkey sausages, sliced
   ½ inch thick

In 10-inch skillet combine cabbage, cauliflower, carrots, and broth; cover and cook over medium-high heat until vegetables are tender-crisp, 8 to 10 minutes. Add sausage and stir to combine; cook until sausages are heated through, 3 to 4 minutes longer.

MAKES 2 SERVINGS

Each serving provides: 2 Protein Exchanges; 2¾ Vegetable Exchanges;
   10 calories Optional Exchange
Per serving: 160 calories; 12 g protein; 8 g fat; 10 g carbohydrate; 55 mg
   calcium; 745 mg sodium; 39 mg cholesterol

VARIATION:

Substitute precooked smoked beef sausage for the turkey sausage.

Per serving: 238 calories; 10 g protein; 17 g fat; 11 g carbohydrate; 44 mg
   calcium; 858 mg sodium; 16 mg cholesterol

Jewell Taylor
Ashdown, Arkansas

Spicy Turkey Chili ☻

Both Delma and her husband have been on the Weight Watchers program. Together they have lost nearly 300 pounds. Delma prepares meals that fit the Food Plan for her entire family, including her three small children.

7 ounces ground turkey
½ cup chopped onion
1 cup drained canned Italian tomatoes, seeded and chopped
½ cup *each* tomato sauce and water
2 teaspoons chili powder
1 teaspoon *each* Worcestershire sauce and white wine vinegar
1 bay leaf
¼ teaspoon *each* salt and garlic powder
⅛ teaspoon *each* ground cinnamon, ground allspice, and crushed red pepper

Spray 3-quart saucepan with nonstick cooking spray and heat over medium-high heat; add turkey and onion and, using back of a wooden spoon to crumble meat, cook, stirring occasionally, until turkey is browned, about 5 minutes. Add remaining ingredients and stir well to combine. Reduce heat to low and let simmer, stirring occasionally, until chili is thick, 25 to 30 minutes. Remove bay leaf before serving.

MAKES 2 SERVINGS

Each serving provides: 2½ Protein Exchanges; 2½ Vegetable Exchanges
Per serving: 231 calories; 21 g protein; 11 g fat; 15 g carbohydrate; 97 mg calcium; 981 mg sodium; 67 mg cholesterol

NOTE:
May be frozen for future use; just thaw and reheat.

Delma Caylor
Lebanon, Indiana

Upside-Down Pizza Loaf ©

Karan, a Weight Watchers leader, says the inspiration and encouragement she gets from her members help her maintain her weight. She encourages her members to convert favorite family recipes to the Food Plan. This is one of hers.

2 teaspoons vegetable oil, divided
10 ounces ground turkey
½ cup chopped onion
½ cup plus 1 tablespoon all-purpose flour, divided
1 cup tomato sauce
¼ cup chopped green bell pepper
¼ teaspoon *each* basil leaves and fennel seed
⅛ teaspoon oregano leaves, crumbled
3 ounces mozzarella cheese, shredded
1 egg
½ cup skim milk
½ teaspoon salt
1 tablespoon grated Parmesan cheese

In 10-inch nonstick skillet heat ½ teaspoon oil; add turkey and onion and, using back of a wooden spoon to crumble meat, cook, stirring occasionally, until onion is tender and turkey is no longer pink. Sprinkle mixture with 1 tablespoon flour and stir quickly to combine; cook, stirring constantly, for 1 minute. Gradually stir in tomato sauce; add bell pepper, basil, fennel seed, and oregano and bring to a boil. Reduce heat and cook, stirring frequently, for 1 minute.

Preheat oven to 425°F. Spray 9 x 5 x 3-inch loaf pan with nonstick cooking spray and transfer turkey mixture to pan; sprinkle with mozzarella cheese. In small mixing bowl, using electric mixer, beat egg; add remaining ½ cup flour and 1½ teaspoons oil along with the milk and salt and continue beating until mixture is smooth. Pour batter over turkey loaf and sprinkle with Parmesan cheese; bake until loaf is puffed and golden, 25 to 30 minutes.

MAKES 4 SERVINGS

Each serving provides: 3 Protein Exchanges; ½ Bread Exchange; 1¼ Vegetable Exchanges; ½ Fat Exchange; 40 calories Optional Exchange
Per serving: 322 calories; 23 g protein; 16 g fat; 22 g carbohydrate; 217 mg calcium; 845 mg sodium; 134 mg cholesterol

Karan K. Ehlers
Hettinger, North Dakota

From the Carving Board
Meats

Hearty Vegetable-Beef Soup ⊙

Genevieve is a turnip and parsnip lover, so she created this recipe using vegetables rarely found in soups. Her hobbies are craft work and knitting.

15 ounces beef for stew (1-inch cubes)
1½ quarts water
1 cup *each* mixed vegetable juice, diced parsnips, diced turnips, and chopped green cabbage
½ cup *each* chopped celery and scallions (green onions)
1½ ounces sorted uncooked lentils, rinsed
¾ teaspoon salt
½ garlic clove, minced
⅛ teaspoon pepper
½ cup drained canned sliced mushrooms

On rack in broiling pan broil beef, turning once, until rare and browned, about 5 minutes on each side. Transfer beef to 4-quart saucepan; add remaining ingredients except mushrooms and bring liquid to a boil. Reduce heat to low, cover pan, and let simmer, stirring occasionally, until meat and vegetables are tender, 40 to 50 minutes. Add mushrooms and cook for 1 to 2 minutes longer.

MAKES 4 SERVINGS

Each serving provides: 3½ Protein Exchanges; ½ Bread Exchange; 1¾ Vegetable Exchanges; 15 calories Optional Exchange
Per serving: 279 calories; 30 g protein; 8 g fat; 19 g carbohydrate; 74 mg calcium; 782 mg sodium; 77 mg cholesterol

NOTE:

Freeze extra portions of this hearty soup in individual containers and you'll always have this meal-in-a-bowl available. Just reheat and eat!

Genevieve E. Jerabek
Paynesville, Minnesota

German Stew

Apples are common in German cooking, and stews are a German favorite as well. After the meat is browned and vegetables sautéed, finish Donna's hearty stew recipe in a slow cooker—you'll have an extra-tender dish.

1¼ pounds beef for stew
  (1-inch cubes)
1 tablespoon plus 1 teaspoon
  vegetable oil
1 medium carrot (about 4
  ounces), pared and grated
½ cup chopped onion
2 garlic cloves, minced
2 small apples, cored, pared,
  and grated
1½ cups water
½ cup dry red table wine
2 packets instant beef broth
  and seasoning mix
1 small bay leaf
½ teaspoon thyme leaves
¼ teaspoon salt
Dash pepper, or to taste

On rack in broiling pan broil beef 5 to 6 inches from heat source, turning occasionally, until browned on all sides and rare, 4 to 6 minutes; set aside.

In 4-quart saucepan heat oil over medium heat; add carrot, onion, and garlic and sauté, stirring occasionally, until vegetables are softened, 2 to 3 minutes. Add beef and remaining ingredients and stir to combine thoroughly. Reduce heat to low, cover, and let simmer, stirring occasionally, for 25 to 30 minutes. Remove cover and continue cooking, stirring often, until meat is fork-tender, 15 to 20 minutes longer. Remove bay leaf before serving.

MAKES 4 SERVINGS

Each serving provides: 4 Protein Exchanges; ¾ Vegetable Exchange; 1 Fat Exchange; ½ Fruit Exchange; 35 calories Optional Exchange
Per serving: 361 calories; 35 g protein; 16 g fat; 14 g carbohydrate; 39 mg calcium; 579 mg sodium; 103 mg cholesterol

Donna Newton
Burnaby, British Columbia,
Canada

Simply Bananas

Banana-Date Muffins
Breakfast in a Glass—I
Oatmeal 'n' Raisin Muffins

Date-Stuffed Pastries
Cheese Pancakes with
Pineapple Topping

Ratatouille-Pasta Gratinée
Most Delicious Cauliflower

Cashew Chicken

Battered Leeks

Banana Cake with Coconut Topping

Beef 'n' Broccoli Stir-Fry ◖

A visiting Japanese family prepared this dish for Barbara and her family. Barbara liked it so much she adapted it to fit the Food Plan. Married and the mother of a teenage daughter, Barbara enjoys bowling and oil painting.

1 tablespoon peanut *or* vegetable oil
2 cups blanched broccoli florets*
1 cup blanched diagonally sliced carrots (thin slices)*
½ cup onion wedges (thin wedges)
6 ounces broiled boneless sirloin steak, cut into thin strips
1 tablespoon plus 1½ teaspoons rosé light wine
1 tablespoon reduced-sodium soy sauce
½ teaspoon cornstarch
¼ teaspoon granulated sugar
⅛ teaspoon salt

In 10-inch skillet or a wok heat oil; add broccoli, carrots, and onion and cook, stirring quickly and frequently, until vegetables are tender-crisp and onions are browned. Stir in beef strips. In small bowl combine remaining ingredients, stirring to dissolve cornstarch; add to beef mixture and cook, stirring constantly, until sauce is thickened, 2 to 3 minutes.

MAKES 2 SERVINGS

*Instead of blanching, the vegetables may be steamed for 2 minutes.

Each serving provides: 3 Protein Exchanges; 3½ Vegetable Exchanges; 1½ Fat Exchanges; 15 calories Optional Exchange
Per serving: 312 calories; 32 g protein; 14 g fat; 15 g carbohydrate; 79 mg calcium; 553 mg sodium; 77 mg cholesterol

SERVING SUGGESTION:

Serve each portion over ½ cup cooked noodles or long-grain rice. Add 1 Bread Exchange to Exchange Information.

Per serving with noodles: 411 calories; 35 g protein; 15 g fat; 34 g carbohydrate; 87 mg calcium; 554 mg sodium; 102 mg cholesterol
With rice: 422 calories; 34 g protein; 14 g fat; 40 g carbohydrate; 89 mg calcium; 553 mg sodium; 77 mg cholesterol

Barbara "Fette" Diebert
Madera, California

Chinese Steak ◑

Susan's mother whipped this up one day, and Susan spiced it up with extra seasonings. When she's not cooking, Susan enjoys boating on the lake near her home.

10 ounces boneless beef steak
    (sirloin, top round, etc.)
¼ teaspoon *each* garlic
    powder and minced pared
    ginger root
1 teaspoon *each* vegetable
    and peanut oil
1 cup diagonally sliced celery
½ cup chopped green bell
    pepper
1 medium tomato, cut into
    8 wedges
¼ cup canned ready-to-serve
    beef broth
2 tablespoons reduced-
    sodium soy sauce
1 teaspoon cornstarch
½ cup drained canned button
    mushrooms
Dash pepper, or to taste
1 cup cooked long-grain rice
    (hot)

Season steak with garlic and ginger; on rack in broiling pan broil steak, turning once, until rare, about 3 minutes on each side. Transfer to cutting board and cut into thin slices; set aside.

In 12-inch nonstick skillet or a wok combine oils and heat over high heat; add celery and bell pepper and cook, stirring quickly and frequently, until tender-crisp, 1 to 2 minutes; add tomato and continue stir-frying for 1 minute. Add beef slices and stir-fry for 1 minute longer. Combine broth, soy sauce, and cornstarch, stirring to dissolve cornstarch; add to beef mixture along with mushrooms and pepper and cook, stirring constantly, until sauce has thickened and vegetables are cooked through, 2 to 3 minutes. Serve over hot rice.

MAKES 2 SERVINGS

Each serving provides: 4 Protein Exchanges; 1 Bread Exchange; 3 Vegetable
    Exchanges; 1 Fat Exchange; 10 calories Optional Exchange
Per serving with sirloin: 442 calories; 42 g protein; 14 g fat; 34 g carbohy-
    drate; 55 mg calcium; 1,027 mg sodium; 103 mg cholesterol
With top round: 422 calories; 41 g protein; 12 g fat; 34 g carbohy-
    drate; 55 mg calcium; 1,024 mg sodium; 103 mg cholesterol

Susan H. Hawkins
North Monmouth, Maine

Steak Champignon ◐

Red wine, sour cream, and mushrooms turn an ordinary steak into a gourmet meal that's so simple to prepare.

1 tablespoon margarine
1 cup sliced mushrooms
2 tablespoons dry red table wine
3 tablespoons sour cream
2 boneless beef steaks (5 ounces each)

In 8-inch nonstick skillet heat margarine over medium heat until bubbly and hot; add mushrooms and sauté until lightly browned. Reduce heat to low; add wine and cook, stirring frequently, for 2 minutes. Stir in sour cream and cook, stirring constantly, until heated. Remove skillet from heat; set aside and keep sauce warm.

On rack in broiling pan, broil steaks, turning once, until done to taste. Remove steaks to serving platter; pour sauce over steaks or transfer sauce to gravy boat and serve with steaks.

MAKES 2 SERVINGS

Each serving provides: 4 Protein Exchanges; 1 Vegetable Exchange; 1½ Fat Exchanges; 65 calories Optional Exchange
Per serving: 353 calories; 38 g protein; 19 g fat; 3 g carbohydrate; 45 mg calcium; 170 mg sodium; 113 mg cholesterol

Weight Watchers Kitchens

❖◦❖

Beef Pie Mexicali ◐

Brenda, a Weight Watchers leader, adapted this recipe for her members. The result is a Mexican dish that tastes almost like a taco. This active grandmother teaches piano, sings in a choir, and enjoys water skiing and square dancing.

15 ounces ground beef
¾ cup finely chopped onions
1½ teaspoons chili powder
1 teaspoon salt, divided
½ teaspoon ground cumin
⅛ teaspoon pepper
¼ cup drained canned mild
   green chili peppers, cut into
   thin strips
1 cup plus 2 tablespoons all-
   purpose flour
1½ teaspoons double-acting
   baking powder
2 tablespoons margarine
1½ cups skim milk
3 eggs
3 ounces Cheddar *or*
   Monterey Jack cheese,
   shredded
1½ cups *each* diced tomatoes
   and shredded lettuce

On rack in broiling pan broil beef 5 to 6 inches from heat source, turning once, for 2½ to 3 minutes on each side. Crumble beef and transfer to medium mixing bowl; add onions, chili powder, ½ teaspoon salt, and the cumin and pepper and mix well.

Preheat oven to 350°F. Spray 10 x 10 x 2-inch baking dish with nonstick cooking spray and spread mixture evenly in dish; top with chili peppers and set aside.

In medium mixing bowl combine flour, baking powder, and remaining ½ teaspoon salt; with pastry blender or 2 knives used scissors-fashion, cut in margarine until mixture resembles coarse meal. Add milk and eggs and, using wire whisk, beat until batter is smooth; pour over meat mixture and bake until topping is puffed and lightly browned, 35 to 40 minutes. Sprinkle with cheese and bake until lightly browned, 3 to 5 minutes. Serve with tomatoes and lettuce.

MAKES 6 SERVINGS

Each serving provides: 3 Protein Exchanges; 1 Bread Exchange; 1¼ Vegetable Exchanges; 1 Fat Exchange; ¼ Milk Exchange
Per serving with Cheddar cheese: 441 calories; 27 g protein; 25 g fat; 26 g carbohydrate; 280 mg calcium; 722 mg sodium; 206 mg cholesterol
With Monterey Jack cheese: 437 calories; 27 g protein; 24 g fat; 26 g carbohydrate; 284 mg calcium; 710 mg sodium; 204 mg cholesterol

Brenda B. Gordon
Salt Lake City, Utah

German-Style Stuffed Meat Loaf

The classic Reuben sandwich was the inspiration for Cheryl's hearty meat loaf. Cheryl is a homemaker and mother of three who has lost 88 pounds on the Weight Watchers program.

7 ounces ground beef *or* veal
1 egg, beaten
1 slice rye bread, toasted and made into crumbs
2 tablespoons *each* minced onion, pickle relish, and reduced-calorie Thousand Island dressing (30 calories per tablespoon)
1 teaspoon Worcestershire sauce
Dash to ⅛ teaspoon pepper
½ cup drained sauerkraut,* chopped
2 ounces Swiss cheese, shredded, divided

Preheat oven to 350°F. In 1-quart bowl combine all ingredients except sauerkraut and cheese, mixing thoroughly; on sheet of wax paper spread mixture to form a 6 x 8-inch rectangle. Spread sauerkraut over rectangle, leaving 1-inch border on all sides; sprinkle sauerkraut with half of cheese and, starting from short end, roll up meat jelly-roll fashion. Press open ends to seal; transfer to rack in roasting pan† and bake for 30 minutes. Sprinkle loaf with remaining cheese and continue baking until cheese is melted, 2 to 3 minutes.

MAKES 2 SERVINGS

*Use the sauerkraut that is packaged in plastic bags and stored in the refrigerator section of the supermarket; it is usually crisper and less salty than the canned.
†If using veal, rack is not necessary; bake in 8 x 8 x 2-inch baking pan.

Each serving provides: 4 Protein Exchanges; ½ Bread Exchange; ½ Vegetable Exchange; 60 calories Optional Exchange
Per serving with beef: 472 calories; 32 g protein; 28 g fat; 21 g carbohydrate; 323 mg calcium; 832 mg sodium; 230 mg cholesterol
With veal: 412 calories; 33 g protein; 21 g fat; 21 g carbohydrate; 323 mg calcium; 819 mg sodium; 235 mg cholesterol

Cheryl J. Usher
Perryopolis, Pennsylvania

Ground Beef "Stroganoff" ☺

Pamela has the distinction of being the only Weight Watchers leader in her town. When she was a member, she had to travel 30 miles to British Columbia to attend meetings. This recipe is a long-time favorite that Pamela serves often.

1 tablespoon plus 1 teaspoon margarine, divided
2 tablespoons all-purpose flour
1 cup evaporated skimmed milk
1 tablespoon Worcestershire sauce
1 teaspoon salt, divided
⅛ teaspoon white pepper, or to taste
½ cup minced onion
2 garlic cloves, minced
2 cups sliced mushrooms
1 pound cooked ground beef, crumbled
1 cup plain low-fat yogurt
1 tablespoon chopped fresh parsley

In small saucepan heat 1 tablespoon margarine over medium heat until bubbly and hot; add flour and mix well. Using wire whisk, gradually stir in milk and cook, stirring constantly, until mixture is smooth; stir in Worcestershire sauce, ½ teaspoon salt, and the pepper. Reduce heat to low and let simmer, stirring frequently, until sauce is thick, 10 to 15 minutes.

While sauce is simmering, in 12-inch non-stick skillet heat remaining teaspoon margarine over medium heat until bubbly and hot; add onion and garlic and sauté until onion is softened, 1 to 2 minutes. Add mushrooms and sauté, stirring occasionally, for 2 to 3 minutes; stir in beef and remaining ½ teaspoon salt. Reduce heat to low and add sauce and yogurt; stir to combine thoroughly. Cook until beef is heated through, 1 to 2 minutes *(do not boil)*; serve sprinkled with parsley.

MAKES 4 SERVINGS

Each serving provides: 4 Protein Exchanges; 1¼ Vegetable Exchanges; 1 Fat Exchange; 1 Milk Exchange; 15 calories Optional Exchange
Per serving: 519 calories; 40 g protein; 31 g fat; 19 g carbohydrate; 319 mg calcium; 827 mg sodium; 113 mg cholesterol

Pamela L. Baldwin
Republic, Washington

Heavenly Hamburger ⊖ ◑

Cheese, olives, and noodles turn ordinary ground beef into a celestial creation that Mary and her daughters enjoy. Mary has lost weight on the Weight Watchers program and feels that the support she receives from the women at her workplace has really helped.

⅓ cup *each* chopped onion
  and celery
¾ cup canned Italian
  tomatoes (with liquid);
  drain, seed, and chop
  tomatoes, reserving liquid
4 ounces cooked ground beef,
  crumbled
6 pitted black olives, sliced
⅛ teaspoon salt
Dash pepper
2 ounces American cheese,
  diced
½ cup cooked egg noodles
  (medium width)

Spray 8-inch nonstick skillet with nonstick cooking spray and set over medium heat; add onion and celery and cook, stirring occasionally, until vegetables are softened, 2 to 3 minutes. Add tomatoes, reserved liquid, beef, olives, salt, and pepper and mix well; cook, stirring occasionally, until beef is heated through and vegetables are tender, 5 to 7 minutes. Add cheese and noodles and cook, stirring frequently, until cheese is melted and noodles are heated, 2 to 3 minutes.

MAKES 2 SERVINGS

Each serving provides: 3 Protein Exchanges; ½ Bread Exchange; 1½ Vegetable Exchanges; 15 calories Optional Exchange
Per serving: 388 calories; 25 g protein; 25 g fat; 17 g carbohydrate; 235 mg calcium; 828 mg sodium; 92 mg cholesterol

Mary L. Kochheiser
Fresno, California

Whole Wheat Beef 'n' Pepper Pizza ©

Debra suggests adding various "extras"—mushrooms, onions, green bell peppers—but don't stop there. Try black olives, sausage, or extra cheese for a real pizzeria-style "special."

¾ cup whole wheat flour
½ cup skim milk
2 eggs
1 teaspoon oregano leaves
¾ teaspoon salt, divided
8 ounces cooked ground beef
  (rare), crumbled
¼ cup *each* diced onion and
  green bell pepper
⅛ teaspoon pepper
1 cup tomato sauce
6 ounces mozzarella cheese,
  coarsely shredded

Preheat oven to 425°F. Spray 13 x 9 x 2-inch glass baking dish with nonstick cooking spray and set aside. In bowl combine flour, milk, eggs, oregano, and ½ teaspoon salt and beat until smooth; pour into sprayed dish and sprinkle evenly with beef, vegetables, pepper, and remaining ¼ teaspoon salt. Bake for 20 minutes; top pizza with tomato sauce, sprinkle with cheese, and bake until cheese is melted and crust browned, 10 to 15 minutes.

MAKES 4 SERVINGS

Each serving provides: 4 Protein Exchanges; 1 Bread Exchange; 1¼ Vegetable Exchanges; 10 calories Optional Exchange
Per serving: 451 calories; 32 g protein; 26 g fat; 24 g carbohydrate; 308 mg calcium; 1,029 mg sodium; 224 mg cholesterol

Debra Sather
Northwood, Iowa

Veal Stew Italian Style

The longer a stew is simmered, the tenderer the meat will be. Follow Donna's recipe for a tender and delicious dish.

1 tablespoon plus 1 teaspoon olive *or* vegetable oil
1¼ pounds boned veal shoulder, cut into 1-inch cubes
6 garlic cloves, minced
1 cup tomato sauce
½ cup canned Italian tomatoes (with liquid); drain, seed, and chop tomatoes, reserving liquid
⅓ cup dry white table wine
2 rosemary sprigs, chopped, *or* ¼ teaspoon rosemary leaves, crushed
½ teaspoon salt
Dash pepper

In 3- or 4-quart saucepan heat oil over medium-high heat; add veal and sauté, turning frequently, until browned on all sides, 3 to 5 minutes. Reduce heat to low, add garlic, and continue to sauté for 1 minute; add remaining ingredients and stir to combine. Cover and let simmer, stirring occasionally, until veal is tender, 45 to 50 minutes.

MAKES 4 SERVINGS

Each serving provides: 4 Protein Exchanges; 1¼ Vegetable Exchanges; 1 Fat Exchange; 20 calories Optional Exchange
Per serving: 333 calories; 29 g protein; 19 g fat; 8 g carbohydrate; 45 mg calcium; 789 mg sodium; 101 mg cholesterol

SERVING SUGGESTION:

Serve each portion of this savory stew over ½ cup cooked pasta or long-grain rice. Add 1 Bread Exchange to Exchange Information.

Per serving with pasta: 410 calories; 31 g protein; 19 g fat; 24 g carbohydrate; 50 mg calcium; 790 mg sodium; 101 mg cholesterol
With rice: 444 calories; 31 g protein; 19 g fat; 33 g carbohydrate; 55 mg calcium; 789 mg sodium; 101 mg cholesterol

Donna Newton
Burnaby, British Columbia, Canada

Pineapple-Veal Rolls

Rita's love for cooking and baking goes back to her seventh-grade cooking class. Today she uses her culinary skills to help others, baking and delivering food to nonambulatory residents in the apartment building where she lives. A friend gave Rita the inspiration for this recipe; she added the fruit.

1 tablespoon plus 1 teaspoon margarine, divided
1 cup drained canned pineapple chunks (no sugar added), divided
¼ cup chopped scallions (green onions)
1 cup cooked long-grain rice
1 tablespoon minced fresh parsley
½ teaspoon salt
⅛ teaspoon pepper
4 veal cutlets (5 ounces each), pounded to ⅛-inch thickness
⅔ cup pineapple juice (no sugar added)
2 teaspoons cornstarch
¼ cup canned ready-to-serve chicken broth
¾ cup drained canned button mushrooms

In 10-inch nonstick skillet heat 1 teaspoon margarine over medium heat until bubbly and hot; add ½ cup pineapple and the scallions and sauté until scallions are soft and pineapple is lightly browned, 1 to 2 minutes. Add rice, parsley, salt, and pepper, mixing well; cook, stirring frequently, until rice is heated through, 2 to 3 minutes. Mound ¼ of rice mixture onto each cutlet; fold narrow ends of each cutlet over filling, then fold remaining sides over to enclose (envelope-style). Secure each roll with a toothpick.

In same skillet heat remaining margarine over medium heat until bubbly and hot; add veal and cook, turning occasionally, until browned, 4 to 6 minutes. Transfer to plate and discard toothpicks.

Combine pineapple juice and cornstarch, stirring to dissolve cornstarch; pour into skillet, add broth, and stir to combine. Return veal rolls to skillet; add mushrooms and remaining ½ cup pineapple, cover, and cook over low heat, stirring occasionally, until sauce is thickened, 5 to 10 minutes.

MAKES 4 SERVINGS, 1 VEAL ROLL EACH

Each serving provides: 4 Protein Exchanges; ½ Bread Exchange; ½ Vegetable Exchange; 1 Fat Exchange; 1 Fruit Exchange; 10 calories Optional Exchange
Per serving: 404 calories; 33 g protein; 16 g fat; 28 g carbohydrate; 40 mg calcium; 579 mg sodium; 115 mg cholesterol

Rita Starr Conlin
Hartford, Connecticut

Veal Madeira

This classic veal dish is elegant enough for a dinner party. Wild mushrooms and artichoke hearts add sweetness, as does the addition of Madeira wine.

1 tablespoon all-purpose flour
Dash *each* **salt and pepper**
10 ounces veal cutlets
1 tablespoon margarine,
  divided
¼ cup *each* **medium-sweet**
  Madeira wine and minced
  shallots
1 garlic clove, minced
1 cup sliced wild mushrooms
  (e.g., porcini, oyster) *or*
  regular mushrooms
1 medium tomato, blanched,
  peeled, seeded, and
  chopped
½ cup *each* **thawed frozen**
  artichoke hearts and
  canned ready-to-serve beef
  broth

On sheet of wax paper or a paper plate combine flour, salt, and pepper; dredge veal in seasoned flour, coating all sides and reserving any remaining flour mixture.

In 12-inch skillet heat 2 teaspoons margarine until bubbly and hot; add veal and brown quickly on both sides. Remove veal to plate and set aside. To same skillet add wine and bring to a boil. Continue cooking over high heat, stirring occasionally, until alcohol evaporates, about 1 minute; pour over veal.

Wipe skillet clean; add remaining teaspoon margarine and heat until bubbly and hot. Add shallots and garlic and sauté for 1 minute; add mushrooms and cook until mushrooms release liquid, about 2 minutes. Sprinkle any reserved seasoned flour over vegetables and quickly stir to combine; add tomato, artichokes, and broth and bring liquid to a boil. Reduce heat to low and cook until mixture thickens slightly, about 3 minutes. Return veal and wine to skillet and let mixture simmer until flavors are blended and veal is heated through, about 2 minutes.

MAKES 2 SERVINGS

Each serving provides: 4 Protein Exchanges; 2¾ Vegetable Exchanges; 1½ Fat Exchanges; 75 calories Optional Exchange
Per serving: 383 calories; 32 g protein; 19 g fat; 15 g carbohydrate; 43 mg calcium; 490 mg sodium; 101 mg cholesterol

Weight Watchers Kitchens

❖·❖

Veal Parmigiana with Spinach Noodles

Spinach noodles, fast becoming a nationwide favorite, give Cathy's classic Italian dish color and flavor.

24 saltines, made into crumbs
1 ounce grated Parmesan cheese, divided
Dash pepper
15 ounces veal cutlets
1 egg, beaten
2 tablespoons reduced-calorie margarine (tub), divided
1 tablespoon vegetable oil
1 cup tomato sauce
½ teaspoon oregano leaves
2 ounces mozzarella cheese, shredded
2 cups cooked spinach noodles (hot)

In large bowl combine cracker crumbs, ¾ ounce Parmesan cheese, and the pepper, mixing well. Dip 1 veal cutlet into egg, then dredge in cracker mixture, coating all sides; transfer to plate. Repeat with remaining cutlets, coating evenly.

In 12-inch nonstick skillet combine 2 teaspoons margarine and the oil and heat over medium-high heat until margarine is bubbly and hot; add veal and cook, turning once, until lightly browned, 1 to 2 minutes on each side. Remove to plate and set aside.

Preheat oven to 375°F. In small bowl combine tomato sauce and oregano. In 12 x 8 x 2-inch baking dish spread ¼ cup sauce; arrange cutlets in single layer in dish. Spread with remaining sauce; sprinkle with mozzarella. Bake until lightly browned, 10 to 15 minutes.

In medium mixing bowl combine noodles, remaining margarine, and remaining Parmesan cheese, tossing to mix. Transfer noodle mixture to platter and top with veal mixture.

MAKES 4 SERVINGS

Each serving provides: 4 Protein Exchanges; 2 Bread Exchanges; 1 Vegetable Exchange; 1½ Fat Exchanges
Per serving: 497 calories; 33 g protein; 26 g fat; 32 g carbohydrate; 212 mg calcium; 892 mg sodium; 181 mg cholesterol

Cathy D. Howell
Bloomington, Indiana

Rolled Veal Loaf Italienne

This Nielson family favorite is festive enough for company dinners—Michelle thinks rolled meats are easy to put together, and she enjoys using the leftovers for cold sandwiches.

2 pounds ground veal
4 slices white bread, made
    into crumbs
½ cup finely chopped onion
1 egg, beaten
6 garlic cloves, minced
1 tablespoon *each* Italian-
    style seasoning and
    chopped fresh parsley
1 teaspoon *each* salt, oregano
    leaves, and chili powder
¼ teaspoon pepper
6 ounces mozzarella cheese,
    shredded
1 cup finely chopped
    mushrooms

In large mixing bowl combine all ingredients except cheese and mushrooms, mixing well.

Preheat oven to 350°F. On 24 x 12-inch sheet of wax paper, shape meat mixture into a 20 x 9-inch rectangle, about ¼ inch thick; sprinkle rectangle evenly with cheese, leaving a 1-inch border on all sides. Top cheese with mushrooms and, starting from narrow end, lift wax paper and roll meat jelly-roll fashion, removing paper as you roll; pinch open ends of roll to seal. Spray 9 x 5 x 3-inch loaf pan with nonstick cooking spray and transfer loaf to pan; bake until meat is cooked through, 55 minutes to 1 hour.

MAKES 8 SERVINGS

Each serving provides: 4 Protein Exchanges; ½ Bread Exchange; ¼ Vegetable Exchange
Per serving: 299 calories; 29 g protein; 15 g fat; 9 g carbohydrate; 146 mg calcium; 491 mg sodium; 137 mg cholesterol

Michelle Nielson
Marion, Iowa

Veal Pie with Spaghetti Crust

Connie discovered an interesting recipe and changed it so that it would fit the Food Plan. She's also shared it with other Weight Watchers members. A homemaker who enjoys oil painting, Connie also collects cookbooks; she suggests that this dish is also delicious with ground buffalo.

1 tablespoon plus 1 teaspoon margarine, divided
2 cups cooked spaghetti (warm)
1 egg, beaten
2 tablespoons grated Parmesan cheese
²/₃ cup low-fat cottage cheese
½ cup *each* diced onion and green bell pepper
5 ounces cooked ground veal, crumbled
1 cup canned Italian tomatoes (with liquid); drain and chop tomatoes, reserving liquid
¼ cup tomato sauce
1 teaspoon *each* granulated sugar and oregano leaves
½ teaspoon salt
Dash *each* garlic powder and pepper
4 ounces mozzarella cheese, shredded

Spray 9-inch pie pan with nonstick cooking spray and set aside. In small flameproof container melt 1 tablespoon margarine. In 1-quart bowl combine spaghetti, egg, Parmesan cheese, and melted margarine, mixing well; press spaghetti mixture over bottom and up sides of sprayed pan to form a crust. Carefully spread cottage cheese over crust.

Preheat oven to 350°F. In 8-inch nonstick skillet heat remaining margarine over medium-high heat until bubbly and hot; add onion and bell pepper and sauté until onion is translucent. Add remaining ingredients except mozzarella and stir to combine. Reduce heat to low and let simmer until flavors are blended, about 10 minutes. Spread mixture evenly over cottage cheese and bake until bubbly and hot, 15 to 20 minutes. Sprinkle pie with mozzarella cheese and bake until cheese is melted and lightly browned, about 5 minutes longer. Remove from oven and let stand for 5 minutes before slicing.

MAKES 4 SERVINGS

Each serving provides: 3 Protein Exchanges; 1 Bread Exchange; 1¼ Vegetable Exchanges; 1 Fat Exchange; 20 calories Optional Exchange
Per serving with veal: 358 calories; 26 g protein; 17 g fat; 25 g carbohydrate; 253 mg calcium; 856 mg sodium; 130 mg cholesterol
With buffalo: 330 calories; 29 g protein; 14 g fat; 25 g carbohydrate; 249 mg calcium; 833 mg sodium; 108 mg cholesterol

Connie Enerson
Hettinger, North Dakota

Zucchini-Veal Pizza

Break away from the ordinary with Renee's unique zucchini-crust pizza. A gardener, Renee also sews, paints, and bikes.

4 cups shredded zucchini
2 teaspoons salt, divided
2 eggs
¼ teaspoon *each* onion and garlic powders
4 ounces *each* shredded mozzarella and Cheddar cheese, divided
2 teaspoons olive oil
8 ounces ground veal
½ cup *each* chopped green bell pepper and mushrooms
¼ cup chopped onion
2 garlic cloves, minced
1 cup tomato sauce
1 teaspoon oregano leaves
½ teaspoon Italian-style seasoning
Dash pepper
1 tablespoon grated Parmesan cheese

In colander sprinkle zucchini with 1 teaspoon salt; let stand 10 minutes. Rinse under running cold water, squeezing out moisture.

Preheat oven to 400°F. In medium bowl beat together eggs, onion powder, and garlic powder; add zucchini and 2 ounces each mozzarella and Cheddar, mixing well. Spray 14 x 10-inch baking pan with nonstick cooking spray and press zucchini mixture over bottom of pan; bake until set, 8 to 10 minutes.

In 10-inch nonstick skillet heat oil over medium heat; add veal and, using back of a wooden spoon to crumble meat, cook, stirring occasionally, until browned. Remove to plate, leaving juices in skillet; add bell pepper, mushrooms, onion, and garlic to skillet and sauté until softened, 2 to 3 minutes. Return veal to skillet and add tomato sauce, seasonings, and remaining salt; cook, stirring occasionally, until veal is thoroughly cooked, 4 to 5 minutes.

Spread veal mixture evenly over crust; top with remaining mozzarella and Cheddar and sprinkle with Parmesan. Bake at 400°F. until crust is lightly browned, 15 to 20 minutes.

MAKES 4 SERVINGS

Each serving provides: 4 Protein Exchanges; 3½ Vegetable Exchanges; ½ Fat Exchange; 10 calories Optional Exchange
Per serving: 401 calories; 30 g protein; 26 g fat; 12 g carbohydrate; 432 mg calcium; 1,363 mg sodium; 233 mg cholesterol

Renee M. Swenson
Fargo, North Dakota

Pork Calvados

Try this version of a classic French dish—pork cutlets in a mildly seasoned creamy sauce. Heavenly!

10 ounces pork cutlets
2 teaspoons margarine
¼ cup sliced onion
¼ cup apple brandy (calvados)
2 tablespoons canned ready-to-serve chicken broth
2 teaspoons thawed frozen concentrated apple juice
1 small apple
1 tablespoon heavy cream
Dash *each* salt, pepper, and ground nutmeg

On rack in broiling pan broil cutlets 2 inches from heat source, turning once, about 3 minutes on each side. Remove cutlets to work surface and cut into 1-inch pieces.

In 1- or 2-quart saucepan heat margarine over medium heat until bubbly and hot; add onion and sauté until translucent, about 2 minutes. Add pork pieces and cook, stirring frequently, for 1 minute; add brandy, chicken broth, and concentrated apple juice and stir to combine. Reduce heat to low, cover saucepan, and let simmer until pork is fork-tender, about 20 minutes.

Core and pare apple; cut into ½-inch-thick slices. Add apple slices to pork mixture and cook until slices are soft, 8 to 10 minutes; stir in cream and seasonings.

MAKES 2 SERVINGS

Each serving provides: 4 Protein Exchanges; ¼ Vegetable Exchange; 1 Fat Exchange; ½ Fruit Exchange; 115 calories Optional Exchange
Per serving: 464 calories; 31 g protein; 23 g fat; 21 g carbohydrate; 28 mg calcium; 261 mg sodium; 112 mg cholesterol

Weight Watchers Kitchens

Fruited Pork Chops

Ruby's fruity pork chop dinner is sure to please your entire family. Ruby, who has two children and four grandchildren, loves to knit, sew, and crochet. She is also a seasoned traveler who has been to every state except Alaska.

2 pork shoulder or loin chops (6 ounces each)
½ cup thinly sliced carrot
⅓ cup unfermented apple cider (no sugar added)
¼ cup *each* sliced onion and celery
½ small mango, pared, pitted, and diced
½ small apple, cored and diced
1 tablespoon golden raisins
1 cup cooked long-grain rice (hot)
Italian (flat-leaf) parsley sprigs

On rack in broiling pan broil pork chops 6 inches from heat source, turning once, until rare, 2 to 3 minutes on each side. Remove from broiler and set aside.

Preheat oven to 350°F. In 8 x 8 x 2-inch baking dish combine carrot, cider, onion, celery, mango, apple, and raisins; top with pork chops. Cover and bake until pork chops are fork-tender and vegetables are thoroughly cooked, 30 to 40 minutes. Serve over hot rice and garnish with parsley.

MAKES 2 SERVINGS

Each serving provides: 4 Protein Exchanges; 1 Bread Exchange; 1 Vegetable Exchange; 1½ Fruit Exchanges
Per serving: 505 calories; 31 g protein; 20 g fat; 51 g carbohydrate; 48 mg calcium; 109 mg sodium; 111 mg cholesterol

Ruby Van Ness
Brazil, Indiana

Pork Chops with Apple Kraut

The recipe from which this was adapted came from Germany and has been in the Kaul family for about 110 years. Albertina, a Weight Watchers leader, weigher, and receptionist, has two sons, seven grandsons, and one great-granddaughter. She enjoys camping, hiking, hunting, and fishing.

4 pork shoulder or loin chops
  (6 ounces each)
1 tablespoon all-purpose flour
2 cups drained sauerkraut*
2 small apples, cored and
  diced
½ cup diced onion
1 teaspoon caraway seed
1 tablespoon plus 1 teaspoon
  Dijon-style mustard
1 teaspoon *each* firmly
  packed brown sugar and
  prepared horseradish
½ teaspoon salt
⅛ teaspoon pepper

On rack in broiling pan broil pork chops 6 inches from heat source, turning once, until rare, 2 to 3 minutes on each side. Remove from broiler and set aside.

Preheat oven to 350°F. Spoon flour into a 20 x 14-inch plastic baking bag and shake to coat inside of bag; set bag in 13 x 9 x 2-inch baking dish. In medium bowl combine sauerkraut, apples, onion, and caraway seed; spread mixture evenly in bag.

In small bowl combine mustard, sugar, horseradish, salt, and pepper; spread a thin coating of mixture on both sides of each pork chop. Arrange chops in bag over sauerkraut mixture and seal bag as manufacturer directs; cut 6 slits in top of bag. Bake until chops are cooked throughout and tender, 45 to 50 minutes.

MAKES 4 SERVINGS

*Use the sauerkraut that is packaged in plastic bags and stored in the refrigerator section of the supermarket; it is usually crisper and less salty than the canned.

Each serving provides: 4 Protein Exchanges; 1¼ Vegetable Exchanges; ½ Fruit Exchange; 20 calories Optional Exchange
Per serving: 354 calories; 32 g protein; 17 g fat; 19 g carbohydrate; 74 mg calcium; 1,068 mg sodium; 102 mg cholesterol

Albertina C. Kaul
Great Falls, Montana

Sweet-and-Sour Pork ◑

Ethel, who lost 45 pounds on the Weight Watchers program, works as a receptionist one meeting per week. She likes the outdoors, handicrafts, and developing new recipes to fit the Food Plan.

**8 ounces boned cooked pork,
   cut into 1-inch cubes**
**2 cups canned pineapple
   chunks (no sugar added)**
¾ cup green bell pepper strips
**½ cup *each* sliced celery
   and mushrooms**
**¼ cup sliced onion (separated
   into rings)**
**⅔ cup pineapple juice
   (no sugar added)**
¼ cup rice vinegar
**1 tablespoon plus 1 teaspoon
   cornstarch**
1 tablespoon soy sauce*
¼ teaspoon salt

In 2-quart microwave-safe casserole combine pork cubes, pineapple chunks, bell pepper, celery, mushrooms, and onion rings; toss to combine.

In small bowl combine pineapple juice, vinegar, cornstarch, soy sauce, and salt, stirring to dissolve cornstarch; pour over pork mixture. Cover with plastic wrap and microwave on High for 10 minutes,† stirring once or twice during cooking, until thoroughly heated. Let stand 5 minutes before serving.

MAKES 4 SERVINGS

Each serving provides: 2 Protein Exchanges; 1 Vegetable Exchange; 1½ Fruit
    Exchanges; 10 calories Optional Exchange
Per serving: 260 calories; 17 g protein; 8 g fat; 31 g carbohydrate; 41 mg
    calcium; 522 mg sodium; 51 mg cholesterol

*Reduced-sodium soy sauce may be substituted. Reduce calories to 259, calcium to 38 mg, and sodium to 342 mg.
†Cooking time may be different in your microwave oven. To help ensure good results, be sure to check for doneness while cooking.

*Ethel Scott
Balderson, Ontario, Canada*

Ham 'n' Cabbage Stew ☉

Barbara is an award-winning cook whose husband collects antique stoves. In fact, Barbara does all her cooking on a 1912 cast-iron gas stove, and she learned to cook on a wood-burning stove. This stew, says Barbara, is a good way to use up fresh garden vegetables.

1 tablespoon plus 1 teaspoon margarine
½ cup diced onion
1 garlic clove, minced
8 ounces cubed cooked ham (1-inch cubes)
½ cup sliced mushrooms
4 cups shredded green cabbage
2 cups sliced carrots (1-inch-thick slices)
1 bay leaf
¼ teaspoon *each* caraway seed and pepper
2 cups water
2 packets instant beef broth and seasoning mix
1 tablespoon cornstarch, dissolved in 2 tablespoons water

In 5-quart saucepot or Dutch oven heat margarine until bubbly and hot; add onion and garlic and sauté until onion is softened. Add ham and mushrooms and sauté for 2 minutes; add cabbage, carrots, bay leaf, caraway seed, and pepper and continue sautéing for 5 minutes longer. Stir in water and broth mix; bring to a boil. Reduce heat, cover, and let simmer, stirring occasionally, for 30 minutes. Stir in dissolved cornstarch and let simmer, uncovered, until mixture thickens, about 5 minutes. Remove bay leaf before serving.

MAKES 4 SERVINGS

Each serving provides: 2 Protein Exchanges; 3½ Vegetable Exchanges; 1 Fat Exchange; 15 calories Optional Exchange
Per serving: 181 calories; 14 g protein; 7 g fat; 15 g carbohydrate; 64 mg calcium; 1,133 mg sodium; 30 mg cholesterol

Barbara Cadigan
Duluth, Minnesota

Ham-Yam Mountain ⓒⓘ

One of our youngest contributors, Tabitha is still in her teens. This is how her grandmother used up leftovers from Easter dinner.

1 slice boned cooked ham (3 ounces)
1 canned pineapple slice (no sugar added)
3 ounces peeled cooked yam or sweet potato, mashed
½ teaspoon firmly packed brown sugar
⅛ teaspoon ground cinnamon
1 teaspoon margarine

Preheat oven to 350°F. Spray shallow individual baking dish with nonstick cooking spray; set ham slice in dish and top with pineapple slice. Spread mashed yam (or sweet potato) over pineapple, sprinkle with brown sugar and cinnamon, and dot with margarine. Bake until heated through, about 15 minutes.

MAKES 1 SERVING

Each serving provides: 3 Protein Exchanges; 1 Bread Exchange; 1 Fat Exchange; ½ Fruit Exchange; 10 calories Optional Exchange
Per serving: 300 calories; 19 g protein; 9 g fat; 36 g carbohydrate; 34 mg calcium; 1,076 mg sodium; 45 mg cholesterol

VARIATION:

Omit brown sugar. Sprinkle yam (or sweet potato) with cinnamon, dot with margarine, and top with 2 medium marshmallows (½ ounce). Bake until marshmallows melt and mixture is heated through, about 15 minutes. Increase Optional Exchange to 50 calories.

Per serving: 337 calories; 20 g protein; 9 g fat; 45 g carbohydrate; 34 mg calcium; 1,081 mg sodium; 45 mg cholesterol

Tabitha LeClere
Hortonville, New York

Jambalaya

Lynda firmly believes that to lose weight you must have faith in yourself. A staunch supporter of the Weight Watchers program, she created this adaptation of a Southern favorite to make dieting more interesting.

2 teaspoons margarine
½ cup diced onion
1 small garlic clove, minced
1 medium tomato, blanched, peeled, seeded, and chopped
½ medium green bell pepper, seeded and diced
1 teaspoon all-purpose flour
1 packet instant chicken broth and seasoning mix, dissolved in 1 cup warm water
4 ounces diced boiled ham
2 ounces uncooked regular long-grain rice
1 tablespoon chopped fresh parsley
Dash to ⅛ teaspoon thyme leaves, crushed
Dash ground red pepper or hot sauce
6 small shrimp, shelled and deveined
6 small oysters, shucked and rinsed (reserve oyster liquid)

In 10-inch nonstick skillet heat margarine until bubbly and hot; add onion and garlic and sauté until onion is translucent. Add tomato and bell pepper and sauté for 1 minute longer. Sprinkle flour over vegetables and stir quickly to combine; cook, stirring constantly, for 1 minute. Stirring constantly, gradually add dissolved broth mix; add ham, rice, and seasonings and bring mixture to a boil. Reduce heat, cover, and let simmer, stirring occasionally to prevent rice from sticking or burning, until rice is tender, 15 to 20 minutes. Add shrimp, oysters, and reserved oyster liquid and toss to combine; cover and cook until shrimp turn pink and edges of oysters curl, 2 to 3 minutes.

MAKES 2 SERVINGS

Each serving provides: 4 Protein Exchanges; 1 Bread Exchange; 2 Vegetable Exchanges; 1 Fat Exchange; 10 calories Optional Exchange
Per serving: 313 calories; 25 g protein; 8 g fat; 34 g carbohydrate; 93 mg calcium; 1,212 mg sodium; 87 mg cholesterol

VARIATION:

Canadian-style bacon or very lean cooked smoked ham may be substituted for the boiled ham.

Per serving with Canadian-style bacon: 320 calories; 25 g protein; 9 g fat; 34 g carbohydrate; 93 mg calcium; 1,329 mg sodium; 85 mg cholesterol
With smoked ham: 294 calories; 23 g protein; 7 g fat; 33 g carbohydrate; 90 mg calcium; 1,246 mg sodium; 84 mg cholesterol

Lynda M. Kuehn
Quesnel, British Columbia, Canada

Micro "Monte Carlo" Sandwich ◑

Rhoda, whose hobbies are needlepoint, painting, and crafts, likes to adapt recipes to the Weight Watchers food plan. This microwave special is a wonderful quick meal.

1 pita bread (1 ounce)
2 teaspoons *each* **reduced-calorie mayonnaise and country Dijon-style mustard**
1 ounce *each* **julienne-cut baked Virginia ham and Swiss cheese (thin strips)**
1 thin tomato slice

Using a sharp knife, cut halfway around edge of pita; open to form pocket. Spread mayonnaise inside onto one half of pita; spread mustard over other half. Fill pita with ham, cheese, and tomato. Wrap in paper towels and microwave on Medium-High until sandwich is hot and cheese is melted, about 2 minutes.* Remove towels before serving.

MAKES 1 SERVING

*Cooking time may be different in your microwave oven. To help ensure good results, be sure to check for doneness while cooking.

Each serving provides: 2 Protein Exchanges; 1 Bread Exchange; ⅛ Vegetable Exchange; 1 Fat Exchange
Per serving: 275 calories; 17 g protein; 13 g fat; 22 g carbohydrate; 280 mg calcium; 969 mg sodium; 44 mg cholesterol

VARIATION:

For a delicious sandwich prepared in a conventional oven or toaster-oven, wrap sandwich in foil and bake at 350°F. until sandwich is hot and cheese is melted, about 10 minutes.

Rhoda Blumenthal
Middletown, New York

Lamb Chops Diable ◐

A spicy sauce with just a hint of sweetness turns ordinary lamb chops into a special dinner. Try barbecuing these in the summertime.

1 garlic clove, chopped
Dash *each* salt and pepper
½ teaspoon oregano leaves
2 tablespoons lemon juice
1 teaspoon *each* Dijon-style mustard and honey
12 ounces lamb loin or shoulder chops (½ to ¾ inch thick)
2 tablespoons plain dried bread crumbs

Using a mortar and pestle, combine garlic, salt, and pepper, mashing to form a smooth paste; add oregano leaves, mashing to combine. Add lemon juice, mustard, and honey and stir until mixture is smooth and well combined.

Arrange lamb chops on rack in broiling pan and brush 1 side with half of the garlic mixture; broil 2 inches from heat source for 3 minutes. Turn chops over; brush with remaining garlic mixture and broil until chops are medium-rare, about 3 minutes longer. Sprinkle chops with bread crumbs and broil until crumbs are lightly browned, about 30 seconds.

MAKES 2 SERVINGS

Each serving provides: 4 Protein Exchanges; 40 calories Optional Exchange
Per serving: 258 calories; 33 g protein; 9 g fat; 10 g carbohydrate; 32 mg calcium; 268 mg sodium; 114 mg cholesterol

Weight Watchers Kitchens

Lamb Curry

Tara, a trained chef who specializes in ethnic cuisines, prepares curry the authentic Indian way—without curry powder. Instead, she uses a blend of seasonings to produce the traditional curry flavor.

1¼ pounds boned lamb shoulder, cut into 1-inch cubes
1 tablespoon plus 1 teaspoon vegetable oil
1½ medium bananas, peeled and diced
1 small apple, cored, pared, and diced
½ cup chopped onion
6 garlic cloves, minced
2 cups canned ready-to-serve chicken broth (at room temperature)
1 tablespoon *each* ground cumin and ground coriander
1 teaspoon *each* chili powder and ground red pepper
½ teaspoon *each* ground cinnamon and ground cardamom
1 cup plain low-fat yogurt
2 cups cooked long-grain rice (hot)

On rack in broiling pan broil lamb, turning once, until rare and browned on all sides; set aside.

In 12-inch nonstick skillet heat oil over medium heat; add fruits, onion, and garlic and sauté, stirring occasionally, until fruits and onion are softened and lightly browned, 2 to 3 minutes.

Transfer fruit mixture to blender container; add broth and seasonings and process until smooth. Return mixture to skillet, add cooked lamb, and stir well; bring to a boil. Reduce heat, cover, and let simmer, stirring occasionally, until lamb is fork-tender, 25 to 30 minutes. Remove from heat and let cool to lukewarm, 10 to 15 minutes. Stir in yogurt, set over low heat, and cook, stirring frequently, until heated through, 3 to 5 minutes *(do not boil);* serve over hot rice.

MAKES 4 SERVINGS

Each serving provides: 4 Protein Exchanges; 1 Bread Exchange; ¼ Vegetable Exchange; 1 Fat Exchange; 1 Fruit Exchange; ½ Milk Exchange; 20 calories Optional Exchange
Per serving: 512 calories; 38 g protein; 18 g fat; 47 g carbohydrate; 171 mg calcium; 663 mg sodium; 117 mg cholesterol

Tara Camille Stephenson
San Francisco, California

Chicken Liver-Vegetable Medley ◑◑

Although liver has never been one of Eileen's favorite foods, she found that experimenting can produce wonderful results, like this recipe. Now she doesn't mind eating liver at all when it's prepared this way. Eileen is a secretary who plays guitar in her spare time and enjoys cooking.

1½ teaspoons vegetable oil, divided
5 ounces chicken livers
½ cup sliced onion
¼ cup *each* sliced mushrooms and diced green bell pepper
1 to 2 small garlic cloves, minced
1 teaspoon all-purpose flour
½ cup water
2 tablespoons tomato sauce
1 packet instant chicken broth and seasoning mix
1 medium tomato, cut into wedges
½ cup cooked spaghetti
Dash pepper, or to taste

In 10-inch nonstick skillet heat 1 teaspoon oil over high heat; add livers and sauté until no longer red, 1 to 2 minutes. Remove from skillet and set aside.

To same skillet add remaining ½ teaspoon oil and heat; add onion, mushrooms, bell pepper, and garlic and sauté for 1 minute; sprinkle vegetables with flour and cook, stirring, for 1 minute longer. Gradually stir in water; add tomato sauce and broth mix, stir to combine, and bring to a boil. Reduce heat and let simmer until liquid thickens, 1 to 2 minutes; add tomato wedges, spaghetti, pepper, and reserved livers and stir to combine. Cover and cook until mixture is heated through and liver is cooked throughout, 1 to 2 minutes *(do not overcook)*.

MAKES 1 SERVING

Each serving provides: 4 Protein Exchanges; 1 Bread Exchange; 4½ Vegetable Exchanges; 1½ Fat Exchanges; 20 calories Optional Exchange
Per serving: 410 calories; 32 g protein; 13 g fat; 41 g carbohydrate; 63 mg calcium; 1,144 mg sodium; 622 mg cholesterol

Eileen L. Mendelson
Brooklyn, New York

Liver and Vegetables ⊖ ◑

Karen, a legal secretary, prepares this for lunch on Saturdays. It's her version of one of her mother's recipes. Karen keeps fit by walking or, when it's too cold, by exercising indoors on her mini-trampoline.

1 cup *each* sliced carrots
   and celery
¾ cup water
1 packet instant beef broth
   and seasoning mix
5 ounces beef liver, cut into
   strips
1 tablespoon Worcestershire
   sauce
1 cup tomato juice
1 teaspoon taco seasoning
   mix
½ teaspoon firmly packed
   brown sugar

In 1-quart saucepan combine carrots, celery, water, and broth mix; cook until vegetables are tender-crisp. Remove saucepan from heat and set aside.

Spray 10-inch nonstick skillet with nonstick cooking spray and heat; add liver and Worcestershire sauce and cook, stirring constantly, until liver is no longer red, 1 to 2 minutes. Add vegetables and cooking liquid along with remaining ingredients and bring to a boil. Reduce heat and let simmer, stirring occasionally, until flavors are well blended, about 15 minutes.

MAKES 1 SERVING

Each serving provides: 4 Protein Exchanges; 4 Vegetable Exchanges; 1 Fruit
   Exchange; 20 calories Optional Exchange
Per serving: 357 calories; 35 g protein; 6 g fat; 43 g carbohydrate; 109 mg
   calcium; 2,436 mg sodium; 425 mg cholesterol

Karen J. Sprouls
Georgetown, Illinois

Liver Chinese-Style ◐

Nancy is a graduate home economist who knows that liver is a good source of iron, but she just couldn't get excited about eating it. That is, not until she combined it with the Chinese-style cuisine she loves.

½ medium green bell pepper, seeded and cut into thin strips
½ cup *each* sliced onion (separated into rings) and mushrooms
1 small garlic clove, minced
½ teaspoon grated pared ginger root *or* dash to ⅛ teaspoon ground ginger
4 ounces beef *or* calf liver, cut into 2 x ½-inch strips
1 tablespoon *each* reduced-sodium soy sauce and dry sherry
Dash pepper
½ cup cooked long-grain rice (hot)

Spray 9- or 10-inch nonstick skillet with non-stick cooking spray and heat over medium-high heat. Add vegetables and cook, stirring quickly and frequently, until tender-crisp *(be careful not to burn)*; stir in garlic and ginger, then push vegetables to one side of skillet. Add liver to center of skillet and cook, stirring quickly and frequently, until liver is no longer red, 1 to 2 minutes. Combine liver and vegetables, add soy sauce and sherry, and continue to cook and stir until liver is cooked throughout, about 1 minute longer *(do not overcook)*. Season with pepper and serve over hot rice.

MAKES 1 SERVING

Each serving provides: 3 Protein Exchanges; 1 Bread Exchange; 3 Vegetable Exchanges; 15 calories Optional Exchange
Per serving with beef liver: 350 calories; 28 g protein; 5 g fat; 43 g carbohydrate; 49 mg calcium; 766 mg sodium; 340 mg cholesterol
With calf liver: 350 calories; 27 g protein; 6 g fat; 42 g carbohydrate; 49 mg calcium; 695 mg sodium; 340 mg cholesterol

Nancy S. Preston
Hampton, Virginia

Liver with Apple and Onion ⊙ ◑

Curry powder adds interest to this tasty liver dish, which Carol developed by chance. It's delicious served over rice or noodles. Carol, a director of nursing services for a nursing home, raises quarter horses on her Idaho farm.

1 teaspoon vegetable oil
1 small apple, cored and thinly sliced
½ cup diced onion
5 ounces liver (beef, calf, lamb, *or* pork), cut into 2-inch-long strips
1 tablespoon reduced-sodium soy sauce
⅛ to ¼ teaspoon curry powder, or to taste

In 10-inch nonstick skillet heat oil; add apple and onion and sauté until onion is translucent. Add liver and cook, stirring constantly, until liver is no longer red, 1 to 2 minutes. Add soy sauce and curry powder and cook, continuing to stir, until liver is cooked throughout, about 1 minute longer (*do not overcook*).

MAKES 1 SERVING

Each serving provides: 4 Protein Exchanges; 1 Vegetable Exchange; 1 Fat Exchange; 1 Fruit Exchange
Per serving with beef liver: 340 calories; 30 g protein; 11 g fat; 31 g carbohydrate; 42 mg calcium; 802 mg sodium; 425 mg cholesterol
With calf liver: 340 calories; 29 g protein; 12 g fat; 29 g carbohydrate; 43 mg calcium; 712 mg sodium; 425 mg cholesterol
With lamb liver: 335 calories; 32 g protein; 11 g fat; 27 g carbohydrate; 45 mg calcium; 682 mg sodium; 425 mg cholesterol
With pork liver: 332 calories; 33 g protein; 10 g fat; 27 g carbohydrate; 44 mg calcium; 732 mg sodium; 427 mg cholesterol

Carol Hackney
Grangeville, Idaho

❖❖❖

Liver Patties ℂ

Audrey, an executive secretary and Weight Watchers member, shows us an inventive way to enjoy liver. The idea came from her mother, who prepared a similar dish when Audrey was a child. It makes a great meal for children of all ages.

1 pound 2 ounces liver (beef, calf, or chicken), finely chopped *(do not puree)*

1 cup *each* finely diced onions and green bell pepper

6 slices reduced-calorie rye, wheat, white, *or* multi-grain bread (40 calories per slice), toasted and made into crumbs

1 egg, lightly beaten

1 teaspoon salt

½ teaspoon pepper, or to taste

2 tablespoons reduced-calorie margarine (tub), divided

In 2-quart bowl combine all ingredients except margarine, mixing thoroughly (mixture will be sticky); cover and refrigerate until chilled (when chilled, mixture will be firmer and easier to handle).

Shape chilled liver mixture into 6 equal patties. In 10-inch skillet heat 1 tablespoon margarine over medium-high heat until bubbly and hot; gently transfer patties to skillet and cook until browned on bottom. Add remaining tablespoon margarine to skillet and heat until bubbly and hot; turn patties over. Reduce heat to medium and cook until patties are browned on other side and cooked throughout *(do not overcook)*.

MAKES 6 SERVINGS, 1 PATTY EACH

Each serving provides: 2½ Protein Exchanges; ½ Bread Exchange; ¾ Vegetable Exchange; ½ Fat Exchange

Per serving with beef liver: 202 calories; 20 g protein; 6 g fat; 17 g carbohydrate; 43 mg calcium; 635 mg sodium; 301 mg cholesterol

With calf liver: 202 calories; 20 g protein; 7 g fat; 16 g carbohydrate; 43 mg calcium; 582 mg sodium; 301 mg cholesterol

With chicken livers: 189 calories; 19 g protein; 6 g fat; 15 g carbohydrate; 46 mg calcium; 587 mg sodium; 419 mg cholesterol

Audrey Marks
Safety Harbor, Florida

On the Side
Side Dishes and Sauces

Easy-to-Prepare Pickles ⊙

Mmm . . . homemade pickles. It's so easy when you follow Florine's recipe. For a decorative look, score the cucumber skin with the tines of a fork before slicing.

2 cups water
1 cup white wine vinegar
Granulated low-calorie
**   sweetener with aspartame**
**   to equal 6 teaspoons sugar**
2 teaspoons *each* onion flakes
**   and celery seed**
1 teaspoon salt
½ teaspoon garlic powder
2 medium cucumbers, cut into
**   ⅛-inch-thick slices**

In 1-quart jar that has a tight-fitting cover combine all ingredients except cucumbers, stirring well to dissolve sweetener and salt. Add cucumber slices to vinegar mixture, cover tightly, and refrigerate for 36 hours.

MAKES 16 SERVINGS

Each serving provides: ¼ Vegetable Exchange
Per serving: 7 calories; 0.4 g protein; trace fat; 1 g carbohydrate; 9 mg
    calcium; 141 mg sodium; 0 mg cholesterol

Florine Powell
Tampa, Florida

Asparagus with Chopped Egg and "Butter" Sauce ◐

Rita's gourmet delight will please your friends and family alike. She likes to make this dish in the spring when fresh asparagus is in season. Rita is a homemaker and mother of three.

16 large asparagus spears
1 quart water
1 small onion (about 2 ounces), cut into quarters
1 teaspoon salt (optional)
2 eggs, hard-cooked and finely minced
2 tablespoons *each* reduced-calorie margarine (tub), melted, and lemon juice
1 tablespoon minced fresh parsley
¼ teaspoon salt
Dash ground nutmeg

Break off woody ends of asparagus; using a vegetable peeler, pare each spear, beginning halfway down spear and scraping toward trimmed end. In 10-inch skillet combine water, asparagus, onion, and salt, if desired; bring to a boil. Reduce heat and let simmer until asparagus is tender, 3 to 5 minutes. Using slotted spoon, transfer asparagus to warmed serving plate, discarding onion and cooking liquid; set aside and keep warm.

In small bowl combine remaining ingredients and spoon over warm asparagus.

MAKES 2 SERVINGS

Each serving provides: 1 Protein Exchange; 1¼ Vegetable Exchanges; 1½ Fat Exchanges
Per serving without salt: 180 calories; 12 g protein; 12 g fat; 10 g carbohydrate; 79 mg calcium; 501 mg sodium; 274 mg cholesterol
If salt is used, increase calcium to 86 mg and sodium to 1,567 mg.

VARIATION:

For a smooth sauce, combine all ingredients for sauce in blender container and process until smooth. Pour sauce over warm asparagus.

Rita Schackmann
Newton, Illinois

Artichoke Casserole

Ruth has enjoyed this casserole since she was a small child in Louisiana. She adapted the recipe when she began the Weight Watchers program. Ruth, who has two grown children, has returned to school to work on her associate's degree.

9-ounce package frozen
    artichoke hearts (quarters),
    cooked (about 2 cups)*
2 slices white bread
2 ounces grated Parmesan
    cheese
2 teaspoons onion flakes
¼ teaspoon garlic powder
2 teaspoons *each* vegetable
    oil and water

Preheat oven to 350°F. Spray 1-quart casserole with nonstick cooking spray; arrange artichokes in casserole and set aside.

In blender container process bread into crumbs; add cheese, onion flakes, and garlic powder and, using an on-off motion, process until well combined. Add crumb mixture to casserole and toss to combine with artichokes. In measuring cup or small bowl combine oil and water, stirring rapidly; immediately drizzle over casserole and bake until golden, 20 to 30 minutes.

MAKES 2 SERVINGS

*2 cups drained canned artichoke hearts may be substituted, but do not cook before placing in casserole.

Each serving provides: 1 Protein Exchange; 1 Bread Exchange; 2 Vegetable Exchanges; 1 Fat Exchange
Per serving: 288 calories; 17 g protein; 14 g fat; 24 g carbohydrate; 438 mg calcium; 710 mg sodium; 23 mg cholesterol

Ruth Harris
Westville, Illinois

Broccoli Casserole

Sandy revised an old family recipe to fit the Food Plan, and the result is a delicious casserole she serves for family, company, and potluck dinners. Sandy, who has three sons, enjoys sewing and ceramics.

4 ounces Cheddar cheese, shredded
1 cup cooked long-grain rice
½ cup *each* drained canned sliced mushrooms, diced onion, and skim milk
1 tablespoon plus 1 teaspoon reduced-calorie margarine
2 packages (10 ounces each) frozen chopped broccoli, thawed (about 4 cups)
1 teaspoon salt

Preheat oven to 350°F. Spray 2-quart casserole with nonstick cooking spray; set aside.

In 3-quart saucepan combine all ingredients except broccoli and salt and cook over medium heat, stirring constantly, until cheese and margarine are melted. Add broccoli and salt and cook, stirring frequently, until broccoli is heated, about 2 minutes. Turn into sprayed casserole and bake until mixture is heated throughout and broccoli is tender, about 30 minutes.

MAKES 4 SERVINGS

Each serving provides: 1 Protein Exchange; ½ Bread Exchange; 2½ Vegetable Exchanges; ½ Fat Exchange; 10 calories Optional Exchange
Per serving: 246 calories; 14 g protein; 12 g fat; 22 g carbohydrate; 336 mg calcium; 894 mg sodium; 30 mg cholesterol

VARIATION:

Substitute Swiss cheese or pasteurized process cheese spread for the Cheddar.

Per serving with Swiss cheese: 238 calories; 15 g protein; 10 g fat; 23 g carbohydrate; 404 mg calcium; 792 mg sodium; 27 mg cholesterol
With cheese spread: 213 calories; 12 g protein; 8 g fat; 25 g carbohydrate; 310 mg calcium; 1,146 mg sodium; 22 mg cholesterol

Sandy McPherson
Indianapolis, Indiana

Stir-Fried Cabbage ○◐

Paulette and her husband like to read cookbooks and experiment with recipes. Try her crunchy cabbage recipe as an accompaniment to your next lunch or dinner.

1 tablespoon plus 1 teaspoon
  reduced-calorie margarine
  (tub)
⅔ cup diagonally sliced celery
2 cups shredded green
  cabbage
½ cup chopped red or green
  bell pepper
⅓ cup chopped onion
1 tablespoon plus 1 teaspoon
  soy sauce*
Dash pepper, or to taste

In 10-inch nonstick skillet heat margarine over high heat until bubbly and hot; add celery and cook, stirring quickly and frequently, for 1 minute. Add cabbage, bell pepper, and onion and continue to stir-fry until vegetables are tender-crisp, 2 to 3 minutes; add soy sauce and pepper, stir well, and cook for 1 minute longer.

MAKES 4 SERVINGS

Each serving provides: 1¾ Vegetable Exchanges; ½ Fat Exchange
Per serving: 40 calories; 1 g protein; 2 g fat; 5 g carbohydrate; 33 mg
  calcium; 508 mg sodium; 0 mg cholesterol

*Reduced-sodium soy sauce may be substituted. Reduce calories to 39, calcium to 28 mg, and sodium to 268 mg.

Paulette J. Howe
Hugo, Minnesota

Carrots à la Française ◐

Elizabeth lives in a rural area not too far from Mount St. Helens. She has been to Europe many times and brought this recipe back from France, where it was served by her son's mother-in-law. Bon appétit!

1 cup shredded carrots
1 garlic clove, minced
1 tablespoon lemon juice
1 teaspoon *each* Dijon-style
   mustard and olive *or*
   vegetable oil
⅛ teaspoon *each* salt
   and pepper

In small bowl combine carrots and garlic. In small jar with tight-fitting cover or small bowl combine remaining ingredients; cover and shake well or stir to mix thoroughly. Pour lemon mixture over carrot-garlic mixture and toss to coat.

MAKES 2 SERVINGS

Each serving provides: 1 Vegetable Exchange; ½ Fat Exchange
Per serving: 51 calories; 1 g protein; 3 g fat; 7 g carbohydrate; 20 mg calcium; 234 mg sodium; 0 mg cholesterol

Elizabeth Berry
Woodland, Washington

Spiced Apple-Carrot Bake ◑◐

Marie likes to try new and different things. For this recipe, she took a few ordinary ingredients, combined them in an unusual way, and created a side dish that adds spice to any meal.

1 tablespoon firmly packed light brown sugar
¼ teaspoon ground ginger
⅛ teaspoon ground nutmeg
2 cups diagonally sliced cooked carrots (tender-crisp)
4 small apples, cored and thinly sliced
1 tablespoon plus 1 teaspoon reduced-calorie margarine (tub)

Preheat oven to 350°F. In small bowl combine sugar, ginger, and nutmeg; set aside.

Spray 1½-quart casserole with nonstick cooking spray; arrange ½ cup carrots in casserole, top with ¼ of the apple slices, and sprinkle with ¼ of the sugar mixture. Repeat layers 3 more times, ending with sugar mixture; dot with margarine and bake until carrots and apples are tender and topping is lightly browned, 15 to 20 minutes.

MAKES 4 SERVINGS

Each serving provides: 1 Vegetable Exchange; ½ Fat Exchange; 1 Fruit Exchange; 15 calories Optional Exchange
Per serving: 127 calories; 1 g protein; 3 g fat; 28 g carbohydrate; 35 mg calcium; 93 mg sodium; 0 mg cholesterol

Marie Twigg
Cumberland, Maryland

Breaded Cauliflower ⊙◑

Nancy enjoyed fried vegetables before joining Weight Watchers and wanted to continue having them while following the Food Plan, so she created this delicious version.

2 cups cooked cauliflower
   florets (tender-crisp),
   cooled
1 egg, beaten
3 tablespoons seasoned dried
   bread crumbs
1 teaspoon grated Parmesan
   cheese
2 teaspoons reduced-calorie
   margarine (tub)
2 garlic cloves, minced

In medium mixing bowl combine cauliflower and egg, mixing well to coat cauliflower with egg. In small bowl combine bread crumbs and cheese; sprinkle over cauliflower and toss to coat.

In 10-inch nonstick skillet heat margarine over medium-high heat until bubbly and hot; add garlic and sauté until softened, about 1 minute. Spread cauliflower in a single layer over bottom of skillet and cook, turning occasionally, until lightly browned on all sides, 4 to 6 minutes.

MAKES 2 SERVINGS

Each serving provides: ½ Protein Exchange; ½ Bread Exchange; 2 Vegetable Exchanges; ½ Fat Exchange; 5 calories Optional Exchange
Per serving: 134 calories; 7 g protein; 6 g fat; 15 g carbohydrate; 74 mg calcium; 396 mg sodium; 138 mg cholesterol

Nancy Sanders
Youngstown, Ohio

Cauliflower au Gratin ©

Searching for a new dish to prepare for her in-laws, Bonnie adapted this recipe to fit the Food Plan and it proved to be a hit. In her spare time, Bonnie enjoys knitting, sewing, fishing, and swimming.

2 tablespoons plus 2 teaspoons reduced-calorie margarine (tub)
2 tablespoons all-purpose flour
2 cups skim milk
½ teaspoon salt
Dash *each* white pepper and ground nutmeg
2 cups cauliflower florets, blanched
4 ounces Cheddar cheese, shredded

In 1-quart saucepan heat margarine over medium heat until bubbly and hot; add flour and stir quickly to combine. Stirring constantly, gradually add milk; stir in salt, pepper, and nutmeg. Reduce heat to low and cook, stirring frequently, until sauce is smooth and thickened, 10 to 15 minutes.

Preheat oven to 350°F. In 2-quart casserole arrange cauliflower florets; top with sauce and sprinkle with cheese. Bake until cheese is melted and lightly browned, 15 to 20 minutes.

MAKES 4 SERVINGS

Each serving provides: 1 Protein Exchange; 1 Vegetable Exchange; 1 Fat Exchange; ½ Milk Exchange; 15 calories Optional Exchange
Per serving: 222 calories; 13 g protein; 14 g fat; 13 g carbohydrate; 373 mg calcium; 605 mg sodium; 32 mg cholesterol

VARIATION:

Substitute Swiss cheese or Muenster cheese for the Cheddar.

Per serving with Swiss cheese; 214 calories; 14 g protein; 12 g fat; 13 g carbohydrate; 441 mg calcium; 503 mg sodium; 29 mg cholesterol
With Muenster cheese: 212 calories; 13 g protein; 13 g fat; 13 g carbohydrate; 372 mg calcium; 608 mg sodium; 30 mg cholesterol

Bonnie Kermicle
Dundas, Illinois

Most Delicious Cauliflower

Our chef tells us this comes from an old Italian recipe that has been handed down in her family from her grandfather.

½ cup part-skim ricotta cheese
1 cup cauliflower florets
½ teaspoon salt
1 teaspoon *each* olive oil and margarine
¼ cup diced onion
1 small garlic clove, minced
1 cup cooked elbow macaroni
1 tablespoon chopped fresh parsley, divided
Dash freshly ground pepper
1 tablespoon plus 1 teaspoon plain dried bread crumbs, lightly toasted
2 teaspoons grated Parmesan cheese
½ ounce toasted almonds, finely ground
Italian (flat-leaf) parsley sprig

In order to eliminate chill, remove ricotta cheese from refrigerator and let stand 30 minutes before using.

In 1-quart saucepan add cauliflower and salt to 1½ cups boiling water; return to a boil and cook until tender, about 10 minutes. Drain cauliflower, reserving ¾ cup cooking liquid.

In 9-inch skillet combine oil and margarine and heat over medium heat until margarine is bubbly and hot; add onion and garlic and sauté for 1 minute *(do not brown)*. Add ¾ cup drained cauliflower and, using a fork or potato masher, mash cauliflower; add macaroni, reserved cooking liquid, and 2 teaspoons chopped parsley and stir to combine.

To serve, spoon macaroni mixture into serving bowl; top with ricotta cheese and sprinkle with remaining teaspoon chopped parsley, the pepper, bread crumbs, Parmesan cheese, and ground almonds. Arrange remaining ¼ cup cauliflower over ricotta mixture and garnish with parsley sprig.

MAKES 2 SERVINGS

Each serving provides: 1 Protein Exchange; 1 Bread Exchange; 1¼ Vegetable Exchanges; 1 Fat Exchange; 75 calories Optional Exchange
Per serving: 291 calories; 14 g protein; 14 g fat; 29 g carbohydrate; 250 mg calcium; 723 mg sodium; 21 mg cholesterol

Weight Watchers Kitchens

Green Beans Amandine

Add a touch of Spain to your meal with this colorful side dish.

1 medium red bell pepper
2 tablespoons margarine
1 ounce sliced almonds
2 garlic cloves, minced
1 teaspoon minced fresh
    parsley
¼ teaspoon salt
Dash freshly ground pepper
3 cups trimmed and halved
    green beans, cooked until
    tender

Preheat broiler. On baking sheet broil pepper 3 to 4 inches from heat source, turning frequently, until charred on all sides; transfer pepper to brown paper bag and let stand until cool enough to handle.

Fit strainer into small bowl and peel pepper over strainer; remove and discard stem end and seeds, allowing juice from pepper to drip through strainer into bowl. Cut pepper into thin strips and set aside pepper and juice.

In 10- or 12-inch nonstick skillet heat margarine over medium heat until bubbly and hot; add almonds, garlic, parsley, salt, and ground pepper and sauté until almonds are golden, 2 to 3 minutes. Add pepper strips, juice from pepper, and green beans and cook, stirring occasionally, until vegetables are heated through, 2 to 3 minutes.

MAKES 4 SERVINGS

Each serving provides: 2 Vegetable Exchanges; 1½ Fat Exchanges; 45 calories Optional Exchange
Per serving: 125 calories; 3 g protein; 10 g fat; 9 g carbohydrate; 57 mg calcium; 209 mg sodium; 0 mg cholesterol

Weight Watchers Kitchens

❖•

Green Beans Provençale ◖

A friend gave Gail the idea for this recipe; the extra spices are her own innovative touch. Gail runs a junior dress company and, in her spare time, enjoys styling for photographic and video shoots.

2 teaspoons vegetable oil
½ cup sliced onion
2 garlic cloves, minced
2 cups canned whole tomatoes (with liquid); drain, seed, and chop tomatoes, reserving liquid
2 tablespoons chopped fresh parsley
1 teaspoon *each* basil leaves, salt, and granulated sugar
½ teaspoon oregano leaves
⅛ teaspoon pepper
4 cups trimmed and halved green beans
½ cup sliced mushrooms

In 4-quart saucepan heat oil over medium heat; add onion and garlic and sauté until onion is softened, about 1 minute. Add remaining ingredients except green beans and mushrooms and stir to combine; bring to a boil. Reduce heat to low, add green beans, and cook, stirring frequently, until beans are tender-crisp, 5 to 10 minutes; add mushrooms and continue cooking until mushrooms are cooked through, 3 to 5 minutes longer.

MAKES 4 SERVINGS

Each serving provides: 3½ Vegetable Exchanges; ½ Fat Exchange; 5 calories Optional Exchange
Per serving: 96 calories; 4 g protein; 3 g fat; 17 g carbohydrate; 98 mg calcium; 754 mg sodium; 0 mg cholesterol

Gail S. Grossman
New York, New York

Eggplant Parmigiana Ⓒ

With a background in home economics, Mary's a natural in the kitchen. She improvises so that her dishes, such as this Italian classic, fit the Food Plan. Mary, a busy mother and grandmother, is a Senior Service Director for her county.

2 teaspoons vegetable oil, divided
½ cup *each* chopped onion and green bell pepper
1½ cups canned Italian tomatoes (with liquid); drain, seed, and puree tomatoes, reserving liquid
½ teaspoon oregano leaves
¼ teaspoon *each* garlic powder and salt
Dash pepper
1 tiny eggplant (about 8 ounces), pared and cut crosswise into 8 rounds (about ½ inch thick each)
2 ounces *each* grated Parmesan and shredded mozzarella cheese

In 1-quart saucepan heat 1 teaspoon oil over medium heat; add onion and bell pepper and sauté 1 to 2 minutes. Add tomatoes, reserved liquid, and seasonings and mix well. Reduce heat to low and let simmer, stirring occasionally, until mixture is thickened, 20 to 25 minutes; set aside.

Preheat oven to 400°F. Using ½ teaspoon oil, brush 1 side of each eggplant slice with an equal amount of oil; on nonstick baking sheet arrange slices oiled-side up and bake until browned, about 10 minutes. Turn slices over and brush each with ⅛ of the remaining oil; bake 10 minutes longer. On sheet of wax paper dredge slices in Parmesan, evenly coating both sides and reserving any remaining cheese.

In shallow 2-quart casserole spread ⅓ of the reserved tomato mixture; top with 4 eggplant slices, in a single layer. Repeat layers, ending with sauce. Sprinkle with any remaining Parmesan and top with mozzarella; bake at 400°F. until cheese is lightly browned, 15 to 20 minutes.

MAKES 4 SERVINGS

Each serving provides: 1 Protein Exchange; 2 Vegetable Exchanges; ½ Fat Exchange
Per serving: 168 calories; 10 g protein; 10 g fat; 11 g carbohydrate; 322 mg calcium; 602 mg sodium; 22 mg cholesterol

Mary Whitmer
Hettinger, North Dakota

Jerusalem Artichoke Sauté ◖

Carolyn loves to try new foods, such as Jerusalem artichokes. Also known as sun chokes, they add wonderful crunch and texture to any dish. Carolyn is a cook at a grade school. She is married and has three children and one grandson.

1 cup sliced Jerusalem artichokes (⅛-inch-thick slices)
1 tablespoon plus 1½ teaspoons distilled white vinegar, combined with 2 cups water
1 tablespoon plus 1 teaspoon reduced-calorie margarine (tub)
2 ounces boiled ham, diced
¼ cup chopped onion
½ cup sliced mushrooms
Dash paprika

In medium mixing bowl combine artichokes with vinegar-water mixture; set aside.

In 10-inch nonstick skillet heat margarine over medium heat until bubbly and hot; add ham and onion and cook until onion is softened, 1 to 2 minutes. Drain artichokes, discarding liquid, and rinse under running cold water; using paper towels, pat dry. Add artichokes and mushrooms to skillet and cook, stirring occasionally, until artichokes are tender-crisp, 3 to 4 minutes. Transfer to serving dish and sprinkle with paprika.

MAKES 2 SERVINGS

Each serving provides: 1 Protein Exchange; 1¾ Vegetable Exchanges; 1 Fat Exchange
Per serving: 144 calories; 8 g protein; 6 g fat; 16 g carbohydrate; 19 mg calcium; 422 mg sodium; 15 mg cholesterol

Carolyn Spellman
Columbus, Indiana

Scalloped Jicama

Genie is originally from Florida, but now lives in Texas with her husband and three daughters. She likes to cook and experiment with new and different foods such as jicama. If you like potatoes, you'll love jicama.

4 cups pared and thinly sliced jicama
2 tablespoons plus 2 teaspoons reduced-calorie margarine (tub)
2 tablespoons all-purpose flour
1 cup skim milk
½ cup *each* evaporated skimmed milk and diced onion
1 teaspoon salt
⅛ teaspoon white pepper
4 ounces Cheddar cheese, shredded, divided

In 5-quart saucepot or Dutch oven bring 3 quarts water to a boil; add jicama and cook over high heat until tender-crisp, 15 to 20 minutes.

While jicama is cooking, in 1-quart saucepan heat margarine over medium heat until bubbly and hot; add flour and stir quickly to combine. Stirring constantly, gradually add skim milk, continuing to stir until mixture is smooth; stir in evaporated milk, onion, and seasonings. Reduce heat to low and let simmer, stirring occasionally, until mixture is thickened, 10 to 15 minutes. Add 3 ounces cheese to saucepan and cook, stirring constantly, until cheese is melted, 1 to 2 minutes. Remove saucepan from heat and set aside.

Preheat oven to 375°F. Spray 2-quart casserole with nonstick cooking spray. Drain jicama and arrange ¼ of slices in casserole; top with ¼ of the cheese sauce. Repeat layers 3 more times, ending with sauce; sprinkle with remaining 1 ounce cheese and bake until cheese is lightly browned, 25 to 30 minutes.

MAKES 4 SERVINGS

Each serving provides: 1 Protein Exchange; 2¼ Vegetable Exchanges; 1 Fat Exchange; ½ Milk Exchange; 15 calories Optional Exchange
Per serving: 264 calories; 14 g protein; 14 g fat; 22 g carbohydrate; 400 mg calcium; 882 mg sodium; 32 mg cholesterol

Genie McCook
Texarkana, Texas

Kohlrabi au Gratin ©

Nan is a good friend of one of our other winners, Eileen Claeys. A homemaker and mother of two, Nan enjoys cooking, crafts, poetry, and genealogy.

2 cups cooked sliced pared
    kohlrabi (tender-crisp)
1 tablespoon lemon juice
2 tablespoons plus 2 tea-
    spoons reduced-calorie
    margarine (tub), divided
2 tablespoons all-purpose
    flour
1 cup skim milk
½ cup evaporated skimmed
    milk
2 tablespoons onion flakes
½ teaspoon salt
Dash white pepper, or to taste
4 ounces American cheese,
    shredded
2 slices white bread, made
    into crumbs

In medium bowl combine kohlrabi and lemon juice.

In 1-quart saucepan heat 2 tablespoons margarine over medium heat until bubbly and hot; add flour and stir quickly. Stirring constantly, gradually add skim milk, continuing to stir until mixture is smooth; stir in evaporated milk and seasonings. Reduce heat to low and let simmer, stirring occasionally, until sauce is thickened, 10 to 15 minutes; stir in cheese and cook until cheese is melted, 1 to 2 minutes longer. Add to kohlrabi and toss to coat thoroughly; set aside.

Preheat oven to 350°F. In small flame-proof container melt remaining margarine; in small bowl combine crumbs with melted margarine, mixing well. Spray 2-quart casserole with nonstick cooking spray; add kohlrabi mixture. Sprinkle evenly with crumbs and bake until topping is lightly browned, 25 to 35 minutes.

MAKES 4 SERVINGS

Each serving provides: 1 Protein Exchange; ½ Bread Exchange; 1 Vegetable Exchange; 1 Fat Exchange; ½ Milk Exchange; 15 calories Optional Exchange
Per serving: 258 calories; 14 g protein; 14 g fat; 22 g carbohydrate; 377 mg calcium; 904 mg sodium; 29 mg cholesterol

Nan G. Christensen
Park View, Iowa

Mushroom Curry ◑

This Western adaptation of a specialty from Sri Lanka is excellent with poultry. Coconut, grapes, and raisins are wonderful garnishes for this interesting dish. Marilyn and her family love its spicy but not "super-hot" flavor.

2 teaspoons margarine
⅓ cup sliced onion
1 teaspoon minced pared
   ginger root
¼ teaspoon *each* crushed
   basil leaves, dillseed,
   crushed marjoram leaves,
   crushed thyme leaves, and
   minced fresh parsley
⅛ teaspoon ground turmeric
1½ cups small whole mush-
   rooms (stems trimmed)
⅔ cup small cauliflower
   florets
1 medium tomato, seeded
   and diced
1 teaspoon lemon juice
½ bay leaf
½ teaspoon curry powder
1 cup cooked long-grain rice
   (hot)
Italian (flat-leaf) parsley
   (whole leaves and shredded)

In 8- or 9-inch nonstick skillet heat margarine over medium heat until bubbly and hot; add onion and ginger and sauté until onion is softened, about 1 minute. Stir in basil, dillseed, marjoram, thyme, minced parsley, and turmeric, mixing well; add mushrooms, cauliflower, tomato, lemon juice, bay leaf, and curry powder and stir to combine. Reduce heat to low, cover, and let simmer, stirring frequently, until vegetables are tender, 8 to 10 minutes.

To serve, arrange rice in serving bowl; remove and discard bay leaf from curry mixture and spoon curry over rice. Garnish with Italian parsley.

MAKES 2 SERVINGS

Each serving provides: 1 Bread Exchange; 3½ Vegetable Exchanges; 1 Fat Exchange
Per serving: 197 calories; 5 g protein; 5 g fat; 35 g carbohydrate; 53 mg calcium; 62 mg sodium; 0 mg cholesterol

Marilyn I. N. Beyer
Lincoln, Nebraska

Mushroom "Stroganoff" ◑

Rita culled ingredients from several recipes and came up with an exciting way to serve this versatile vegetable. Several of Rita's recipes have appeared in the Wednesday food column of a Hartford newspaper.

1⅓ cups cottage cheese
½ cup plain low-fat yogurt
½ teaspoon salt
¼ teaspoon *each* pepper and
    Worcestershire sauce
1 tablespoon plus 1 teaspoon
    margarine
¼ cup diced onion
2 garlic cloves, minced
2 cups halved mushrooms
1 tablespoon chopped fresh
    parsley *or* 1 teaspoon
    parsley flakes
2 cups cooked egg noodles
    (medium width), hot

In blender container combine cheese, yogurt, salt, pepper, and Worcestershire, processing just until smooth; set aside.

In 10-inch nonstick skillet heat margarine until bubbly and hot; add onion and garlic and sauté until onion is translucent. Add mushrooms and parsley and cook, stirring occasionally, for 5 minutes; remove skillet from heat and stir in cheese mixture. Return to heat and cook just until mixture is heated through, about 1 minute *(do not boil)*. Serve over hot noodles.

MAKES 4 SERVINGS

Each serving provides: 1 Protein Exchange; 1 Bread Exchange; 1⅛ Vegetable
    Exchanges; 1 Fat Exchange; ¼ Milk Exchange
Per serving: 239 calories; 14 g protein; 9 g fat; 26 g carbohydrate; 114 mg
    calcium; 628 mg sodium; 37 mg cholesterol

Rita Starr Conlin
Hartford, Connecticut

Stuffed Spanish Onions

Kathy loves the Weight Watchers program and has lost 26 pounds following it. This favorite of hers is especially good with a roast, meat loaf, or steak.

3 medium sweet Spanish onions (3- to 4-inch diameter each)
2 quarts water
10-ounce package frozen chopped broccoli, cooked according to package directions (about 2 cups)
3 ounces grated Parmesan cheese
¼ cup reduced-calorie mayonnaise
2 tablespoons *each* lemon juice, reduced-calorie margarine (tub), and all-purpose flour
Dash salt
1½ cups skim milk
3 ounces Monterey Jack cheese, shredded
¼ teaspoon paprika

Peel onions and cut each through stem ends into halves (do not remove stem ends; they help to hold onion halves together). In 4-quart saucepan bring water to a boil; add onions. Reduce heat and let simmer until onions are tender, 10 to 12 minutes. Drain well. Scoop pulp from each onion half, leaving about ½-inch-thick shell; reserve shells. Chop enough pulp to measure 1 cup; transfer chopped pulp to medium mixing bowl and add broccoli, Parmesan, mayonnaise, and lemon juice. Mix well and set aside.

In 10-inch skillet heat margarine until bubbly and hot; add flour and salt and stir quickly. Stirring, gradually add milk; bring just to a boil. Reduce heat and let simmer, stirring frequently, until smooth and thickened; add Monterey Jack and cook, stirring constantly, until melted.

Preheat oven to 375°F. Fill shells with onion mixture and set in 8 x 8 x 2-inch baking dish. Top with sauce; sprinkle with paprika. Bake until sauce is bubbly, about 15 minutes.

MAKES 6 SERVINGS, ½ ONION EACH

Each serving provides: 1 Protein Exchange; 2 Vegetable Exchanges; 1½ Fat Exchanges; ¼ Milk Exchange; 10 calories Optional Exchange
Per serving: 242 calories; 14 g protein; 14 g fat; 17 g carbohydrate; 431 mg calcium; 523 mg sodium; 28 mg cholesterol

Kathy Dionne
Coeur d'Alene, Idaho

Caraway Sauerkraut ⊝ ◑

Both Joanne, in New York, and her aunt Marylou, in Florida, are Weight Watchers leaders who swap recipes and tips with each other. Joanne is an executive secretary who enjoys aerobics and traveling. This German side dish is a snap to prepare and goes especially well with pork.

2 teaspoons margarine
1 tablespoon all-purpose flour
1 cup sauerkraut (with juice)*
1 teaspoon caraway seed

In small saucepan heat margarine over medium heat until bubbly and hot; add flour and cook, stirring constantly, for 1 minute. Add sauerkraut and caraway seed; mix well. Reduce heat to low, cover pan, and let simmer, stirring occasionally, until mixture is thickened and heated through, 4 to 6 minutes.

MAKES 2 SERVINGS

*Use the sauerkraut that is packaged in plastic bags and stored in the refrigerator section of the supermarket; it is usually crisper and less salty than the canned.

Each serving provides: 1 Vegetable Exchange; 1 Fat Exchange; 25 calories Optional Exchange
Per serving: 74 calories; 2 g protein; 4 g fat; 9 g carbohydrate; 45 mg calcium; 825 mg sodium; 0 mg cholesterol

Joanne Landry
Staten Island, New York

Breaded Spinach ☻◑

Here's a unique way to serve an old standby. Gizella's mother-in-law serves spinach with bread crumbs and that idea blossomed into this delicious side dish, turning ordinary spinach into something really special.

1 tablespoon plus 1 teaspoon
  reduced-calorie margarine
  (tub)
3 tablespoons plain dried
  bread crumbs
¼ teaspoon *each* garlic
  powder and salt
2 teaspoons grated Parmesan
  cheese
Dash pepper
1 pound spinach leaves,
  trimmed, washed well, and
  drained

In 10-inch nonstick skillet heat margarine over medium heat until bubbly and hot; add bread crumbs, garlic powder, and salt and cook, stirring frequently, until crumbs are lightly browned, 1 to 2 minutes. Transfer to small bowl, add cheese and pepper, and mix well; set aside and keep warm.

Spray same skillet with nonstick cooking spray and heat over medium heat; add spinach and cook, stirring frequently, until spinach is wilted and thoroughly cooked, 1 to 2 minutes. Transfer to serving platter and top with crumb mixture.

MAKES 2 SERVINGS, ABOUT 1 CUP EACH

Each serving provides: ½ Bread Exchange; 2 Vegetable Exchanges; 1 Fat
  Exchange; 10 calories Optional Exchange
Per serving: 120 calories; 7 g protein; 5 g fat; 14 g carbohydrate; 282 mg
  calcium; 576 mg sodium; 2 mg cholesterol

Gizella Troha
Euclid, Ohio

Baked Squash

Paul is an accountant who lost nearly 50 pounds on the Program, and now feels younger and healthier than ever. He invented this recipe one Thanksgiving when his wife was away and he had to cook for himself and his son.

1 tablespoon plus 1 teaspoon
   reduced-calorie margarine
   (tub)
1 small apple, cored and diced
¼ cup dry white table wine
2 tablespoons dark raisins
1 butternut squash (about
   2 pounds)*
1 tablespoon plus 1 teaspoon
   firmly packed dark brown
   sugar
Celery leaves

Preheat oven to 350°F. In 9-inch skillet heat margarine over medium heat until bubbly and hot; add apple and sauté until lightly browned, 1 to 2 minutes. Add wine and raisins and cook until liquid has evaporated, 2 to 3 minutes. Remove from heat and set aside.

Cut squash lengthwise into quarters, discarding seeds and membranes. In 10 x 10 x 2-inch baking dish arrange squash quarters, cut-side up. Spoon ¼ of apple mixture into seed cavity of each quarter; sprinkle each quarter with 1 teaspoon sugar. Fill baking dish with water to a depth of about ½ inch; cover and bake until squash is fork-tender, 40 to 45 minutes. Arrange squash on serving platter and garnish with celery leaves.

MAKES 4 SERVINGS, 1 STUFFED SQUASH QUARTER EACH

*A 2-pound butternut squash will yield about 1 pound (2 cups) cooked pulp.

Each serving provides: 1 Bread Exchange; ½ Fat Exchange; ½ Fruit Exchange; 35 calories Optional Exchange
Per serving: 121 calories; 1 g protein; 2 g fat; 25 g carbohydrate; 56 mg calcium; 47 mg sodium; 0 mg cholesterol

Paul A. Banquer
Akron, Ohio

Honey-Cinnamon Winter Squash ◓ ◑

Francis developed this recipe as an alternative to pumpkin pie, and he thinks it's better tasting, too. A high school science teacher, Francis is also a Weight Watchers leader who lost over 60 pounds.

**1 butternut squash (about
   2 pounds)***
2 tablespoons *each* **margarine
   and honey**
⅛ teaspoon *each* **ground
   cinnamon and salt**
**Dash ground nutmeg,
   or to taste**
½ cup water

Cut squash in half lengthwise and discard seeds and membranes; score cut surface of each squash half in a crisscross pattern, being careful not to cut through shell.

In 10 x 10 x 2-inch microwave-safe baking dish arrange halves, cut-side up; fill seed cavity of each half with 1 tablespoon margarine and 1 tablespoon honey. Sprinkle halves evenly with cinnamon, salt, and nutmeg and pour water into baking dish; microwave on High for 1 minute.† Baste halves with honey mixture and microwave on High until pulp is soft, 10 to 15 minutes longer,† basting every 5 minutes.

To serve, cut each half lengthwise into halves and top each portion with an equal amount of any remaining pan juices.

MAKES 4 SERVINGS, 1 SQUASH QUARTER EACH

*A 2-pound butternut squash will yield about 1 pound
   (2 cups) cooked pulp.
†Cooking time may be different in your microwave
   oven. To help ensure good results, check the instructions accompanying your unit regarding length of
   time to cook butternut squash.

Each serving provides: 1 Bread Exchange; 1½ Fat Exchanges; 30 calories
   Optional Exchange
Per serving: 129 calories; 1 g protein; 6 g fat; 21 g carbohydrate; 51 mg
   calcium; 141 mg sodium; 0 mg cholesterol

*Francis John Marone
Bridgeton, New Jersey*

Tropical Spaghetti Squash ◑

Dorothy is a Weight Watchers leader who enjoys experimenting in the kitchen. Her squash dish makes a great "take-along" for brown-bag lunches.

1 cup cooked spaghetti
    squash (hot)
½ cup drained canned
    crushed pineapple
    (no sugar added)
¼ cup *each* finely chopped
    red and green bell peppers
2 teaspoons reduced-calorie
    margarine (tub), melted
¼ teaspoon salt
Dash ground nutmeg

In medium bowl combine all ingredients, mixing well. Serve immediately or cover and refrigerate until chilled.

MAKES 2 SERVINGS

Each serving provides: 1½ Vegetable Exchanges; ½ Fat Exchange; ½ Fruit
    Exchange
Per serving: 83 calories; 1 g protein; 2 g fat; 16 g carbohydrate; 29 mg
    calcium; 326 mg sodium; 0 mg cholesterol

Dorothy L. Young
Shawnee, Kansas

Squash, Tomato, and Onion Casserole ☻

Marilyn's elegant, easy-to-fix casserole is as delicious as it is colorful. Try it for a company dinner. Your guests will think you spent hours preparing it. We won't tell if you won't.

2 medium zucchini (about
    5 ounces each), cut into
    ¼-inch-thick slices
1 medium yellow straightneck
    or crookneck squash
    (about 5 ounces), cut into
    ¼-inch-thick slices
1 medium tomato, cut into
    8 slices
1 medium onion (about 4
    ounces), sliced and
    separated into rings
2 tablespoons plus 2
    teaspoons reduced-calorie
    margarine (tub)
1 tablespoon *each* grated
    Parmesan cheese and
    chopped fresh parsley
½ teaspoon *each* basil leaves
    and grated lemon peel
¼ teaspoon *each* salt
    and pepper

Preheat oven to 350°F. In bottom of shallow 1½-quart casserole arrange zucchini and yellow squash in a single layer, overlapping slices slightly; top with tomato slices, then onion rings. Dot vegetables evenly with margarine and sprinkle evenly with remaining ingredients; bake until vegetables are tender, 25 to 30 minutes.

MAKES 4 SERVINGS

Each serving provides: 2½ Vegetable Exchanges; 1 Fat Exchange; 10 calories Optional Exchange
Per serving: 72 calories; 2 g protein; 5 g fat; 7 g carbohydrate; 51 mg calcium; 245 mg sodium; 1 mg cholesterol

Marilyn K. Yarmon
Augusta, Georgia

Swiss Chard with Pine Nuts and Raisins

This unusual Mediterranean-style side dish uses Swiss chard, a vegetable similar in texture to spinach.

6 cups Swiss chard
2 quarts water
2 teaspoons olive oil
1 ounce pignolias (pine nuts)
¼ cup *each* dark raisins and finely chopped onion
2 garlic cloves, minced
1 tablespoon *each* dry sherry and lemon juice
¼ teaspoon salt
Dash pepper

Using sharp knife, remove leaves from stems of Swiss chard; carefully pare stems, discarding tough outer skin. In 4-quart saucepan bring water to a boil; add pared stems and cook until slightly tender, 3 to 4 minutes. Add leaves and cook until stems are tender and leaves are wilted, 3 to 4 minutes. Drain and cut stems and leaves into thin strips; pat dry with paper towels and set aside.

In 10- or 12-inch nonstick skillet heat oil over medium heat; add pignolias, raisins, onion, and garlic and sauté, stirring often, until onion is tender and pignolias are golden, 2 to 3 minutes. Add sherry, lemon juice, salt, pepper, and Swiss chard and sauté until mixture is heated through and flavors are blended, 3 to 4 minutes longer.

MAKES 4 SERVINGS

Each serving provides: 3⅛ Vegetable Exchanges; ½ Fat Exchange; ½ Fruit Exchange; 45 calories Optional Exchange
Per serving: 106 calories; 3 g protein; 6 g fat; 12 g carbohydrate; 41 mg calcium; 253 mg sodium; 0 mg cholesterol

Weight Watchers Kitchens

Bacon-Cream Tomatoes ◑

Tomatoes aren't just for salads. Here, a simple tomato becomes an elegant side dish when topped with sour cream and bacon.

2 medium tomatoes
1 teaspoon vegetable oil, divided
1 tablespoon plus 1½ teaspoons sour cream
1 slice crisp bacon, crumbled
4 small parsley leaves

Using top of a paring knife or a tomato corer, remove core of each tomato; cut tomatoes horizontally into halves.

In 8- or 10-inch skillet heat ½ teaspoon oil; set tomato halves in skillet, cut-side down, and cook until lightly browned, 1 to 2 minutes.

While tomatoes are cooking, in small bowl combine sour cream and bacon. Carefully turn tomatoes over and spoon an equal amount of sour cream mixture onto each tomato half. Add remaining ½ teaspoon oil to pan; cover and cook until thoroughly heated, 2 to 3 minutes longer. Remove tomato halves to serving platter and garnish each with a parsley leaf.

MAKES 2 SERVINGS

Each serving provides: 2 Vegetable Exchanges; ½ Fat Exchange; 50 calories Optional Exchange
Per serving: 85 calories; 2 g protein; 6 g fat; 6 g carbohydrate; 22 mg calcium; 66 mg sodium; 7 mg cholesterol

Weight Watchers Kitchens

Italian Vegetables ◐

Daryl is a Weight Watchers leader and an active member of several local clubs. She also enjoys macramé and crocheting. Her vegetable recipe is delicious, whether cooked indoors or outdoors on a grill.

2 tablespoons plus 2 teaspoons reduced-calorie margarine (tub)

2 medium zucchini (about 5 ounces each), cut into ¼-inch-thick slices

1 small eggplant (about 12 ounces), cut into ½-inch cubes

1 medium green bell pepper, seeded and cut into thin strips

½ cup thinly sliced onion

12 cherry tomatoes, cut into halves

8 pimiento-stuffed green olives, cut into halves

1 teaspoon salt

½ teaspoon oregano leaves

⅛ teaspoon *each* garlic powder and pepper, or to taste

In 12-inch nonstick skillet heat margarine over high heat until bubbly and hot; add zucchini, eggplant, bell pepper, and onion and sauté until vegetables are softened, 2 to 3 minutes. Add tomatoes and remaining ingredients and stir to combine thoroughly. Reduce heat to medium-low, cover skillet, and cook, stirring occasionally, until vegetables are tender-crisp, 4 to 6 minutes.

MAKES 4 SERVINGS

Each serving provides: 3¼ Vegetable Exchanges; 1 Fat Exchange; 10 calories Optional Exchange

Per serving: 93 calories; 3 g protein; 5 g fat; 11 g carbohydrate; 61 mg calcium; 826 mg sodium; 0 mg cholesterol

VARIATION:

Here's how to prepare this delicious vegetable side dish outdoors. Divide all ingredients equally onto four 15-inch-long pieces heavy-duty foil; fold foil tightly to enclose, making 4 packets. Barbecue over hot coals for 8 to 10 minutes, turning packets occasionally.

Daryl J. Byford
Knoxville, Tennessee

Savory Vegetable Mélange ◑

Both Ellen, in Maine, and one of her three daughters, in Florida, have lost weight on the Weight Watchers program. Ellen works with retarded children, and likes to paint, golf, fish, and hunt. Her recipe is a filling side dish that goes well with any meal.

4 cups trimmed and halved green beans
½ cup *each* **chopped onion and water**
1 packet instant chicken broth and seasoning mix
½ teaspoon salt
¼ teaspoon tarragon leaves, crushed
Dash pepper, or to taste
2 cups sliced mushrooms
2 medium tomatoes, seeded and cut into 8 wedges each

In 4-quart saucepan combine green beans, onion, water, broth mix, and seasonings; cover and cook over medium-high heat until beans are just tender, 4 to 6 minutes. Add mushrooms and tomatoes, cover, and cook until vegetables are tender-crisp, 3 to 4 minutes longer.

MAKES 4 SERVINGS

Each serving provides: 4¼ Vegetable Exchanges; 3 calories Optional Exchange
Per serving: 64 calories; 4 g protein; 0.5 g fat; 14 g carbohydrate; 55 mg calcium; 495 mg sodium; 0 mg cholesterol

Ellen Dow
Gouldsboro, Maine

Sweet-and-Sour Veggies ◖

Bored with the same old vegetables? So was Renee, until she came up with this tasty way to enjoy them! Renee, who is an identical triplet, does silk flower arrangements for weddings and other occasions.

1 cup *each* sliced onions and sliced mushrooms
1 medium green bell pepper, seeded and cut into thin strips
½ cup *each* sliced carrot, chopped celery, and tomato sauce
1 tablespoon soy sauce*
½ cup canned crushed pineapple (no sugar added)

Spray 10-inch skillet with nonstick cooking spray; add onions, mushrooms, bell pepper, carrot, and celery and cook over medium heat, stirring occasionally, until vegetables are tender-crisp, about 5 minutes. Reduce heat to low, stir in tomato sauce and soy sauce, and let simmer for 3 minutes; add pineapple and stir to combine; cook until heated through, about 1 minute longer.

MAKES 4 SERVINGS

Each serving provides: 2½ Vegetable Exchanges; 15 calories Optional Exchange
Per serving: 62 calories; 2 g protein; 0.4 g fat; 14 g carbohydrate; 33 mg calcium; 537 mg sodium; 0 mg cholesterol

*Reduced-sodium soy sauce may be substituted. Reduce calories to 61, calcium to 30 mg, and sodium to 357 mg.

Renee Van Krevelen
Robbinsdale, Minnesota

Basque Potatoes ℃

Mary's filling potato side dish is easy on the budget. Currently a Weight Watchers member, Mary is active in the PTA, church choir, and her neighborhood watch. She is married and has two children.

2 teaspoons margarine
½ cup *each* chopped celery, chopped onion, and grated carrot
2 garlic cloves, minced
12 ounces diced pared potatoes
1 packet instant beef broth and seasoning mix, dissolved in 1 cup boiling water
1 tablespoon minced fresh parsley
½ teaspoon salt
Dash pepper

In 10-inch nonstick skillet heat margarine over medium-high heat until bubbly and hot; add celery, onion, carrot, and garlic and sauté, stirring occasionally, until vegetables are softened, 1 to 2 minutes. Add remaining ingredients, mixing well. Reduce heat to low, cover, and let simmer until potatoes are fork-tender, 15 to 20 minutes.

MAKES 4 SERVINGS

Each serving provides: 1 Bread Exchange; ¾ Vegetable Exchange; ½ Fat Exchange; 3 calories Optional Exchange
Per serving: 104 calories; 3 g protein; 2 g fat; 20 g carbohydrate; 27 mg calcium; 506 mg sodium; 0 mg cholesterol

Mary T. Duncan
Susanville, California

❖❖❖❖❖❖❖❖❖❖❖❖❖❖❖❖❖❖❖❖❖❖❖❖❖❖❖❖❖❖❖❖❖❖❖❖❖❖❖

Crisped Baked Potatoes ☺

This is a terrific way to use up leftover boiled potatoes, according to Marilyn. She's an enthusiastic member of Weight Watchers and thinks her leader is just "the greatest." Marilyn's hobbies? Her five beautiful grandchildren.

6 ounces cooked whole new potatoes, chilled
1 tablespoon plus 1 teaspoon reduced-calorie margarine (tub)
1 tablespoon soy sauce*
¼ teaspoon salt-free low-pepper no-garlic herb seasoning
Dash pepper

Preheat oven to 400°F. Cut each potato into 4 wedges and transfer to small bowl; set aside.

In small saucepan or metal measuring cup melt margarine; add soy sauce and stir to combine. Pour margarine mixture over potatoes and toss to coat thoroughly. Transfer potatoes to nonstick baking sheet, brushing with any remaining margarine mixture. Sprinkle with seasonings and bake until crisp, about 1 hour.

MAKES 2 SERVINGS

Each serving provides: 1 Bread Exchange; 1 Fat Exchange
Per serving: 114 calories; 2 g protein; 4 g fat; 18 g carbohydrate; 14 mg calcium; 749 mg sodium; 0 mg cholesterol

*Reduced-sodium soy sauce may be substituted. Reduce calories to 113, calcium to 7 mg, and sodium to 388 mg.

Marilyn L. Cohen
Champaign, Illinois

Creamy Fruit Salad

Chicken Enchiladas

*Easy But Elegant
Chicken Supreme*

Shrimp Creole

Ricotta Dip   Caper Sauce or Dressing   Clam Spread

Cheddar-Onion Hors d'Oeuvres   Creamed Pimiento Cheese
Stuffed Pasta Shells

Chinese Chicken Salad

Greek Country Salad
Arabian Pocket Bread

Chocolate-Strawberry Frozen Pie

Potato Pancake ⊙◑

Julie and her husband each lost 75 pounds on the Weight Watchers program. Julie works as a receptionist/weigher as well. Her potato pancake recipe was created when she and her husband had a craving for hash brown potatoes.

3 ounces pared potato, finely grated
¼ teaspoon onion flakes
1 tablespoon all-purpose flour
¼ teaspoon *each* double-acting baking powder and salt
⅛ teaspoon pepper
1 ounce Cheddar cheese, shredded

In small bowl combine potato and onion flakes; stir in flour, baking powder, salt, and pepper.

Spray 10-inch nonstick skillet with nonstick cooking spray and heat. Spread potato mixture over bottom of pan and cook over medium heat until underside is brown and crisp, about 10 minutes. Using pancake turner, turn pancake over and cook until other side is brown. Sprinkle cheese over pancake; remove from heat, cover, and let stand until cheese melts, about 2 minutes.

MAKES 1 SERVING

Each serving provides: 1 Protein Exchange; 1 Bread Exchange; 30 calories Optional Exchange
Per serving: 212 calories; 10 g protein; 10 g fat; 22 g carbohydrate; 269 mg calcium; 826 mg sodium; 30 mg cholesterol

Julie D. Slaughter
Marion, Iowa

Twice-Baked Potato

Jean has often made these cheese-stuffed potatoes, which she developed while following the Food Plan. She has two daughters and enjoys gardening.

2 teaspoons margarine
¼ cup *each* finely chopped
    mushrooms and scallions
    (green onions)
2 ounces Gouda cheese,
    shredded
1 tablespoon chopped fresh
    Italian (flat leaf) parsley *or*
    1 teaspoon parsley flakes
¼ teaspoon salt
Dash white pepper
1 baked potato (6 ounces)

In small skillet heat margarine until bubbly and hot; add mushrooms and scallions and sauté until vegetables are tender. Remove from heat and stir in cheese, parsley, salt, and pepper; set aside.

Cut potato in half lengthwise. Scoop out pulp from potato halves, leaving about ¼-inch-thick shells; mash pulp and reserve shells. Combine potato pulp with cheese mixture; spoon half of mixture into each reserved shell. Set stuffed potato halves on nonstick baking sheet and broil until potato is thoroughly heated and browned, 5 to 8 minutes.

MAKES 2 SERVINGS

Each serving provides: 1 Protein Exchange; 1 Bread Exchange; ½ Vegetable Exchange; 1 Fat Exchange
Per serving: 234 calories; 9 g protein; 12 g fat; 23 g carbohydrate; 221 mg calcium; 555 mg sodium; 32 mg cholesterol

VARIATION:

Substitute Swiss or Cheddar cheese for the Gouda.

Per serving with Swiss cheese: 239 calories; 10 g protein; 12 g fat; 24 g carbohydrate; 295 mg calcium; 397 mg sodium; 26 mg cholesterol
With Cheddar cheese: 247 calories; 9 g protein; 13 g fat; 23 g carbohydrate; 227 mg calcium; 499 mg sodium; 30 mg cholesterol

Jean Parman
Sonoma, California

Pilaf with Fruits and Almonds ◑

A wonderful complement to chicken or turkey, this rice dish is festive enough for a holiday meal. For variety, substitute your favorite dried fruits or nuts for the ones called for in the recipe.

1 tablespoon plus 1 teaspoon margarine
½ ounce blanched almonds, chopped
4 dried apricot halves, cut into thin strips
2 large pitted prunes, cut into thin strips
2 tablespoons dark *or* golden raisins
1½ cups water
4 ounces uncooked regular long-grain rice
2 teaspoons honey
¼ teaspoon salt

In 1½-quart nonstick saucepan heat margarine over medium heat until bubbly and hot; add almonds, apricots, prunes, and raisins and sauté until almonds are lightly browned, about 3 minutes. Stir in remaining ingredients and bring to a boil. Reduce heat, cover, and let simmer until liquid is absorbed and rice is tender, about 20 minutes.

MAKES 4 SERVINGS

Each serving provides: 1 Bread Exchange; 1 Fat Exchange; ½ Fruit Exchange; 45 calories Optional Exchange
Per serving: 202 calories; 3 g protein; 6 g fat; 35 g carbohydrate; 24 mg calcium; 183 mg sodium; 0 mg cholesterol

Weight Watchers Kitchens

Holiday Dressing for Poultry

Irene created this dish after some experimentation, and liked it so much she shared it with other Weight Watchers members. Irene, who is retired, enjoys working with elderly and handicapped individuals, helping them to be self-sufficient. She also loves the "great outdoors."

1 packet instant chicken
    broth and seasoning mix
1 cup water
2 cups diced eggplant
1 cup sliced asparagus
½ cup diced onion
¼ cup *each* diced green bell
    pepper and diced celery
1 teaspoon rubbed sage
¼ teaspoon *each* pepper and
    ground cinnamon
4 slices whole wheat bread,
    cut into ½-inch cubes

Preheat oven to 350°F. In 2½-quart saucepan sprinkle broth mix over water and bring to a boil. Reduce heat; add remaining ingredients except bread cubes and stir to combine. Cover pan and cook, stirring occasionally, until vegetables are tender, 4 to 5 minutes. Remove from heat, add bread cubes, and mix well. Spray 1½-quart casserole with nonstick cooking spray and spread mixture evenly in casserole; bake until lightly browned, 20 to 25 minutes.

MAKES 4 SERVINGS

Each serving provides: 1 Bread Exchange; 2 Vegetable Exchanges; 3 calories Optional Exchange
Per serving: 87 calories; 4 g protein; 1 g fat; 17 g carbohydrate; 58 mg calcium; 339 mg sodium; 1 mg cholesterol

Irene Batton
Meadville, Missouri

Southern Corn Bread ◐◑

An assistant professor of voice at the University of Montevallo, Jo Anne likes to cook for her family when she visits them in Washington State. She prepares recipes that fit the Food Plan and gets a round of applause from her entire family.

1½ ounces uncooked self-rising white cornmeal mix
2 tablespoons plus 2 teaspoons instant nonfat dry milk powder
1 teaspoon double-acting baking powder
Granulated sugar substitute to equal 2 teaspoons sugar*
1 egg, beaten with ¼ cup water

Preheat oven to 425°F. Spray 1-quart casserole with nonstick cooking spray; set aside. Using a fork, in small bowl combine dry ingredients; pour in beaten egg and stir with fork just until dry ingredients are moistened. Transfer to sprayed casserole and bake for 12 to 15 minutes (until top of bread is lightly browned and a knife, inserted in center, comes out dry). Remove from oven and let cool slightly; serve warm.

MAKES 2 SERVINGS

*Do not use low-calorie sweetener with aspartame in this recipe; it may lose sweetness during baking.

Each serving provides: ½ Protein Exchange; 1 Bread Exchange; ¼ Milk Exchange
Per serving: 137 calories; 7 g protein; 3 g fat; 20 g carbohydrate; 272 mg calcium; 565 mg sodium; 138 mg cholesterol

SERVING SUGGESTION:

Cut corn bread into squares and serve with margarine or preserves.

Jo Anne Dawson
Montevallo, Alabama

Yogurt Corn Bread 🄲

When Daryl joined Weight Watchers, she couldn't have the corn bread the rest of her family ate every night. Once cornmeal was added to the Food Plan, however, Daryl developed a recipe the whole family could enjoy.

1 tablespoon plus 1 teaspoon vegetable oil
3 ounces uncooked self-rising white cornmeal mix, divided
1 tablespoon plus 1 teaspoon self-rising flour
1½ teaspoons granulated sugar
½ teaspoon baking soda
Dash salt (optional)
1 cup plain low-fat yogurt

Preheat oven to 400°F. In 6-inch cast-iron or nonstick skillet that has a metal or removable handle add oil; bake until hot, about 2 minutes.

While oil is heating, in small bowl combine all but 1 teaspoon cornmeal, the flour, sugar, baking soda, and, if desired, salt; stir in yogurt. Carefully remove skillet from oven; pour hot oil into cornmeal mixture, stirring to combine. Sprinkle remaining teaspoon cornmeal over bottom of skillet and spoon in cornmeal mixture; smooth surface of mixture. Bake at 400°F. until golden brown, 25 to 30 minutes; serve hot.

MAKES 4 SERVINGS

Each serving provides: 1 Bread Exchange; 1 Fat Exchange; ½ Milk Exchange; 20 calories Optional Exchange
Per serving without salt: 165 calories; 5 g protein; 6 g fat; 23 g carbohydrate; 192 mg calcium; 456 mg sodium; 3 mg cholesterol
If salt is used, increase sodium to 489 mg.

Daryl J. Byford
Knoxville, Tennessee

Freezer Tomato Sauce ©

*Rhonda found the perfect way to use those freshly harvested garden tomatoes.
If your crop is really abundant, just double the recipe. Store the sauce in
handy ½- or 1-cup portions.*

**10 large tomatoes, blanched,
   peeled, seeded, and
   chopped
4 cups chopped onions
2 cups chopped carrots
2 tablespoons chopped fresh
   Italian (flat-leaf) parsley
2 to 3 small garlic cloves,
   chopped
1 teaspoon salt
½ to 1 teaspoon oregano
   leaves, crumbled
Granulated sugar substitute
   to equal 1 to 1½ teaspoons
   sugar (optional)***

In 4-quart saucepan combine all ingredients except sugar substitute; set over low heat. Bring to a simmer and cook until carrots are soft, 30 to 40 minutes, stirring occasionally to prevent burning. Let cool slightly.

In blender container process 2 cups of tomato mixture until smooth; transfer sauce to 3-quart bowl and repeat procedure with remaining tomato mixture, processing 2 cups at a time. If sauce is slightly bitter, stir in sugar substitute. Measure sauce into plastic freezer bags or freezer containers and label with date and amount; store in freezer until needed.

YIELDS 2½ QUARTS SAUCE

*Since tomato sauce is generally heated before using, do not use low-calorie sweetener with aspartame in this recipe; it may lose sweetness during cooking.

Each ½-cup serving provides: 2⅛ Vegetable Exchanges
Per ½ cup: 35 calories; 1 g protein; 0.3 g fat; 8 g carbohydrate; 20 mg calcium; 123 mg sodium; 0 mg cholesterol

*Rhonda Brilz
Lanigon, Saskatchewan,
Canada*

Orange-Pineapple Sauce ◖

Jan is enthusiastic about developing her own recipes to fit the Food Plan. She recommends serving this sauce over dietary frozen dessert, part-skim ricotta cheese mixed with sliced bananas, or even chicken. Jan's hobbies include needlework and costume-making.

½ cup orange juice
 (no sugar added)
⅓ cup pineapple juice
 (no sugar added)
2 teaspoons honey
2 teaspoons cornstarch,
 dissolved in 1 tablespoon
 water

In small saucepan combine juices and honey; over medium heat and stirring constantly, bring to a boil. Stir in dissolved cornstarch and cook, stirring, until sauce is thickened. Serve hot or at room temperature.

MAKES 4 SERVINGS, ABOUT ¼ CUP EACH

Each serving provides: ½ Fruit Exchange; 15 calories Optional Exchange
Per serving: 40 calories; 0.3 g protein; trace fat; 10 g carbohydrate; 5 mg
 calcium; 0.7 mg sodium; 0 mg cholesterol

Jan M. Cherry
Seattle, Washington

Pico de Gallo (Mexican Sauce) ⊖⊕

Mexico and music rank high on the list of Imogene's interests. A former resident of Mexico, she loves the cuisine of that country, including this zippy sauce. It's called Pico de Gallo (rooster's beak) because of its color. Imogene is a pianist and the mother of three children, all musicians.

4 medium tomatoes, blanched, peeled, seeded, and quartered
½ cup chopped onion
¼ cup cilantro leaves (Chinese parsley)
3 tablespoons lemon juice, or to taste
2 small serrano chili peppers, seeded
1 teaspoon salt

In work bowl of food processor combine all ingredients; using an on-off motion, process until vegetables are finely chopped *(do not puree).*

MAKES 8 SERVINGS, ABOUT ¼ CUP EACH

Each serving provides: 1¼ Vegetable Exchanges
Per serving: 21 calories; 1 g protein; 0.2 g fat; 5 g carbohydrate; 14 mg calcium; 283 mg sodium; 0 mg cholesterol

SERVING SUGGESTIONS:

1. For superb Salsa, serve sauce chilled or at room temperature; it's a wonderful accompaniment for corn chips.
2. For tasty Taco Sauce, in 1-quart saucepan cook sauce over medium heat, stirring occasionally, for 15 to 20 minutes.
3. For delicious Mexican Rice, prepare sauce as for Taco Sauce (see above); top each ½-cup portion hot cooked long-grain rice with 1 serving of sauce. Add 1 Bread Exchange to Exchange Information.

Per serving: 133 calories; 3 g protein; 0.3 g fat; 30 g carbohydrate; 24 mg calcium; 283 mg sodium; 0 mg cholesterol

Imogene Williams
Dallas, Texas

Royal Barbecue Sauce ☾◑

For a dish fit for a king, spread Faye's sauce over skinned chicken and broil or bake, then pour any pan juices remaining in pan over the cooked poultry.

⅓ cup ketchup
1 tablespoon *each* Worcestershire sauce and distilled
   white vinegar
2 teaspoons *each* vegetable
   oil and firmly packed dark
   brown sugar
½ to ¾ teaspoon powdered
   mustard
⅛ teaspoon salt
Dash *each* ground red pepper
(optional) and black pepper

In small saucepan combine all ingredients and, over high heat, bring to a boil. Reduce heat to low and let simmer, stirring frequently, until flavors are well blended, 5 to 10 minutes.

MAKES 4 SERVINGS, ABOUT 2 TABLESPOONS EACH

Each serving provides: ½ Fat Exchange; 30 calories Optional Exchange
Per serving: 58 calories; 0.7 g protein; 2 g fat; 9 g carbohydrate; 8 mg
   calcium; 346 mg sodium; 0 mg cholesterol

Faye George
Brainerd, Minnesota

Walnut Sauce ◑

Thick and delicious, this sauce keeps for up to a week in the refrigerator; be sure to store it in a covered container. When ready to use, just heat and spoon over cooked chicken breasts, veal, or pork chops. An elegant touch for any meal!

1 tablespoon plus 1 teaspoon margarine
2 tablespoons minced onion
1 garlic clove, minced
2 teaspoons all-purpose flour
1 cup water
1 packet instant chicken broth and seasoning mix
1 ounce shelled walnuts, very finely ground
2 teaspoons red wine vinegar
⅛ teaspoon ground cinnamon
Dash *each* ground cloves, ground red pepper, salt, and pepper
2 teaspoons chopped fresh parsley

In small saucepan heat margarine until bubbly and hot; add onion and garlic and sauté until softened. Add flour and cook, stirring constantly, for 2 minutes. Gradually stir in water; add broth mix and, continuing to stir, bring mixture to a boil. Continue to stir and cook until mixture thickens slightly; stir in remaining ingredients. Reduce heat to low and let sauce simmer, stirring occasionally, until flavors are blended, about 5 minutes. Serve immediately or let cool, then transfer to container, cover, and refrigerate until ready to use.

MAKES 4 SERVINGS

Each serving provides: 1 Fat Exchange; 55 calories Optional Exchange
Per serving: 91 calories; 2 g protein; 8 g fat; 4 g carbohydrate; 13 mg calcium; 288 mg sodium; 0 mg cholesterol

Weight Watchers Kitchens

From the Sweet Shop
Desserts

Chocolate Soufflé

An elegant French classic, this soufflé gets its special flavor from the addition of orange liqueur.

2 teaspoons margarine
⅓ cup plus 2 teaspoons
   all-purpose flour
¼ cup granulated sugar
⅛ teaspoon salt
2 cups skim milk, divided
2 ounces semisweet chocolate
   chips
2 tablespoons orange liqueur
1 teaspoon vanilla extract
4 eggs, separated
⅛ teaspoon cream of tartar

Spread bottom and sides of 1½-quart soufflé dish with margarine; set aside.

In small bowl combine flour, sugar, and salt; gradually stir in 1 cup milk. Continue to stir until mixture is smooth; set aside.

In double boiler combine chocolate and remaining cup milk; cook over boiling water, stirring occasionally, until chocolate melts. Stir flour mixture into chocolate mixture and continue to cook, stirring constantly, until mixture thickens. Stir in liqueur and vanilla. Remove from heat and let stand until mixture is lukewarm, about 15 minutes.

Preheat oven to 350°F. Using electric mixer, in large mixing bowl beat egg yolks until thick and lemon colored, about 5 minutes; stir in chocolate mixture. Using clean beaters, in 2-quart bowl beat egg whites with cream of tartar until stiff but not dry. Lightly stir ¼ of beaten whites into chocolate mixture; fold in remaining whites. Gently transfer mixture to prepared soufflé dish. Set dish in 8 x 8 x 2-inch baking pan and pour boiling water into pan to a depth of about 1 inch; bake until firm, about 1¼ hours. Serve immediately.

MAKES 8 SERVINGS

Each serving provides: ½ Protein Exchange; ¼ Milk Exchange; 115 calories Optional Exchange
Per serving: 163 calories; 6 g protein; 6 g fat; 19 g carbohydrate; 93 mg calcium; 112 mg sodium; 138 mg cholesterol

Weight Watchers Kitchens

Raspberry-Meringue Bread Pudding

The original version of this recipe was a specialty of Geraldine's grandmother. By altering the ingredients, Geraldine turned it into a meringue pudding that she could eat while on the Food Plan. She enjoys quilting, camping, and decorating wedding cakes.

2 slices reduced-calorie white bread (40 calories per slice), cut into small cubes
½ cup skim milk
1 egg
Granulated sugar substitute to equal 2 teaspoons sugar*
½ teaspoon vanilla extract
Dash ground nutmeg
1 tablespoon plus 1 teaspoon reduced-calorie raspberry spread (16 calories per 2 teaspoons)
1 egg white (at room temperature)
1 teaspoon granulated sugar
⅛ teaspoon cream of tartar

Preheat oven to 350°F. Spray two 6-ounce custard cups with nonstick cooking spray; place half of bread cubes into each cup and set aside.

In small mixing bowl combine milk, whole egg, sweetener, vanilla, and nutmeg and beat until thoroughly combined; pour half of mixture into each custard cup, making sure bread cubes are thoroughly moistened. Set cups in 4 x 4 x 2-inch baking dish and pour enough hot water into dish to come halfway up sides of custard cups; bake for 25 to 30 minutes (until a knife, inserted in center of pudding, comes out clean). Remove baking dish from oven and custard cups from water bath; spread 2 teaspoons raspberry spread evenly over top of each pudding and set aside.

Increase oven temperature to 400°F. Using electric mixer, in small mixing bowl beat egg white until soft peaks form; add remaining ingredients and beat until stiff but not dry. Spread half of meringue over each bread pudding, making sure meringue touches edges of pudding. Return custard cups to oven and bake until meringue is lightly browned, 2 to 3 minutes. Remove from oven and let cool for at least 10 minutes before serving. Serve warm or chilled.

MAKES 2 SERVINGS

*Do not use low-calorie sweetener with aspartame in

(continued)

this recipe because it may lose some sweetness during baking.

Each serving provides: ½ Protein Exchange; ½ Bread Exchange; ¼ Milk Exchange; 35 calories Optional Exchange
Per serving: 139 calories; 9 g protein; 3 g fat; 19 g carbohydrate; 111 mg calcium; 186 mg sodium; 138 mg cholesterol

Geraldine M. Fuson
Gladstone, Oregon

Pineapple Pudding

Married, with two children, Stevi works in a school lunchroom. She made a similar dessert at the school and changed the ingredients so she could enjoy it while following the Food Plan. Stevi has lost 60 pounds on the Weight Watchers program.

8 graham crackers (2½-inch squares), made into fine crumbs
1 tablespoon plus 1 teaspoon margarine, softened
2 cups skim milk
1 envelope (four ½-cup servings) reduced-calorie vanilla pudding mix
2 cups canned pineapple chunks (no sugar added)
1 cup thawed frozen dairy whipped topping

Preheat oven to 350°F. In small mixing bowl combine crumbs and margarine, mixing thoroughly. Press mixture into bottom of 8 x 8 x 2-inch nonstick baking pan; bake until lightly browned, about 10 minutes. Remove pan from oven and set aside to cool.

Using 2 cups skim milk, prepare pudding according to package directions; let cool slightly. Carefully pour pudding over cooled crumbs and top with pineapple; spread whipped topping over pudding, cover lightly, and refrigerate until chilled.

MAKES 8 SERVINGS

Each serving provides: ½ Bread Exchange; ½ Fat Exchange; ½ Fruit Exchange; ½ Milk Exchange; 25 calories Optional Exchange
Per serving: 147 calories; 3 g protein; 5 g fat; 25 g carbohydrate; 88 mg calcium; 115 mg sodium; 1 mg cholesterol

Stevi Bryant
Spartanburg, South Carolina

Baked Rice Pudding

Joyce works in a cookie factory and has become accustomed to the smell of fresh-baked cookies. She sometimes takes a serving of this pudding to work, and when she does, it looks so good that people can't believe she's on a weight-reduction program. In her spare time, Joyce enjoys swimming and roller skating.

1 cup *each* cooked long-grain
    rice and skim milk
¼ cup dark raisins
2 eggs
½ teaspoon vanilla extract
⅛ to ¼ teaspoon ground
    nutmeg
Granulated sugar substitute
    to equal 4 teaspoons sugar*
⅛ teaspoon ground cinnamon
    (optional)

In small saucepan combine rice, milk, and raisins and cook over medium heat, stirring to prevent burning or sticking, until mixture comes to a boil. Remove from heat.

Preheat oven to 350°F. In small bowl beat together eggs, vanilla, nutmeg, and sugar substitute; stir in ¼ cup hot rice mixture. Slowly pour egg mixture into remaining rice mixture, stirring rapidly to prevent egg from lumping. Spray 1-quart casserole with non-stick cooking spray; turn rice mixture into casserole and, if desired, sprinkle with cinnamon. Set casserole in 8 x 8 x 2-inch baking pan and pour water into pan to a depth of about 1 inch; bake for 15 to 20 minutes (until a knife, inserted in center of pudding, comes out clean; pudding will be loose). Remove baking pan from oven and casserole from water bath. Let pudding cool slightly and serve warm, or cool completely, cover, and refrigerate until chilled.

MAKES 2 SERVINGS

*Do not use low-calorie sweetener with aspartame in this recipe; it may lose sweetness during baking.

Each serving provides: 1 Protein Exchange; 1 Bread Exchange; 1 Fruit Exchange; ½ Milk Exchange
Per serving: 296 calories; 13 g protein; 6 g fat; 47 g carbohydrate; 198 mg calcium; 135 mg sodium; 276 mg cholesterol

Joyce E. Wills
Burlington, Iowa

Apple-Cinnamon Bread Pudding

Anna believes imagination is an important ingredient in cooking, and her apple dessert is proof of that. Married, with two daughters, Anna enjoys sewing, needlework, crafts, and gardening. She lost 58 pounds on the Weight Watchers program.

3 slices white bread, cut into cubes
1½ cups skim milk
3 large eggs
2 tablespoons granulated sugar
2 tablespoons margarine, melted, divided
½ teaspoon *each* ground cinnamon and vanilla extract
¼ teaspoon *each* ground nutmeg and salt
3 small apples, cored and thinly sliced
2 tablespoons caramel topping

Spread bread cubes on a baking sheet; bake at 275°F., stirring once, until bread is dry, about 10 minutes. Remove from oven and set aside; increase oven temperature to 350°F.

Using electric mixer, in medium bowl beat together milk, eggs, sugar, 1 tablespoon margarine, the cinnamon, vanilla, nutmeg, and salt until combined; add bread cubes and stir to combine.

Spray shallow 1½- or 2-quart casserole with nonstick cooking spray; pour in bread mixture. Arrange apple slices in rows over bread mixture, overlapping slices slightly, and brush evenly with remaining margarine. Set casserole in baking pan that is slightly larger than casserole and pour hot water into pan to a depth of about ½ inch; bake for 45 to 55 minutes (until a knife, inserted in center of pudding, comes out clean). Remove baking pan from oven and casserole from water bath; set casserole on wire rack and let cool for 15 to 20 minutes. Serve topped with caramel topping.

MAKES 6 SERVINGS

Each serving provides: ½ Protein Exchange; ½ Bread Exchange; 1 Fat Exchange; ½ Fruit Exchange; ¼ Milk Exchange; 40 calories Optional Exchange
Per serving: 200 calories; 6 g protein; 7 g fat; 27 g carbohydrate; 111 mg calcium; 262 mg sodium; 139 mg cholesterol

Anna M. Schmidgall
Fairbury, Illinois

❖❖

Apricot "Foldovers"

A former Weight Watchers leader who lost 40 pounds on the Program, Kathryn adapted her favorite traditional Christmas cookie recipe to fit the Food Plan. Her members were ecstatic when she gave them the recipe; they felt it was a great creation and a tremendous find.

4 dried apricot halves, finely chopped
2 tablespoons golden raisins, finely chopped
2 teaspoons *each* granulated sugar and reduced-calorie apricot spread (16 calories per 2 teaspoons)
4 ready-to-bake refrigerated buttermilk flaky biscuits (1 ounce each)*
½ teaspoon confectioners' sugar

Preheat oven to 400°F. In small bowl combine all ingredients except biscuits and confectioners' sugar; set aside.

Carefully separate each biscuit into 4 thin layers of dough. Spoon an equal amount of apricot mixture onto center of each layer of dough and fold each in half, turnover style; using the tines of a fork, press edges to seal. Transfer "foldovers" to nonstick baking sheet and bake until golden brown, 8 to 10 minutes; transfer to wire rack to cool.

To serve, using a small tea strainer, sift an equal amount of confectioners' sugar over each "foldover."

MAKES 4 SERVINGS, 4 "FOLDOVERS" EACH

*Keep biscuits refrigerated until ready to use. Separate dough into layers as soon as it is removed from the refrigerator; it will be difficult to work with if allowed to come to room temperature.

Each serving provides: 1 Bread Exchange; ½ Fruit Exchange; 15 calories Optional Exchange
Per serving: 120 calories; 2 g protein; 4 g fat; 22 g carbohydrate; 4 mg calcium; 294 mg sodium; 0 mg cholesterol

Kathryn Gniadek
Cheshire, Connecticut

Date-Stuffed Pastries

Geraldine has a positive attitude about weight loss: she concentrates on what she can have, not on what she can't have. Here she adapted a favorite pastry recipe to fit the Food Plan. Her husband is her best critic and he thinks these are excellent.

10 pitted dates, finely diced
3 tablespoons water
½ teaspoon granulated sugar
10-ounce package refrigerated
  buttermilk flaky biscuits
  (10 biscuits)
2 tablespoons plus 1 teaspoon
  confectioners' sugar, sifted
2½ teaspoons margarine,
  softened
½ teaspoon vanilla extract

In small saucepan combine dates, water, and sugar; cook over low heat, stirring, until mixture is pasty, about 4 minutes.

Preheat oven to 400°F. Separate biscuits; set 2 biscuits on work surface, overlapping edges by about 1 inch. Using fingers, flatten dough to about ⅛-inch thickness (dough circles should form a figure 8, overlapping at center). Repeat with remaining biscuits, making 4 more figure 8s. Spoon ⅕ of date mixture onto center of bottom circle of each figure 8, then fold top circles over bottom circles, forming 5 date-filled pastries; pinch edges to seal. Using sharp knife or scissors, make 4 evenly spaced cuts, each about ½ inch in length, through top and bottom layers of pinched edge of pastries; spread dough slightly at cuts. Transfer pastries to nonstick baking sheet; bake until golden brown, 8 to 10 minutes. Using a spatula, remove pastries to wire rack to cool.

In small bowl combine confectioners' sugar, margarine, and vanilla, mixing well until smooth; spread over pastries.

MAKES 5 SERVINGS, 1 PASTRY EACH

Each serving provides: 2 Bread Exchanges; ½ Fat Exchange; 1 Fruit Exchange; 30 calories Optional Exchange
Per serving: 248 calories; 3 g protein; 9 g fat; 41 g carbohydrate; 6 mg calcium; 610 mg sodium; 0 mg cholesterol

Geraldine M. Fuson
Gladstone, Oregon

Desirable Cinnamon Rolls

Therese likes to feel that she's not depriving herself while following the Food Plan. Since she loves cinnamon rolls, Therese, a Weight Watchers leader, created her own recipe.

10-ounce package refrigerated buttermilk flaky biscuits (10 biscuits)
1 tablespoon plus 2 teaspoons margarine, melted
1 tablespoon plus 2 teaspoons firmly packed brown sugar, divided
1 teaspoon ground cinnamon
½ cup plus 2 tablespoons dark raisins
1 tablespoon plus 2 teaspoons confectioners' sugar, sifted
2 teaspoons water

Preheat oven to 400°F. Spray 8 x 8 x 2-inch baking pan with nonstick cooking spray; set aside.

Separate biscuits; using fingers, flatten each into 3-inch circle. Brush each circle with an equal amount of the margarine; sprinkle each with ¼ teaspoon brown sugar and an equal amount of the cinnamon, then top each with 1 tablespoon raisins. Roll each circle jelly-roll fashion and arrange in 2 rows, seam-side down, in sprayed pan. Bake until rolls are puffed and golden brown, 8 to 12 minutes. Transfer pan to wire rack and let rolls cool in pan.

In small bowl or cup combine remaining 2½ teaspoons brown sugar and the confectioners' sugar; add water, 1 teaspoon at a time, stirring constantly until mixture is smooth and syrupy. Remove rolls to serving platter; brush each with an equal amount of sugar mixture.

MAKES 10 SERVINGS, 1 ROLL EACH

Each serving provides: 1 Bread Exchange; ½ Fat Exchange; ½ Fruit Exchange; 20 calories Optional Exchange
Per serving: 143 calories; 2 g protein; 5 g fat; 23 g carbohydrate; 10 mg calcium; 318 mg sodium; 0 mg cholesterol

Therese Hill
Lewiston, Idaho

Banana Cake with Coconut Topping

Busy Ethel runs a beauty shop in her home and also sells cakes that she bakes and decorates. This banana cake was originally her mother's recipe and was adapted to the Food Plan. Ethel has two children; daughter Tabitha also has a recipe in this cookbook.

2 very ripe medium bananas, sliced
¼ cup vegetable oil
1 egg
1½ cups cake flour
2 tablespoons plus ½ teaspoon granulated sugar, divided
1 teaspoon *each* double-acting baking powder, vanilla extract, and imitation butter flavor
½ teaspoon baking soda
1 tablespoon plus 1 teaspoon shredded coconut
½ teaspoon ground cinnamon

Preheat oven to 350°F. Spray 8-inch round cake pan or 8 x 8 x 2-inch baking pan with nonstick cooking spray; set aside. In medium mixing bowl combine bananas, oil, and egg; using electric mixer beat until well blended (mixture will contain small lumps of banana). Beat in flour, 1 tablespoon plus 1½ teaspoons sugar, the baking powder, vanilla, butter flavor, and baking soda; pour into sprayed pan and set aside. In small bowl combine coconut, remaining 2 teaspoons sugar, and the cinnamon; sprinkle over batter. Bake for 20 to 25 minutes (until a cake tester, inserted in center, comes out clean). Let cake cool in pan for 5 minutes, then remove to wire rack to cool.

MAKES 8 SERVINGS

Each serving provides: 1 Bread Exchange; 1½ Fat Exchanges; ½ Fruit Exchange; 30 calories Optional Exchange
Per serving: 197 calories; 3 g protein; 8 g fat; 28 g carbohydrate; 37 mg calcium; 116 mg sodium; 34 mg cholesterol

Ethel LeClere
Hortonville, New York

Carrot Cake

Bonnie, a licensed practical nurse, loves being creative with recipes and ingredients, and her carrot cake recipe is a perfect example. She enjoys this cake so much, she even takes it along on camping trips!

4 eggs
3 tablespoons firmly packed
    brown sugar
1 tablespoon plus 1 teaspoon
    vegetable oil
1 teaspoon vanilla extract
1⅓ cups instant nonfat dry
    milk powder
¾ cup whole wheat flour
2 teaspoons *each* baking soda
    and ground cinnamon
3 cups grated carrots
1 cup canned crushed
    pineapple (no sugar added)
¼ cup dark raisins

Preheat oven to 350°F. Spray 8-inch fluted tube pan with nonstick cooking spray and set aside.

In mixing bowl, using electric mixer, beat together eggs, sugar, oil, and vanilla until mixture is light and fluffy; using mixer at low speed, beat in milk powder, flour, baking soda, and cinnamon, beating until thoroughly combined. Add remaining ingredients and stir to combine. Pour batter into sprayed pan and bake 40 to 45 minutes (until a cake tester, inserted in center, comes out clean). Let cake cool in pan for 5 minutes. Remove cake from pan and set on wire rack; let cool for at least 15 minutes.

MAKES 8 SERVINGS

Each serving provides: ½ Protein Exchange; ½ Bread Exchange; ¾ Vegetable Exchange; ½ Fat Exchange; ½ Fruit Exchange; ½ Milk Exchange; 25 calories Optional Exchange
Per serving: 210 calories; 9 g protein; 5 g fat; 32 g carbohydrate; 187 mg calcium; 320 mg sodium; 139 mg cholesterol

Bonnie J. Palakovich
Great Falls, Montana

Cheesecake Bars ⊙

Debra's sweet and creamy creation is a variation of the traditional dessert favorite. Start a tradition of your own by serving these to friends and family.

1⅓ cups cottage cheese
4 eggs
½ cup plain low-fat yogurt
⅓ cup plus 2 teaspoons all-purpose flour
⅓ cup instant nonfat dry milk powder
2 tablespoons plus 2 teaspoons granulated sugar *or* honey
½ to 1 teaspoon grated lemon peel, or to taste
½ teaspoon vanilla *or* almond extract
Dash salt
4 graham crackers (2½-inch squares), made into crumbs, *or* 1½ ounces ready-to-eat crunchy nutlike cereal nuggets

Preheat oven to 325°F. Spray 10 x 6 x 1¾-inch glass baking dish with nonstick cooking spray; set aside.

In blender container combine all ingredients except cracker crumbs (or cereal) and process until smooth; pour mixture into sprayed pan and bake for 20 minutes (mixture will be slightly set). Sprinkle crumbs (or cereal) evenly over cake and continue baking until cake is golden brown and edges pull away from sides of dish, 25 to 30 minutes longer. Let cool, then cover and refrigerate until chilled. To serve, cut into eight 2½ x 3-inch bars.

MAKES 8 SERVINGS, 1 BAR EACH

Each serving provides: 1 Protein Exchange; ½ Bread Exchange; ¼ Milk Exchange; 20 calories Optional Exchange
Per serving with graham crackers and sugar: 147 calories; 10 g protein; 5 g fat; 15 g carbohydrate; 98 mg calcium; 242 mg sodium; 144 mg cholesterol
With graham crackers and honey: 152 calories; 10 g protein; 5 g fat; 17 g carbohydrate; 98 mg calcium; 242 mg sodium; 144 mg cholesterol
With cereal nuggets and sugar: 152 calories; 10 g protein; 5 g fat; 17 g carbohydrate; 99 mg calcium; 255 mg sodium; 144 mg cholesterol
With cereal nuggets and honey: 157 calories; 10 g protein; 5 g fat; 18 g carbohydrate; 99 mg calcium; 255 mg sodium; 144 mg cholesterol

Debra Sather
Northwood, Iowa

Chocolate Sheetcake

Alana enjoys her job as a Weight Watchers leader, especially the friendships she's formed over the years. With her teaching background, she finds that being a leader comes easily to her. The sheetcake recipe from which this was developed came to Alana from a friend. Alana tried several variations before perfecting this one.

2¼ cups all-purpose flour
⅔ cup instant nonfat dry milk powder
⅓ cup plus 2 teaspoons granulated sugar
¼ cup unsweetened cocoa
1 teaspoon *each* double-acting baking powder and baking soda
1 cup water
¾ cup buttermilk
½ cup reduced-calorie mayonnaise
1 teaspoon vanilla extract

Preheat oven to 375°F. Spray 16 x 12 x ¾-inch sheet pan with nonstick cooking spray; set aside.

Onto sheet of wax paper or a paper plate sift together flour, milk powder, sugar, cocoa, baking powder, and baking soda; set aside.

In mixing bowl combine remaining ingredients; using electric mixer, beat sifted ingredients into buttermilk mixture, beating until smooth. Pour batter into prepared pan and bake for 20 minutes (until cake pulls away from sides of pan and a cake tester, inserted in center, comes out clean). Let cake cool in pan 5 minutes; remove cake from pan and set on wire rack to cool.

MAKES 12 SERVINGS

Each serving provides: 1 Bread Exchange; 1 Fat Exchange; ¼ Milk Exchange; 35 calories Optional Exchange
Per serving: 162 calories; 5 g protein; 3 g fat; 29 g carbohydrate; 88 mg calcium; 217 mg sodium; 5 mg cholesterol

Alana Althoff
Addieville, Illinois

Golden Squash Cake

The versatility of summer squash has become well known through such favorites as zucchini bread and ratatouille. But this delicious sour cream cake, with its cream cheese frosting, will surprise even the most ardent squash devotee.

1½ cups all-purpose flour
¾ teaspoon *each* double-acting baking powder and baking soda
¼ teaspoon *each* salt and ground cinnamon
2 eggs
¼ cup granulated sugar
½ cup sour cream
1 teaspoon grated orange peel
½ teaspoon vanilla extract
1 cup grated yellow straight-neck squash
8 pitted dates, chopped
¼ cup confectioners' sugar
2 tablespoons whipped cream cheese
2 teaspoons freshly squeezed orange juice

Preheat oven to 350°F. Onto sheet of wax paper or a paper plate sift together flour, baking powder, baking soda, salt, and cinnamon; set aside.

Using electric mixer at medium speed, in medium mixing bowl beat together eggs and granulated sugar until combined; add sour cream, orange peel, and vanilla and continue beating until thoroughly combined. Add sifted ingredients and mix well; stir in squash and dates.

Spray 1½-quart fluted tube pan with nonstick cooking spray; pour batter into pan. Bake 25 to 30 minutes (until a cake tester, inserted in center, comes out clean). Invert cake onto wire rack and let cool, 15 to 20 minutes.

In small mixing bowl combine confectioners' sugar and cream cheese; add juice and mix well. Set cooled cake on cake platter; drizzle mixture over cake and let harden.

MAKES 8 SERVINGS

Each serving provides: 1 Bread Exchange; ¼ Vegetable Exchange; ½ Fruit Exchange; 120 calories Optional Exchange
Per serving: 219 calories; 5 g protein; 6 g fat; 36 g carbohydrate; 59 mg calcium; 224 mg sodium; 80 mg cholesterol

Weight Watchers Kitchens

Strawberry-Topped Sponge Cake

Losing over 40 pounds has spurred Verda to change her life-style. She now enjoys exercise and physical fitness when she's not conducting a meeting for Weight Watchers or working as a postmaster. This dessert is one of her favorites.

1/3 cup plus 2 teaspoons
  all-purpose flour
1/2 teaspoon double-acting
  baking powder
Dash salt
2 eggs
1 tablespoon plus 1 teaspoon
  granulated sugar
1 tablespoon hot water
1/2 teaspoon vanilla extract
1/2 cup thawed frozen dairy
  whipped topping
1 cup strawberries, sliced

Preheat oven to 350°F. Onto sheet of wax paper or a paper plate sift together flour, baking powder, and salt; set aside.

Using electric mixer, in medium bowl beat together eggs and sugar until thick and lemon colored, 3 to 4 minutes; beat in water and vanilla, then gradually beat in sifted ingredients. Spray 8 x 8 x 2-inch baking pan with nonstick cooking spray; pour in batter and bake 12 to 15 minutes (until lightly browned and a cake tester, inserted in center, comes out clean). Remove cake from pan and set on wire rack to cool.

To serve, cut cake in half making two rectangles, each 8 x 4 inches; transfer 1 rectangle to serving plate. Spread half of whipped topping over top of rectangle; top with half of strawberries. Set remaining rectangle over strawberries; spread top with remaining whipped topping and top with remaining strawberries.

MAKES 4 SERVINGS

Each serving provides: 1/2 Protein Exchange; 1/2 Bread Exchange; 60 calories
  Optional Exchange
Per serving: 136 calories; 4 g protein; 5 g fat; 18 g carbohydrate; 48 mg
  calcium; 131 mg sodium; 137 mg cholesterol

Verda H. Kurtz
Forest City, Missouri

Butterscotch-Peanut Butter Pie

Love butterscotch? Peanut butter? Susan blends these two favorites in a creamy pie she takes to potluck suppers or serves for company. Susan is married to a stockbroker and has two sons, and she's very excited about this cookbook.

8 graham crackers (2½-inch squares), made into fine crumbs
2 tablespoons plus 2 teaspoons reduced-calorie margarine (tub), melted
1 envelope (four ½-cup servings) reduced-calorie butterscotch pudding mix
1 teaspoon unflavored gelatin
2 cups skim milk
¼ cup chunky peanut butter
½ cup thawed frozen dairy whipped topping

Preheat oven to 350°F. In small bowl combine crumbs and margarine, mixing thoroughly; using the back of a spoon, press crumb mixture over bottom and up sides of 9-inch pie plate. Bake for 8 minutes; remove to wire rack and let cool.

In 1-quart saucepan combine pudding mix and gelatin; add milk and cook over low heat, stirring constantly, until mixture comes to a boil. Add peanut butter and stir to combine; remove from heat and let cool to room temperature. Spread pudding mixture over prepared crust; cover and refrigerate until chilled, about 1 hour. Just before serving, spread pie with whipped topping.

MAKES 4 SERVINGS

Each serving provides: 1 Protein Exchange; 1 Bread Exchange; 2 Fat Exchanges; 1 Milk Exchange; 25 calories Optional Exchange
Per serving: 279 calories; 10 g protein; 16 g fat; 27 g carbohydrate; 161 mg calcium; 371 mg sodium; 0 mg cholesterol

Susan K. Larrison
Columbus, Ohio

Chocolate-Cherry Frozen Pie

Attention, chocolate-lovers! Donna and her family would like you to know that you can have delectable chocolate desserts and still lose weight on the Weight Watchers program. Everybody will enjoy this creation, whether or not they're on a weight-loss program.

2 tablespoons plus 1½ teaspoons chocolate syrup
12 graham crackers (2½-inch squares), made into crumbs
18 ounces chocolate dietary frozen dessert, softened
¾ cup thawed frozen dairy whipped topping
12 large fresh or frozen pitted cherries (no sugar added), cut into halves

In small bowl drizzle chocolate syrup over cracker crumbs and, using a fork, stir to combine. Using the back of a spoon, press crumb mixture over bottom and up sides of 9-inch pie plate; set aside.

Using electric mixer, in medium mixing bowl beat frozen dessert until smooth; carefully transfer to graham cracker crust. Cover with plastic wrap and freeze until firm, about 1 hour.

To serve, spread whipped topping over pie, or fit a pastry bag with star tip, fill bag with topping, and decoratively pipe topping onto pie; arrange cherries on top.

MAKES 6 SERVINGS

Each serving provides: 1 Bread Exchange; 1 Fruit Exchange; ½ Milk Exchange; 60 calories Optional Exchange
Per serving: 208 calories; 6 g protein; 5 g fat; 39 g carbohydrate; 158 mg calcium; 179 mg sodium; 2 mg cholesterol

VARIATION:

Chocolate-Strawberry Frozen Pie—Substitute 2 cups strawberries for the cherries. Slice berries, leaving 1 whole, and arrange on top of pie. Increase Optional Exchange to 65 calories.

Per serving: 212 calories; 6 g protein; 5 g fat; 40 g carbohydrate; 163 mg calcium; 179 mg sodium; 2 mg cholesterol

Donna B. Catlin
Williamsfield, Illinois

Lemon-Cheese Pie

The original recipe for this pie called for cream cheese. In trying to come up with a lower-calorie version that fit the Food Plan, Judith substituted part-skim ricotta and, after much experimentation, produced this delicious dessert. Judith's hobbies include knitting, crocheting, and quilting.

16 graham crackers (2½-inch squares), made into crumbs
2 tablespoons plus 2 teaspoons reduced-calorie margarine (tub)
½ cup evaporated skimmed milk
1 envelope (eight ½-cup servings) *or* 2 envelopes (four ½-cup servings each) low-calorie lemon-flavored gelatin (8 calories per ½ cup)
1 cup boiling water
2 cups part-skim ricotta cheese

Preheat oven to 350°F. Spray 9-inch pie plate with nonstick cooking spray; set aside.

In small mixing bowl combine crumbs and margarine, mixing thoroughly; using the back of a spoon, press crumb mixture over bottom and up sides of sprayed pie plate. Bake until crust is crisp and brown, about 10 minutes; remove to wire rack and let cool.

While pie crust is baking and cooling, prepare filling. Pour milk into freezer-safe medium bowl, cover, and freeze until partially frozen, 15 to 20 minutes. Meanwhile, in small mixing bowl dissolve gelatin in boiling water; set aside.

Using an electric mixer, beat partially frozen milk until thick and foamy; gradually beat in dissolved gelatin. Add about ½ cup ricotta cheese to gelatin mixture and beat until combined; add remaining cheese, about ½ cup at a time, beating well after each addition (mixture should be smooth). Pour mixture into cooled crust; cover and refrigerate until set, about 3 hours.

MAKES 8 SERVINGS

Each serving provides: 1 Protein Exchange; 1 Bread Exchange; ½ Fat Exchange; 20 calories Optional Exchange
Per serving: 176 calories; 11 g protein; 8 g fat; 15 g carbohydrate; 219 mg calcium; 235 mg sodium; 20 mg cholesterol

Judith J. Hoffpauir
Morse, Louisiana

❖❖❖

Lemon Pie ☻

This luscious pie is a family favorite handed down from generation to generation, beginning with Norma's grandmother.

¾ **cup plus 1 tablespoon all-purpose flour, divided**
¼ **teaspoon salt**
¼ **cup margarine, divided**
¼ **cup plain low-fat yogurt**
4 **eggs, separated**
½ **cup granulated sugar**
3 **tablespoons lemon juice**
1 **cup evaporated skimmed milk**
1 **teaspoon grated lemon peel**

In mixing bowl combine ¾ cup flour and the salt; with pastry blender, or 2 knives used scissors-fashion, cut in 3 tablespoons margarine until mixture resembles coarse meal. Add yogurt and mix thoroughly; form dough into a ball, wrap in plastic wrap, and refrigerate for at least 1 hour.

Preheat oven to 400°F. Between 2 sheets of wax paper roll dough, forming a 10-inch circle about ⅛ inch thick. Fit dough into 9-inch pie plate; fold under any dough that extends and flute edges. Using a fork, prick bottom and sides of pie shell; bake until lightly browned, 10 to 12 minutes. Remove to wire rack; let cool.

Using electric mixer, in large mixing bowl beat egg yolks with sugar until thick and lemon colored. Beat in lemon juice and remaining flour and margarine; gradually beat in milk and lemon peel.

In separate bowl beat whites until stiff; gently fold into yolk mixture. Pour filling into crust and bake at 350°F. for 30 minutes (until a cake tester, inserted in center, comes out clean). Let cool on wire rack.

MAKES 8 SERVINGS

Each serving provides: ½ Protein Exchange; ½ Bread Exchange; 1½ Fat Exchanges; ¼ Milk Exchange; 70 calories Optional Exchange
Per serving: 215 calories; 7 g protein; 9 g fat; 27 g carbohydrate; 125 mg calcium; 212 mg sodium; 139 mg cholesterol

Norma Perkins
Sheridan, Montana

Mock Coconut Cream Pie ☻

Developed especially for her father, Marilyn's pie is so delicious she serves it to her guests for Thanksgiving dinner. Marilyn is a bookkeeper and homemaker whose interests include real estate, needlepoint, cooking, and volunteer work.

2 cups cooked spaghetti
   squash
1 cup skim milk
4 eggs
½ cup evaporated skimmed
   milk
¼ cup *each* all-purpose flour
   and granulated sugar
2 tablespoons plus 2 tea-
   spoons reduced-calorie
   margarine (tub)
½ teaspoon *each* vanilla
   extract and coconut
   extract
¼ teaspoon double-acting
   baking powder

Preheat oven to 350°F. Spray 9-inch pie plate with nonstick cooking spray; using the back of a spoon, spread squash over bottom and up sides of plate. Set aside.

In blender container combine remaining ingredients and process until smooth; pour over squash and bake for 50 minutes to 1 hour (until a knife, inserted in center, comes out clean). Transfer pie plate to wire rack and let stand for 1 hour. Cover with plastic wrap and refrigerate overnight.

MAKES 8 SERVINGS

Each serving provides: ½ Protein Exchange; ½ Vegetable Exchange; ½ Fat Exchange; ¼ Milk Exchange; 45 calories Optional Exchange
Per serving: 130 calories; 6 g protein; 5 g fat; 15 g carbohydrate; 113 mg calcium; 129 mg sodium; 138 mg cholesterol

Marilyn K. Yarmon
Augusta, Georgia

Pumpkin Pie

Joe lost 75 pounds on the Weight Watchers program, and feels it's the only sound way to shed excess pounds. He loves to cook and often prepares specialties that fit the Food Plan for his children and grandchildren. Here's a favorite—his special pumpkin pie.

4 ready-to-bake brown-and-serve rolls (1 ounce each)

¼ cup reduced-calorie margarine (tub), divided

2 tablespoons *each* all-purpose flour, divided, and skim milk

Granulated sugar substitute to equal 7 teaspoons sugar,* divided

4 eggs

2 cups canned *or* cooked and pureed fresh pumpkin

½ cup evaporated skimmed milk

1 teaspoon *each* pumpkin pie spice and vanilla extract

In work bowl of food processor, using shredding attachment, shred dough; change to steel chopping blade. Cut 2 tablespoons margarine into pieces and add to work bowl along with 1 tablespoon plus 1 teaspoon flour, the skim milk, and sweetener to equal 1 teaspoon sugar and process just until well blended. Shape dough into ball, wrap in plastic wrap, and refrigerate until dough is chilled, about 30 minutes.

Preheat oven to 450°F. Onto sheet of wax paper sprinkle remaining 2 teaspoons flour; set dough onto floured surface, top with second sheet of wax paper, and roll to form a 10-inch circle, about ⅛ inch thick. Carefully remove paper and fit dough into 9-inch pie plate; fold under any dough that extends beyond edge of plate and flute or crimp edges. Using a fork, prick bottom and sides of dough; bake for 8 minutes. Remove pie plate to wire rack and let cool. While pie shell is cooling, prepare filling.

In mixing bowl combine eggs, remaining 2 tablespoons margarine, and sweetener to equal 6 teaspoons sugar and, using electric mixer, beat until well combined; add remaining ingredients and beat until combined. Pour filling into cooled crust and bake at 450°F. for 8 minutes. Reduce oven temperature to 325°F. and continue baking for 35 to 40 minutes longer (until a knife, inserted in center, comes out clean). Remove pie plate to wire rack and let pie cool. Serve at room

(continued)

temperature or cover and refrigerate until chilled.

MAKES 8 SERVINGS

*Do not use low-calorie sweetener with aspartame in this recipe; it may lose sweetness during baking.

Each serving provides: ½ Protein Exchange; ½ Bread Exchange; ½ Vegetable Exchange; ½ Fat Exchange; 30 calories Optional Exchange
Per serving: 154 calories; 6 g protein; 7 g fat; 17 g carbohydrate; 88 mg calcium; 197 mg sodium; 138 mg cholesterol

Joe L. Saia
Helena, Arkansas

Cantaloupe "Ice Cream"

Cheryl's dessert is a thick and creamy confection that's a lot like soft-serve ice cream from the ice cream parlor. Cheryl likes to keep busy; when she's not working, she enjoys aerobics, swimming, reading, sewing, and cooking.

1 cup cantaloupe balls, divided
½ cup evaporated skimmed milk
1 teaspoon vanilla extract
Granulated low-calorie sweetener with aspartame to equal 2 teaspoons sugar
2 mint sprigs

In freezer-safe bowl combine all but 2 cantaloupe balls and the milk; cover with plastic wrap and freeze until ice crystals begin to form, about 20 minutes. Using slotted spoon, remove cantaloupe from milk; set aside. Pour milk into blender container; add vanilla and sweetener and process. With motor running, add frozen cantaloupe balls, 1 at a time, processing after each addition (mixture should be thick and smooth). Divide mixture into 2 glasses. Into each reserved melon ball insert stem of 1 mint sprig; garnish rim of each glass with a melon ball.

MAKES 2 SERVINGS

Each serving provides: ½ Fruit Exchange; ½ Milk Exchange
Per serving: 87 calories; 6 g protein; 0.3 g fat; 15 g carbohydrate; 194 mg calcium; 81 mg sodium; 3 mg cholesterol

Cheryl Mangum
Eastland, Texas

Amaretti-Berry Coupe

Amaretti cookies add crunch to this special dessert. A lovely ending for a dinner party!

½ cup raspberries
2 teaspoons *each* granulated
   sugar and water
1 cup strawberries, cut into
   halves
1 tablespoon orange brandy
1 cup vanilla ice milk
1 amaretti cookie (¼ ounce),
   made into crumbs

In blender container process raspberries until smooth. Fit fine sieve over small saucepan and force raspberry puree through sieve into pan; discard seeds. Add sugar and water to saucepan and cook over medium heat, stirring frequently and skimming foam from surface when necessary, until sauce is thick and reduced by half (about 2 tablespoons), 4 to 5 minutes. Transfer raspberry mixture to small cup or bowl; cover with plastic wrap and refrigerate until chilled, about 1 hour.

In small mixing bowl combine strawberries and brandy; cover with plastic wrap and refrigerate for at least 30 minutes.

To serve, into each of 2 dessert dishes spoon half of the strawberry mixture; top each with ½ cup ice milk, half of the raspberry sauce, and half of the cookie crumbs. Serve immediately.

MAKES 2 SERVINGS

Each serving provides: 1 Fruit Exchange; 175 calories Optional Exchange
Per serving: 184 calories; 4 g protein; 5 g fat; 31 g carbohydrate; 112 mg
   calcium; 54 mg sodium; 9 mg cholesterol

Weight Watchers Kitchens

Instant Fruit "Ice Cream" ◑

Pat and her children really enjoy this dessert. For Pat, it eliminates the temptation to finish off a pint of ice cream.

1 packet (1 serving) reduced-calorie vanilla dairy drink mix, prepared according to package directions
1 cup frozen strawberries (no sugar added)
¼ teaspoon vanilla extract

In blender container process dairy drink, adding a few frozen strawberries at a time, until all berries have been processed and mixture is smooth, scraping down sides of container as necessary. Add extract and process just to combine; spoon into dessert dish and serve immediately.

MAKES 1 SERVING

Each serving provides: 1 Milk Exchange; 1 Fruit Exchange
Per serving: 127 calories; 7 g protein; 0.2 g fat; 25 g carbohydrate; 174 mg calcium; 3 mg sodium; 0 mg cholesterol

VARIATIONS:

1. Other fruits will also make delicious "ice cream." Freeze 1 cup cantaloupe chunks, ½ cup drained canned pineapple chunks (no sugar added), ½ cup drained canned peach slices (no sugar added), or ½ medium banana, sliced, and substitute for the strawberries.

Per serving with cantaloupe: 130 calories; 7 g protein; 0.4 g fat; 25 g carbohydrate; 168 mg calcium; 14 mg sodium; 0 mg cholesterol
With pineapple: 149 calories; 7 g protein; 0.1 g fat; 31 g carbohydrate; 168 mg calcium; 1 mg sodium; 0 mg cholesterol
With peach: 103 calories; 7 g protein; 0.1 g fat; 19 g carbohydrate; 152 mg calcium; 4 mg sodium; 0 mg cholesterol
With banana: 126 calories; 7 g protein; 0.3 g fat; 25 g carbohydrate; 153 mg calcium; 0.6 mg sodium; 0 mg cholesterol

2. Strawberry-flavored reduced-calorie dairy drink mix may be substituted for the vanilla.

Pat Mayer
Lee's Summit, Missouri

Creamy Fruit Salad

Cindy and her mother, Joan, put their heads together and came up with this fresh and fruity dessert. Cindy does aerobics and runs to keep fit; Joan likes to walk. They take turns preparing Sunday dinners that fit the Food Plan.

1 cup *each* **strawberries, quartered, and cantaloupe chunks (reserve 6 whole strawberries)**
1 small apple, cored and chopped
20 small seedless green grapes
½ cup *each* **canned pineapple chunks and mandarin orange sections (no sugar added)**
1½ cups thawed frozen non-dairy whipped topping, divided
2 tablespoons shredded coconut, toasted

In 2-quart bowl combine fruits except whole berries; cover with plastic wrap and refrigerate until well chilled, at least 2 hours.

To serve, into each of 6 parfait or sundae glasses spoon 2 tablespoons whipped topping and top each portion with ¼ cup fruit mixture. Top each portion of fruit with 1 tablespoon whipped topping, then an equal amount of remaining fruit mixture. Spoon 1 tablespoon whipped topping onto each portion of fruit, sprinkle with 1 teaspoon coconut, and garnish with 1 reserved berry.

MAKES 6 SERVINGS

Each serving provides: 1 Fruit Exchange; 60 calories Optional Exchange
Per serving: 116 calories; 1 g protein; 5 g fat; 18 g carbohydrate; 15 mg calcium; 9 mg sodium; 0.1 mg cholesterol

Cindy Underhill
Port Moody, British Columbia, Canada

Joan M. Walsh
New Westminster, British Columbia, Canada

Fruitcake Dessert ◑

Although Ercellene created this dessert especially for Christmas, feel free to enjoy it any time of the year.

4 *each* graham crackers (2½-inch squares) and zwieback, made into crumbs
Dash *each* ground cinnamon and ground cloves
2 small apples, cored and cut into cubes
8 dried apricot halves, diced
4 large pitted prunes, diced
¼ cup dark *or* golden raisins
Zest of ½ small orange,* diced and blanched
Zest of ¼ lemon,* diced and blanched
2 tablespoons reduced-calorie pancake syrup (60 calories per fluid ounce)
¼ cup thawed frozen dairy whipped topping

In small bowl combine graham cracker crumbs, zwieback crumbs, cinnamon, and cloves; set aside.

In 1-quart microwave-safe bowl combine apples, apricots, prunes, and raisins; microwave on High until apples are soft and fruit is moist, 2 to 3 minutes.† Add orange zest, lemon zest, and syrup, tossing until thoroughly coated; let stand 1 to 2 minutes. Add crumb mixture and stir to combine. Divide mixture into four 6-ounce custard cups; top each portion with 1 tablespoon whipped topping.

MAKES 4 SERVINGS

*The zest of the orange and lemon is the peel without any of the pith (white membrane). To remove zest from fruit, use a zester or vegetable peeler; wrap fruit in plastic wrap and refrigerate for use at another time.
†Cooking time may be different in your microwave oven. To help ensure good results, be sure to check for doneness while cooking.

Each serving provides: 1 Bread Exchange; 2 Fruit Exchanges; 30 calories Optional Exchange
Per serving: 185 calories; 2 g protein; 2 g fat; 41 g carbohydrate; 24 mg calcium; 65 mg sodium; 1 mg cholesterol

Ercellene Thomas
Junction City, California

Heavenly Chocolate Banana "Crème" Log ◑

The answer to Kathryn's prayer for something sweet, cool, creamy, and chocolaty, this makes a lovely holiday dessert. Kathryn, a former college calculus teacher, is a busy mother and the wife of a physician.

2 tablespoons part-skim ricotta cheese
½ teaspoon confectioners' sugar
⅛ teaspoon vanilla extract
½ medium banana, peeled and cut lengthwise into 4 equal slices
½ teaspoon *each* chocolate syrup and shredded coconut

In small bowl combine cheese, sugar, and vanilla, mixing well. Set 1 banana slice on a dessert plate; spread with ⅓ of the cheese mixture, top with a banana slice, and spread with half of the remaining cheese mixture. Repeat with remaining banana slices and cheese mixture, ending with banana; spread with chocolate syrup and sprinkle with coconut.

MAKES 1 SERVING

Each serving provides: ½ Protein Exchange; 1 Fruit Exchange; 25 calories Optional Exchange
Per serving: 113 calories; 4 g protein; 3 g fat; 19 g carbohydrate; 88 mg calcium; 43 mg sodium; 10 mg cholesterol

Kathryn Gniadek
Cheshire, Connecticut

Microwave Nutty Apple ☾◑

A legal secretary and Weight Watchers leader, Erma converted a favorite family recipe to fit the Food Plan. She encourages her members to try to do the same with their recipes. Erma, who used to be shy, says that her 44-pound weight loss has helped her to become more outgoing.

4 small Red *or* Golden
   Delicious apples, cored
2 teaspoons firmly packed
   brown sugar, divided
2 tablespoons chunky peanut
   butter
Ground cinnamon

Into each of four 6-ounce custard cups place 1 apple; sprinkle core cavity of each apple with ¼ teaspoon brown sugar, fill each with 1½ teaspoons peanut butter, and top each with ¼ teaspoon brown sugar. Sprinkle each apple with an equal amount of cinnamon and microwave on High for 3 to 4 minutes.*

MAKES 4 SERVINGS, 1 APPLE EACH

*Timing may be different in your microwave oven. To ensure good results, be sure to check for doneness while cooking.

Each serving provides: ½ Protein Exchange; ½ Fat Exchange; 1 Fruit
   Exchange; 10 calories Optional Exchange
Per serving: 118 calories; 2 g protein; 4 g fat; 20 g carbohydrate; 13 mg
   calcium; 39 mg sodium; 0 mg cholesterol

Erma M. Williams
Coeur d'Alene, Idaho

From the Snack Bar
Snacks and Beverages

Peanut Butter Macaroons

Mary Lou wanted something to satisfy her yen for cookies so she developed this recipe. This active grandmother is a Weight Watchers leader who lost 65 pounds. In her spare time, she enjoys boating and fishing with her husband, Cal.

1½ ounces ready-to-eat corn flake cereal

1 ounce uncooked quick *or* old-fashioned oats

3 tablespoons plus 1 teaspoon shredded coconut

2 tablespoons *each* all-purpose flour, granulated sugar, and chunky peanut butter

2 egg whites (at room temperature)

½ teaspoon vanilla extract

⅛ teaspoon salt

Preheat oven to 325°F. In medium mixing bowl combine corn flakes, oats, coconut, flour, and sugar; with pastry blender, or 2 knives used scissors-fashion, cut in peanut butter until mixture is well blended.

Using electric mixer at high speed, in small mixing bowl beat egg whites until stiff but not dry, gradually adding vanilla and salt while beating; fold into peanut butter mixture.

Spray nonstick baking sheet with nonstick cooking spray; drop batter by rounded teaspoonfuls onto sheet, forming 16 equal cookies. Bake until lightly browned, about 20 minutes; using a spatula, remove cookies to wire rack to cool.

MAKES 4 SERVINGS, 4 MACAROONS EACH

Each serving provides: ½ Protein Exchange; 1 Bread Exchange; ½ Fat Exchange; 65 calories Optional Exchange

Per serving: 183 calories; 6 g protein; 6 g fat; 27 g carbohydrate; 10 mg calcium; 274 mg sodium; 0 mg cholesterol

Mary Lou Galloway
Orofino, Idaho

Peanut-Honey Cookies

A favorite old-fashioned cookie. We've substituted peanuts for the usual pecans.

1½ cups all-purpose flour
½ teaspoon baking soda
⅓ cup margarine
¼ cup firmly packed dark
   brown sugar
1 tablespoon honey
1 egg
½ teaspoon vanilla extract
⅛ teaspoon ground cinnamon
2 ounces unsalted shelled
   roasted peanuts, chopped

On sheet of wax paper or a paper plate sift together flour and baking soda; set aside. Preheat oven to 375°F.

Using electric mixer, in large mixing bowl cream margarine; gradually add sugar and honey and beat until light and fluffy. Beat in egg, vanilla, and cinnamon; gradually beat in sifted ingredients and peanuts.

Spray 2 nonstick cookie sheets with nonstick cooking spray. Using half of dough, drop dough by ½ teaspoonfuls onto cookie sheets, forming 24 equal cookies and leaving a space of about 2 inches between each. Using tines of fork, slightly press each cookie to flatten, then press down in opposite direction to create a checkerboard pattern. Bake until cookies are lightly browned, 8 to 10 minutes. Using a spatula, remove cookies to wire rack to cool. Repeat procedure with remaining dough, making 24 more cookies.

MAKES 16 SERVINGS, 3 COOKIES EACH

Each serving provides: ½ Bread Exchange; 1 Fat Exchange; 45 calories Optional Exchange
Per serving: 119 calories; 3 g protein; 6 g fat; 14 g carbohydrate; 11 mg calcium; 76 mg sodium; 17 mg cholesterol

Weight Watchers Kitchens

Pumpkin-Raisin Cookies

These chewy cookies are Rudine's own creation. A homemaker who writes and paints, Rudine has three children and two grandchildren.

3 tablespoons all-purpose
  flour
½ teaspoon *each* baking soda
  and double-acting baking
  powder
1 egg
2 tablespoons firmly packed
  brown sugar
2 teaspoons *each* granulated
  sugar and reduced-calorie
  margarine (tub)
1 teaspoon ground cinnamon
Dash salt
2 tablespoons *each* canned
  pumpkin and dark raisins
1 tablespoon instant nonfat
  dry milk powder

Preheat oven to 325°F. Onto sheet of wax paper or a paper plate sift together flour, baking soda, and baking powder; set aside.

Using electric mixer, in medium mixing bowl beat together egg, sugars, margarine, cinnamon, and salt until light and fluffy; stir in pumpkin, raisins, milk powder, and sifted dry ingredients.

Spray cookie sheet with nonstick cooking spray; drop batter by teaspoonfuls onto sheet, forming 16 equal cookies and leaving a space of about 2 inches between each. Bake until cookies are browned, about 15 minutes. Using a spatula, remove cookies to wire rack to cool.

MAKES 4 SERVINGS, 4 COOKIES EACH

Each serving provides: 100 calories Optional Exchange
Per serving: 105 calories; 3 g protein; 2 g fat; 19 g carbohydrate; 65 mg
  calcium; 235 mg sodium; 69 mg cholesterol

Rudine Mayfield
Kelso, Washington

Oatmeal-Raisin Cookies

Alma revised her husband's favorite cookie recipe so she could eat them. They're so good they are tops with her three young children too. Alma is a Weight Watchers leader who lost 60 pounds while following the Program.

1 cup plus 2 tablespoons
    all-purpose flour
4½ ounces uncooked quick
    or old-fashioned oats
1 teaspoon salt
½ teaspoon baking soda
¼ teaspoon ground cinnamon
½ cup *each* firmly packed
    dark brown sugar and
    thawed frozen concen-
    trated apple juice (no sugar
    added)
¼ cup vegetable oil
1 teaspoon vanilla extract
¾ cup dark raisins
2 egg whites (at room
    temperature)
⅛ teaspoon cream of tartar

In medium mixing bowl combine flour, oats, salt, baking soda, and cinnamon; set aside. Using electric mixer, in small mixing bowl beat together sugar, juice, oil, and vanilla; add to oat mixture and mix well. Stir in raisins and set aside.

Preheat oven to 375°F. Using clean beaters, in separate medium mixing bowl beat egg whites at low speed until foamy; add cream of tartar and continue beating until soft peaks form. Fold beaten whites into oatmeal mixture.

Spray nonstick cookie sheet with nonstick cooking spray; drop batter by heaping teaspoonfuls onto sprayed sheet, forming 12 equal cookies and leaving a space of about 2 inches between each. Bake until edges of cookies are lightly browned, 10 to 12 minutes; using a spatula, remove cookies to wire rack to cool. Repeat procedure 2 more times, spraying cookie sheet with nonstick cooking spray each time and making 24 more cookies.

MAKES 12 SERVINGS, 3 COOKIES EACH

Each serving provides: 1 Bread Exchange; 1 Fat Exchange; 1 Fruit Exchange;
    45 calories Optional Exchange
Per serving: 209 calories; 4 g protein; 5 g fat; 37 g carbohydrate; 24 mg
    calcium; 233 mg sodium; 0 mg cholesterol

Alma M. Beaudry
Spokane, Washington

"Marshmallow" Puffs

Nan updated and changed an old recipe that was handed out by her Weight Watchers leader. She loves to cook and has had several recipes published in a church cookbook.

½ cup instant nonfat dry
  milk powder
2 tablespoons granulated
  sugar
4 egg whites (from large eggs),
  at room temperature
¼ teaspoon cream of tartar
1 teaspoon vanilla extract
¼ teaspoon *each* almond
  extract (optional) and
  ground cinnamon

In small bowl combine milk powder and sugar; set aside.

Using electric mixer, in large mixing bowl beat egg whites until frothy; add cream of tartar and beat until whites hold soft peaks. Gradually add milk mixture and extracts and beat until powder is dissolved and whites are stiff but not dry.

Preheat oven to 275°F. Onto nonstick cookie sheet drop mixture by tablespoon-fuls, forming 12 equal mounds; using the back of a spoon, smooth mounds. Bake in lower third portion of oven until puffs are dry to the touch, 35 to 45 minutes. Sprinkle each puff with an equal amount of cinnamon and remove to wire rack to cool. Serve immediately or store in airtight container until ready to serve.

MAKES 6 SERVINGS, 2 PUFFS EACH

Each serving provides: ¼ Milk Exchange; 35 calories Optional Exchange
Per serving: 50 calories; 4 g protein; trace fat; 8 g carbohydrate; 73 mg
  calcium; 65 mg sodium; 1 mg cholesterol

Nan G. Christensen
Park View, Iowa

Blondies

A unique and luscious change from brownies, these caramel-flavored bar cookies make great snacks and desserts. They need no refrigeration, so pack them to take along to the office, school, or on a picnic.

1 cup plus 2 tablespoons all-purpose flour
1 teaspoon double-acting baking powder
¼ teaspoon salt
¼ cup reduced-calorie margarine (tub)
⅓ cup firmly packed dark brown sugar
1 egg
1½ teaspoons vanilla extract
2 ounces semisweet mini chocolate chips
1½ ounces shelled pecans, chopped

Preheat oven to 350°F. Into small mixing bowl or onto sheet of wax paper sift together flour, baking powder, and salt; set aside.

Using electric mixer, in large mixing bowl cream margarine. Add sugar to margarine and beat at high speed until light and fluffy; beat in egg and vanilla. Reduce speed to low and gradually add sifted ingredients, beating until combined; fold in chocolate chips and pecans.

Spray 6 x 6 x 2-inch baking dish with non-stick cooking spray; spread batter evenly in dish and bake 30 to 35 minutes (until lightly browned and a cake tester, inserted in center, comes out clean). Transfer to wire rack and let cool completely before serving. To serve, cut into six 3 x 2-inch bars.

MAKES 6 SERVINGS, 1 BAR COOKIE EACH

Each serving provides: 1 Bread Exchange; 1 Fat Exchange; 165 calories Optional Exchange
Per serving: 276 calories; 4 g protein; 13 g fat; 37 g carbohydrate; 60 mg calcium; 257 mg sodium; 46 mg cholesterol

Weight Watchers Kitchens

Fruit 'n' Oat Bars

A Weight Watchers leader, Eileen lost over 50 pounds and has kept them off for a number of years. She enjoys converting old recipes and believes you can eat almost anything if you learn to make it the right way.

3 ounces uncooked
    quick oats
1½ ounces *each* ready-to-eat
    shredded wheat cereal,
    crumbled, and crunchy
    nutlike cereal nuggets
1 cup *each* evaporated
    skimmed milk and apple-
    sauce (no sugar added)
½ cup reduced-calorie
    margarine (tub), melted
⅓ cup shredded coconut
¼ cup *each* firmly packed
    brown sugar and golden
    raisins
8 pitted dates, chopped
2 teaspoons ground cinnamon
1 teaspoon baking soda

Preheat oven to 350°F. In large bowl combine oats and ready-to-eat cereals; add remaining ingredients, mixing well. Spray 13 x 9 x 2-inch baking pan with nonstick cooking spray; transfer cereal mixture to pan and bake for 30 minutes (until a cake tester, inserted in center, comes out clean). Remove from pan and let cool on wire rack; to serve, cut into 16 equal bars.

MAKES 16 SERVINGS, 1 BAR EACH

Each serving provides: ½ Bread Exchange; ½ Fat Exchange; ½ Fruit Exchange; 45 calories Optional Exchange
Per serving: 122 calories; 3 g protein; 4 g fat; 20 g carbohydrate; 61 mg calcium; 154 mg sodium; 0.6 mg cholesterol

Eileen J. Welzien
Dike, Iowa

Choco-Nut Bars

This chewy, fudgelike snack is sure to please everyone in your family. To store, wrap each bar in plastic wrap and refrigerate for up to 2 weeks or freeze for up to 1 month.

½ cup dark raisins
3 ounces ready-to-eat crunchy nutlike cereal nuggets
½ ounce *each* unsalted shelled roasted peanuts, chopped, and mini marshmallows
2 teaspoons shredded coconut
½ cup chunky peanut butter
2 ounces semisweet mini chocolate chips

Soak raisins in warm water to cover until plumped; drain, discarding liquid.

Line 9¼ x 5¼ x 3-inch loaf pan with wax paper, allowing ends of paper to extend over sides of pan; set aside. In small bowl combine raisins with remaining ingredients except peanut butter and chocolate chips. In small nonstick saucepan melt peanut butter over low heat, stirring constantly *(be careful not to burn);* add to cereal mixture, stirring to coat. Press mixture into lined loaf pan.

In small nonstick saucepan melt chocolate over low heat, stirring constantly, until smooth *(be careful not to burn).* Spread chocolate over peanut butter mixture, cover pan with plastic wrap, and refrigerate or freeze until mixture is firm.

Using ends of wax paper, gently lift firm mixture out of pan; remove and discard wax paper. Cut mixture into 8 equal bars.

MAKES 8 SERVINGS, 1 BAR EACH

Each serving provides: 1 Protein Exchange; ½ Bread Exchange; 1 Fat Exchange; ½ Fruit Exchange; 55 calories Optional Exchange
Per serving: 214 calories; 7 g protein; 12 g fat; 24 g carbohydrate; 18 mg calcium; 153 mg sodium; trace cholesterol

Weight Watchers Kitchens

Peanut Butter Fudge

Pauline was inspired to create this peanutty snack to combat hunger pangs at the factory where she works. Pauline loves the Weight Watchers program and says it works if you stick to it. She should know—she's lost 80 pounds herself.

1 cup instant nonfat dry
   milk powder
1 tablespoon granulated sugar
1 envelope unflavored gelatin
¾ cup water
⅓ cup plus 2 teaspoons
   smooth peanut butter
¼ cup thawed frozen dairy
   whipped topping
1 tablespoon sunflower seed

In medium heatproof mixing bowl combine milk powder and sugar; set aside.

In small saucepan sprinkle gelatin over water and let stand to soften, about 1 minute; add peanut butter and cook over medium heat, stirring constantly, until peanut butter is melted and gelatin is dissolved. Pour into milk mixture and add whipped topping and sunflower seed; using a wooden spoon, mix until thoroughly combined. Spray 8 x 8 x 2-inch pan with nonstick cooking spray and pour peanut butter mixture into pan; using a spatula, spread into even layer. Cover with plastic wrap and refrigerate for at least 2 hours before serving. To serve, cut fudge into four 2-inch-wide bars, then cut each bar into thirds.

MAKES 6 SERVINGS, 2 PIECES EACH

Each serving provides: 1 Protein Exchange; 1 Fat Exchange; ½ Milk
   Exchange; 30 calories Optional Exchange
Per serving: 164 calories; 10 g protein; 10 g fat; 11 g carbohydrate; 147 mg
   calcium; 142 mg sodium; 2 mg cholesterol

Pauline Fox
Columbus, Indiana

"Gum Drops" ☉

Gertrude makes this version of an old-fashioned favorite at Christmastime for her grandchildren. They love them, and you will, too.

1 envelope (eight ½-cup servings) raspberry-flavored gelatin
1 envelope (eight ½-cup servings) low-calorie raspberry-flavored gelatin (8 calories per serving)
½ cup plus 2 tablespoons water
1 tablespoon plus 1 teaspoon granulated sugar

Spray 8 x 4 x 2-inch pan with nonstick cooking spray; set aside.

In small saucepan combine gelatin with water and stir to dissolve; stirring constantly, bring to a boil. Reduce heat and simmer, stirring constantly, for 2 to 3 minutes; pour into sprayed pan and let cool. Cover with plastic wrap and refrigerate until set, at least 1 hour.

Cut gelatin into eight 1-inch-wide strips, then cut each strip in half crosswise, forming sixteen 2 x 1-inch rectangles; cut 8 rectangles diagonally into halves, forming 16 triangles. Transfer "gum drops" to plastic bag, add sugar, and shake to coat.

MAKES 16 SERVINGS,
1 RECTANGLE OR 2 TRIANGLES EACH

Each serving provides: 60 calories Optional Exchange
Per serving: 63 calories; 1 g protein; 0 g fat; 15 g carbohydrate; 0 mg calcium; 36 mg sodium; 0 mg cholesterol

VARIATION:

Other flavors of gelatin may be substituted for the raspberry-flavored, but be sure to use the same flavor of the regular and low-calorie products. Try cherry, strawberry, orange, lemon, or any other favorite.

Gertrude C. Delaney
Delphi, Indiana

Frozen Chocolate Banana ◔

Alma's recipe is a delightful snack that kids from 2 to 102 will enjoy. Married and the mother of two children, Alma collects art, antiques, plates, and Indian artifacts. She also likes to fish, hike, and garden.

1 medium banana, peeled and cut in half crosswise
2 graham crackers (2½-inch squares), finely crushed
1 teaspoon chocolate syrup

Insert a wooden ice cream bar stick into cut end of each banana half; wrap in wax paper or foil and freeze until hard.

On sheet of wax paper spread half of cracker crumbs; coat 1 banana half with ½ teaspoon syrup, then roll in crumbs. Repeat procedure with remaining banana half. Serve immediately or wrap in moisture- and vapor-resistant wrapping and store in freezer until ready to use.

MAKES 2 SERVINGS, ½ BANANA EACH

Each serving provides: ½ Bread Exchange; 1 Fruit Exchange; 10 calories Optional Exchange
Per serving: 87 calories; 1 g protein; 1 g fat; 21 g carbohydrate; 7 mg calcium; 50 mg sodium; 0 mg cholesterol

VARIATION:

For a nutty chocolate banana, substitute ½ ounce unsalted shelled roasted peanuts, chopped (about 2 tablespoons), for the graham crackers. Roll each banana in ¼ ounce (about 1 tablespoon) chopped nuts. Omit Bread Exchange from Exchange Information and increase Optional Exchange to 55 calories.

Per serving: 101 calories; 3 g protein; 4 g fat; 17 g carbohydrate; 10 mg calcium; 3 mg sodium; 0 mg cholesterol

Alma E. Arnold
Thomson Falls, Montana

Peanut Butter Balls

Jo's love for peanut butter prompted her to develop a satisfying snack that's easy to prepare. An Alaska resident for the past ten years, Jo runs two businesses, is a Weight Watchers leader, and the mother of three.

¼ cup thawed frozen dairy whipped topping
2 tablespoons smooth or chunky peanut butter
1 tablespoon plus 1 teaspoon shredded coconut

In small mixing bowl combine all ingredients; cover and refrigerate for 30 minutes. Roll mixture into 6 equal balls and set each ball into a paper soufflé cup. Set cups on freezer-safe plate, cover with moisture- and vapor-resistant wrapping, and freeze until hardened.

MAKES 2 SERVINGS, 3 BALLS EACH

Each serving provides: 1 Protein Exchange; 1 Fat Exchange; 45 calories Optional Exchange
Per serving: 134 calories; 5 g protein; 11 g fat; 6 g carbohydrate; 6 mg calcium; 94 mg sodium; 0 mg cholesterol

Jo Cropley
Sitka, Alaska

Cardamom-Toasted Popcorn Mix

Barbara loves the taste of cardamom, so she created this crunchy snack. It's perfect for brown-bag lunches at school or work.

2 cups prepared plain
  popcorn
1½ ounces ready-to-eat
  miniature shredded whole
  wheat biscuits
¾ ounce uncooked old-
  fashioned oats
¾ ounce dried apple pieces
2 tablespoons dark raisins
¼ cup water
2 tablespoons granulated
  sugar
1 tablespoon plus 1 teaspoon
  margarine
⅛ to ¼ teaspoon ground
  cardamom
½ teaspoon vanilla extract
¼ teaspoon baking soda

In 2-quart bowl combine popcorn, cereals, and fruit; set aside.

Preheat oven to 250°F. In small saucepan combine water, sugar, margarine, and cardamom. Stirring constantly, bring to a boil and cook for 1 minute *(be careful not to burn)*; remove from heat and stir in vanilla and baking soda. Immediately pour over popcorn mixture and toss to coat; on nonstick baking sheet spread popcorn mixture and bake until toasted, 20 to 25 minutes, turning pieces occasionally to ensure even toasting. Serve warm or at room temperature.

MAKES 4 SERVINGS

Each serving provides: 1 Bread Exchange; 1 Fat Exchange; ½ Fruit
  Exchange; 30 calories Optional Exchange
Per serving: 157 calories; 3 g protein; 5 g fat; 28 g carbohydrate; 12 mg
  calcium; 102 mg sodium; 0 mg cholesterol

Barbara Cadigan
Duluth, Minnesota

❖❖❖

Crunchy Cereal Mix

Pretzels and nuts on a weight-loss plan? Of course! Now you can serve this crunchy snack at your next party, and not go off the Food Plan when you eat some, too.

¼ cup margarine
1 tablespoon Worcestershire sauce
Dash to ⅛ teaspoon hot sauce
4½ ounces *each* ready-to-eat bite-size crispy corn and crispy wheat squares cereals
4 ounces unsalted shelled roasted peanuts
2 ounces thin pretzel sticks
½ teaspoon salt
⅛ teaspoon garlic powder or onion powder

Preheat oven to 325°F. In small metal measuring cup or other small flameproof container melt margarine over low heat *(be careful not to burn)*. Stir in Worcestershire sauce and hot sauce; remove from heat and set aside.

In large bowl combine remaining ingredients; slowly drizzle margarine mixture over cereal mixture, tossing constantly to thoroughly combine. Spread mixture on large baking sheet and bake, stirring occasionally, until mixture is lightly toasted, 25 to 30 minutes.

MAKES 12 SERVINGS, ABOUT ¾ CUP EACH

Each serving provides: 1 Bread Exchange; 1 Fat Exchange; 75 calories Optional Exchange
Per serving: 189 calories; 5 g protein; 9 g fat; 24 g carbohydrate; 16 mg calcium; 404 mg sodium; 0 mg cholesterol

VARIATION:

Substitute blanched almonds or unsalted shelled cashews for the peanuts, or use ⅓ each of peanuts, almonds, and cashews.

Per serving with almonds: 190 calories; 4 g protein; 9 g fat; 24 g carbohydrate; 33 mg calcium; 404 mg sodium; 0 mg cholesterol
With cashews: 187 calories; 4 g protein; 9 g fat; 25 g carbohydrate; 12 mg calcium; 404 mg sodium; 0 mg cholesterol
With peanuts, almonds, and cashews: 189 calories; 4 g protein; 9 g fat; 24 g carbohydrate; 21 mg calcium; 404 mg sodium; 0 mg cholesterol

Weight Watchers Kitchens

Raspberry Cocktail

A refreshing summer drink — try it with brunch or before dinner.

½ cup raspberries*
1 tablespoon black currant
  liqueur
1 cup dry white table wine
4 ice cubes

Chill two 6-ounce glasses. In blender container process raspberries until smooth. Set fine sieve over small saucepan and force raspberry puree through sieve into pan; discard seeds. Add liqueur to saucepan and cook over medium heat, stirring frequently and skimming foam from surface when necessary, until mixture is thickened and reduced by half, 4 to 5 minutes. Transfer raspberry mixture to small cup or bowl; cover with plastic wrap and refrigerate until chilled, about 1 hour.

To serve, divide raspberry mixture into chilled glasses; add ½ cup wine and 2 ice cubes to each glass and stir. Serve immediately.

MAKES 2 SERVINGS

*If fresh raspberries are not available, frozen raspberries (no sugar added) may be used; thaw after measuring.

Each serving provides: ½ Fruit Exchange; 125 calories Optional Exchange
Per serving: 134 calories; 0.4 g protein; 0.2 g fat; 11 g carbohydrate; 17 mg calcium; 6 mg sodium; 0 mg cholesterol

VARIATION:

Raspberry Spritzer — Prepare recipe as directed but use two 10-ounce glasses; add ¼ cup salt-free club soda or seltzer along with the wine and ice to each glass.

Weight Watchers Kitchens

Toasted Almond Cocktail ◑

A sweet and creamy before-dinner cocktail that you and your guests will enjoy.

½ cup low-fat milk
   (1% milk fat)
2 tablespoons amaretto
1 tablespoon *each* coffee
   liqueur and chocolate
   liqueur
2 to 3 ice cubes

Chill two 4-ounce rock glasses. In blender container combine all ingredients and process until smooth and frothy. Divide into chilled glasses and serve.

MAKES 2 SERVINGS

Each serving provides: ¼ Milk Exchange; 105 calories Optional Exchange
Per serving: 108 calories; 2 g protein; 0.7 g fat; 12 g carbohydrate; 75 mg
   calcium; 31 mg sodium; 2 mg cholesterol

Weight Watchers Kitchens

Choco-Banana Supreme ☾

A licensed practical nurse, mother of two, and a grandmother as well, Martha loves chocolate and peanut butter. Her chocolaty shake is so thick and creamy you can eat it with a spoon.

1 cup chilled diet chocolate soda (2 calories per 8 fluid ounces), divided
½ medium banana, peeled
1 packet (1 serving) reduced-calorie chocolate dairy drink mix
1 tablespoon smooth peanut butter, frozen

Into each of 4 sections of ice cube tray pour 2 tablespoons soda (sections should be about ⅔ full); freeze until ice cubes are solid. Wrap banana in plastic freezer wrap and freeze until solid.

In blender container combine remaining ½ cup soda, frozen banana half, dairy drink mix, and peanut butter and process at high speed until smooth, scraping down sides of container as necessary; with motor running add soda cubes, 1 at a time, processing after each addition until ice is dissolved (mixture will be thick). Serve immediately.

MAKES 1 SERVING

Each serving provides: 1 Protein Exchange; 1 Fat Exchange; 1 Fruit Exchange; 1 Milk Exchange; 2 calories Optional Exchange
Per serving: 220 calories; 11 g protein; 10 g fat; 28 g carbohydrate; 209 mg calcium; 143 mg sodium; 0 mg cholesterol

VARIATION:

Peanut butter may be omitted from recipe; omit Protein and Fat Exchanges from Exchange Information.

Per serving: 125 calories; 7 g protein; 1 g fat; 25 g carbohydrate; 203 mg calcium; 67 mg sodium; 0 mg cholesterol

Martha E. Slemons Shilling
Rebersburg, Pennsylvania

Mocha Frappe ◑

Try Lois's answer to an ice cream parlor favorite—it's cool and refreshing. Lois, a Weight Watchers receptionist, loves discovering new recipes and converting old ones. What she has learned at Weight Watchers meetings has inspired Lois to try unusual foods.

1 cup black coffee, chilled
½ medium banana, peeled and cut into chunks
⅓ cup instant nonfat dry milk powder
¼ cup part-skim ricotta cheese
1 tablespoon chocolate syrup
½ teaspoon vanilla extract
Granulated low-calorie sweetener with aspartame to equal 4 teaspoons sugar
5 to 6 ice cubes

Chill two 12-ounce glasses. In blender container combine all ingredients except ice cubes and process until smooth; with motor running add ice cubes, 1 at a time, processing after each addition until ice is dissolved (mixture should be smooth and thick). Pour half of mixture into each chilled glass.

MAKES 2 SERVINGS, ABOUT 1½ CUPS EACH

Each serving provides: ½ Protein Exchange; ½ Fruit Exchange; ½ Milk Exchange; 30 calories Optional Exchange
Per serving: 141 calories; 9 g protein; 3 g fat; 20 g carbohydrate; 227 mg calcium; 106 mg sodium; 12 mg cholesterol

Lois M. Greene
Southbridge, Massachusetts

Mocha Nog ☺◑

This drink is a favorite of Diane's for Christmas breakfast. Her kids love it, too. Diane is a Weight Watchers receptionist who has lost 74 pounds on the Program. Her hobby is sewing.

2 packets (1 serving each) reduced-calorie milk chocolate-flavored hot cocoa mix
2 cups water
1 egg, separated
1 teaspoon instant coffee powder
½ teaspoon vanilla extract

In 1-quart saucepan combine cocoa mix with water, egg yolk, coffee, and vanilla and, using wire whisk, mix well; cook over medium heat, stirring frequently, until thickened, 2 to 4 minutes (*do not boil*). Reduce heat to low and keep warm.

In small mixing bowl, using electric mixer, beat egg white until stiff peaks form. Into each of 2 mugs spoon half of beaten white; pour half of cocoa mixture into each and serve immediately.

MAKES 2 SERVINGS

Each serving provides: ½ Protein Exchange; 1 Milk Exchange
Per serving: 104 calories; 8 g protein; 3 g fat; 11 g carbohydrate; 315 mg calcium; 195 mg sodium; 137 mg cholesterol

Diane L. Hodges
Independence, Missouri

Yogurt Shake ◖◗

This recipe originally called for honey and fruit juice, but Anne decided to substitute fruit cocktail and omit the honey. She likes to prepare enough for the family because they love it as much as she does. Anne keeps fit by walking two miles a day.

1 cup canned fruit cocktail
   (no sugar added)
½ cup *each* water and plain
   low-fat yogurt
⅓ cup instant nonfat dry milk
   powder
2 teaspoons vanilla extract
Granulated low-calorie
   sweetener with aspartame
   to equal 2 teaspoons sugar
3 to 4 ice cubes

Chill two 10-ounce glasses. In blender container combine all ingredients except ice cubes and process until smooth, scraping down sides of container as necessary; with motor running add ice cubes, 1 at a time, processing after each addition until ice is dissolved. Pour half of mixture into each chilled glass and serve with a straw.

MAKES 2 SERVINGS

Each serving provides: 1 Fruit Exchange; 1 Milk Exchange
Per serving: 132 calories; 8 g protein; 1 g fat; 22 g carbohydrate; 248 mg
   calcium; 106 mg sodium; 5 mg cholesterol

NOTE:

You may enjoy a serving of Yogurt Shake when you prepare it, then cover and refrigerate the extra serving. When you're ready to serve it, just process again.

Anne L. Cawker
Oshawa, Ontario, Canada

Orange-Spice Tea Mix ◑

Lise adores Russian tea, which is made with fruit juices, but she wanted a lower-calorie version. After a good deal of experimenting, she came up with this delicious mix, which she drinks often. Lise is a real estate agent and mother of two.

1 cup unsweetened instant
   lemon-flavored iced tea mix
1 tub (eight 8-fluid-ounce
   servings) low-calorie
   orange-flavored drink mix
   (4 calories per serving)
1 teaspoon ground cinnamon
½ teaspoon ground cloves

In jar that has a tight-fitting cover combine all ingredients; cover and shake well to combine. Store in jar until ready to use.

To serve, dissolve 1 teaspoon mixture in 1 cup boiling water.

YIELDS 1⅛ CUPS TEA MIX

Each teaspoon tea mix provides: 2 calories Optional Exchange
Per serving: 3 calories; 0 g protein; 0 g fat; 0.6 g carbohydrate; 0.6 mg
   calcium; 0.1 mg sodium; 0 mg cholesterol

Lise Burnett
Clarksville, Virginia

Appendix

About Weighing and Measuring

- Always take time to measure and weigh ingredients carefully; this is vital to both recipe results and weight control. Don't try to judge amounts by eye.

- To weigh foods, use a scale.

- To measure liquids, use a standard glass or clear plastic measuring cup. Place it on a level surface and read markings at eye level. Fill the cup just to the appropriate marking. To measure less than ¼ cup, use standard measuring spoons.

- To measure dry ingredients, use metal or plastic measuring cups that come in sets of four: ¼ cup, ⅓ cup, ½ cup, and 1 cup. Spoon the ingredients into the cup, then level with the straight edge of a knife or metal spatula. To measure less than ¼ cup, use standard measuring spoons and, unless otherwise directed, level as for measuring cup.

- A dash is about ¹⁄₁₆ of a teaspoon (½ of a ⅛-teaspoon measure or ¼ of a ¼-teaspoon measure).

- In any recipe for more than one serving it is important to mix ingredients well and to divide evenly so that each portion will be the same size.

About Herbs and Spices

- The herbs used in these recipes are dried unless otherwise indicated. If you are substituting fresh herbs, use approximately four times the amount of dried (e.g., 1 teaspoon chopped fresh basil instead of ¼ teaspoon dried basil leaves). If you are substituting ground (powdered) herbs for dried leaves, use approximately half the amount of dried (e.g., ¼ teaspoon ground thyme instead of ½ teaspoon dried thyme leaves).

- If you are substituting fresh spices for ground, use approximately eight times the amount of ground (e.g., 1 teaspoon minced pared ginger root instead of ⅛ teaspoon ground ginger).

- Generally, dried herbs and spices should not be kept for more than a year. Date the container at the time of purchase and check periodically for potency. Usually, if the herb (or spice) is aromatic, it is still potent; if the aroma has diminished, the recipe may require a larger amount of the seasoning.

About Other Ingredients

• We've used fresh vegetables unless otherwise indicated. If you substitute frozen or canned vegetables, it may be necessary to adjust cooking times accordingly.

• When vegetable oil is called for, oils such as safflower, sunflower, soybean, corn, cottonseed, peanut, or any of these combined may be used. Since olive oil and Chinese sesame oil have distinctive flavors, they have been specifically indicated. There are two types of sesame oil: light and dark. The light oil is relatively flavorless and may be used as a substitute for any other vegetable oil. When sesame oil is specified, use the dark variety. This product, made from toasted sesame seeds, has a rich amber color and a characteristic sesame flavor.

• Hot chili peppers require special handling; their volatile oils can make your skin and eyes burn. Wear rubber gloves and be careful not to touch your face or eyes while working with these peppers. Before continuing with the recipe, thoroughly wash your hands, knife, and cutting board to remove all traces of the pepper.

About Sugar Substitutes and Low-Calorie Sweeteners

The use of these items on the Weight Watchers food plan is entirely optional. Natural sweetness is available in the form of fruits and honey. You may also use white and brown sugar, fructose, molasses, syrup, jams, jellies, and preserves. The decision about using sugar substitutes and low-calorie sweeteners should be made by you and your physician.

About the Exchange and Nutrition Information

Each recipe in this book is followed by an Exchange Information statement. This statement provides information as to how one serving of the item prepared from that recipe fits into the Weight Watchers food plan. If you are following the Food Plan, be aware that some of the recipes use ingredients from the Personal Choice® Series. You will find the Exchange Information useful when preparing menus as it will help you keep track of your Exchanges. If you make any changes in the recipes, be sure to adjust the Exchange Information accordingly.

Since many people are concerned about nutrition, on each recipe we have also included the per-serving nutrition analyses for calories, protein, fat, carbohydrate, calcium, sodium, and cholesterol. These figures were calculated using the most up-to-date data available; they will change if the recipe is altered, even if the substitution in ingredients does not affect the Exchange Information.

Nutrition Notes

The foods we eat provide the nutrients we need to stay healthy—about 40 in all, including proteins, fats, carbohydrates, vitamins, minerals, and water. Our bodies use these nutrients for energy, growth, repair of body tissue, and regulation/control of body processes. It is the amount of proteins, fats, and carbohydrates in foods that determines their caloric content.

- Proteins are necessary for building and maintaining body tissue. Best sources of protein: poultry, meat, fish, eggs, milk, and cheese.

- Fats and carbohydrates provide energy and assist other body functions. Fruits, vegetables, cereals, and grains are excellent sources of carbohydrates. Margarine, vegetable oils, poultry, meat, and fish supply fats.

- Sodium is a significant factor in weight control since it affects the body's water balance. Sodium occurs naturally in some foods, and additional amounts are often added in processing prepared foods.

- Calcium builds and maintains strong bones and teeth, and is essential throughout your life to prevent osteoporosis in later years. The best sources of calcium are, of course, milk and other dairy products. But calcium is also found in sardines and salmon (canned with bones); tofu and cooked soybeans; and in certain vegetables and fruits, such as cooked collard, turnip, and mustard greens, broccoli, spinach, and oranges.

- Cholesterol is an essential part of all body tissue and is found in foods of animal origin. However, high blood cholesterol has been associated with increased risk of heart disease. To lower your cholesterol intake, choose low-fat dairy products; trim all visible fat from meats; cook meats on a rack (bake, roast, or broil); select poultry or fish in place of meats.

The objective of daily menu planning is to provide yourself with basic nutrients while staying within your caloric limit. Remember that no single food supplies all the essential nutrients in the amounts needed, and that *variety* is the key to success. The greater the variety of food the less likely you are to develop a deficiency or an excess of any nutrient, and the more interesting and attractive your diet will be.

❖❖❖

Pan Substitutions

It's best to use the pan size that's recommended in a recipe; however, if your kitchen isn't equipped with that particular pan, chances are a substitution will work just as well. The pan size is determined by the volume of food it holds. When substituting, use a pan as close to the recommended size as possible. Food cooked in too small a pan may boil over; food cooked in too large a pan may dry out or burn. To determine the dimensions of a baking pan, measure across the top, between the inside edges. To determine the volume, measure the amount of water the pan holds when completely filled.

When you use a pan that is a different size from the one recommended, it may be necessary to adjust the suggested cooking time. Depending on the size of the pan and the depth of the food in it, you may need to add or subtract 5 to 10 minutes. If you substitute glass or glass-ceramic for metal, it is recommended that the oven temperature be reduced by 25°F.

The following chart provides some common pan substitutions:

Recommended Size	Approximate Volume	Possible Substitutions
8 x 1½-inch round baking pan	1½ quarts	10 x 6 x 2-inch baking dish 9 x 1½-inch round baking pan 8 x 4 x 2-inch loaf pan 9-inch pie plate
8 x 8 x 2-inch baking pan	2 quarts	11 x 7 x 1½-inch baking pan 12 x 7½ x 2-inch baking pan 9 x 5 x 3-inch loaf pan two 8 x 1½-inch round baking pans
13 x 9 x 2-inch baking pan	3 quarts	14 x 11 x 2-inch baking dish two 9 x 1½-inch round baking pans two 8 x 1½-inch round baking pans

Metric Conversions

If you are converting the recipes in this book to metrics, use the following table as a guide:

Temperature

To change degrees Fahrenheit to degrees Celsius, subtract 32° and multiply by five-ninths.

Weight

To change	To	Multiply by
Ounces	Grams	30.0
Pounds	Kilograms	.48

Volume

To Change	To	Multiply by
Teaspoons	Milliliters	5.0
Tablespoons	Milliliters	15.0
Cups	Milliliters	250.0
Cups	Liters	.25
Pints	Liters	.5
Quarts	Liters	1.0
Gallons	Liters	4.0

Length

To Change	To	Multiply by
Inches	Millimeters	25.0
Inches	Centimeters	2.5
Feet	Centimeters	30.0
Yards	Meters	.9

Oven Temperatures

Degrees Fahrenheit	=	Degrees Celsius
250		120
275		140
300		150
325		160
350		180
375		190
400		200
425		220
450		230
475		250
500		260
525		270

Symbol	=	Metric Unit
g		gram
kg		kilogram
ml		milliliter
l		liter
°C		degrees Celsius
mm		millimeter
cm		centimeter
m		meter

Dry and Liquid Measure Equivalents

Teaspoons	Tablespoons	Cups	Fluid Ounces
3 teaspoons	1 tablespoon		½ fluid ounce
6 teaspoons	2 tablespoons	⅛ cup	1 fluid ounce
8 teaspoons	2 tablespoons plus 2 teaspoons	⅙ cup	
12 teaspoons	4 tablespoons	¼ cup	2 fluid ounces
15 teaspoons	5 tablespoons	⅓ cup less 1 teaspoon	
16 teaspoons	5 tablespoons plus 1 teaspoon	⅓ cup	
18 teaspoons	6 tablespoons	⅓ cup plus 2 teaspoons	3 fluid ounces
24 teaspoons	8 tablespoons	½ cup	4 fluid ounces
30 teaspoons	10 tablespoons	½ cup plus 2 tablespoons	5 fluid ounces
32 teaspoons	10 tablespoons plus 2 teaspoons	⅔ cup	
36 teaspoons	12 tablespoons	¾ cup	6 fluid ounces
42 teaspoons	14 tablespoons	1 cup less 2 tablespoons	7 fluid ounces
45 teaspoons	15 tablespoons	1 cup less 1 tablespoon	
48 teaspoons	16 tablespoons	1 cup	8 fluid ounces

Note: Measurements of less than ⅛ teaspoon are considered a Dash or a Pinch.

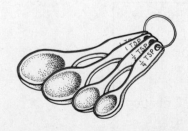

Index

✧✧

✧✧✧

WEIGHT WATCHERS® COOKBOOKS For Your Enjoyment
(0452—0453)

WEIGHT WATCHERS
FAVORITE RECIPES

NAL Hardcover Edition: $17.50 U.S., $24.50 Canada (0-453-01012-1)

WEIGHT WATCHERS®
QUICK START PLUS
PROGRAM® COOKBOOK

Plume Softcover Edition: $9.95 U.S., $13.95 Canada (0-452-25831-6)
NAL Hardcover Edition: $17.50 U.S., $21.50 Canada (0-453-01014-8)

WEIGHT WATCHERS®
NEW INTERNATIONAL COOKBOOK

Plume Softcover Edition: $9.95 U.S., $13.95 Canada (0-452-25951-7)
NAL Hardcover Edition: $18.50 U.S., $24.50 Canada (0-453-01011-3)

WEIGHT WATCHERS®
Fast & Fabulous COOKBOOK

Plume Softcover Edition: $7.95 U.S., $10.50 Canada (0-452-25727-1)
NAL Hardcover Edition: $14.95 U.S., $18.75 Canada (0-453-01008-3)

Buy them at your local bookstore or use this convenient coupon for ordering.

THE NEW AMERICAN LIBRARY, INC.
P.O. Box 999, Bergenfield, New Jersey 07621

Please send me the PLUME and NAL BOOKS I have checked.
I am enclosing $ _____ (please add $1.50 to this order to
cover postage and handling). Send check or money order—no
cash or C.O.D.'s. Prices and numbers are subject to change
without notice.

Name _____

Address _____

City _____ State _____ Zip Code_____

Allow 4-6 weeks for delivery.
This offer is subject to withdrawal without notice.